From Child Art to Visual Language of Youth

From Child Art to Visual Language of Youth
New Models and Tools for Assessment of Learning and Creation in Art Education

Edited by Andrea Kárpáti and Emil Gaul

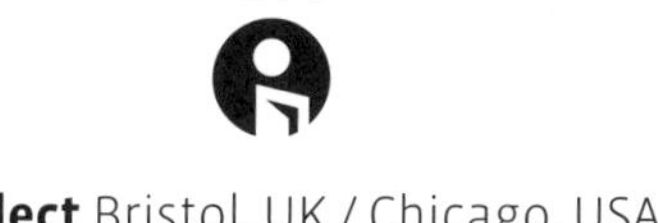

intellect Bristol, UK / Chicago, USA

First published in the UK in 2013 by
Intellect, The Mill, Parnall Road, Fishponds, Bristol, BS16 3JG, UK

First published in the USA in 2013 by
Intellect, The University of Chicago Press, 1427 E. 60th Street,
Chicago, IL 60637, USA

Cover designer: Holly Rose
Copy-editor: Emma Rhys
Production manager: Melanie Marshall/Tom Newman
Typesetting: Contentra Technologies

Print ISBN: 978-1-84150-624-1
ePDF ISBN: 978-1-78320-058-0
ePub ISBN: 978-1-78320-059-7

Printed and bound by Hobbs the Printers Ltd, UK

Contents

Foreword

Rita L. Irwin, The University of British Columbia; President, International Society for Education through Art

On behalf of the International Society for Education through Art (InSEA), it gives me great pleasure to congratulate editors Andrea Kárpáti and Emil Gaul, and their many chapter authors, for compiling an outstanding collection of articles on assessment for learning and the creation of art. At our recent *2011 InSEA World Congress* held in Budapest, Hungary a research pre-conference was dedicated to an intense discussion on assessment, art, and education. InSEA is pleased to endorse this extremely important contribution to the literature that details the diversity of perspectives and debates shared during that event.

It is also important to recall an earlier milestone publication endorsed by InSEA and edited by three prominent art educators and InSEA members, Douglas Boughton, Elliot W. Eisner, and Johan Ligtvoet, entitled *Evaluation and Assessment of Visual Arts Education: International Perspectives* (Boston: Teachers College Press, 1996). That publication was a result of a research conference organized by InSEA and it sparked a great deal of international attention. Seventeen years later, InSEA hopes this new publication will spark as much or more international attention. It is important that we keep these ideas uppermost in the minds of educators and policy makers as change permeates our educational and cultural systems.

As you read through this volume you will experience a diversity of epistemological perspectives on assessment *and* you will experience a diversity of cultural perspectives steeped in local, national, and international sensitivities, traditions, reforms, and debates. It is perhaps in the liminal space of "and" that we, as an international group of art educators, can linger, discuss, imagine, debate, encourage, stress, agree, and disagree on what is taking place and what should take place. This edited volume provides an important springboard for animated discussions around child art, program reform, curriculum development, visual literacy, aesthetic judgment, visual culture, political agendas, and cultural traditions/innovations, among other important ideas on evaluation and assessment. Moreover, with authors representing visual arts education in Finland, France, Germany, Hungary, Japan, Morocco, Portugal, Spain, Switzerland, the Netherlands, Turkey, United Kingdom, and the

United States, readers are invited to consider an important topic from a broad international basis. This is one of the greatest benefits of being connected with InSEA – our network of art educators from the world, willing to learn from one another in order to appreciate, enhance, and strengthen visual arts education worldwide. With that in mind, I want to thank all of you as readers for taking a keen interest in this topic and working to enhance and strengthen visual arts education in your local, national and/or international circles of connection.

Preface

to the collection of studies, From Child Art to Visual Language of Youth:
New Models and Tools for Assessment of Learning and Creation in Art
education

Andrea Kárpáti and Emil Gaul, Editors

In 2012, it is 16 years after *Evaluating and Assessing the Visual Arts in Education* – a collection
of studies and resulting remarks edited by Douglas G. Boughton, Elliot W. Eisner, and Johan
Ligtvoet – was published by Teachers College Press. The seminar, that was supported by the
Paul Getty Trust, the results of which were published in this highly important work, may not
be repeated, but it was the sincere hope of the organizers of the *33ʳᵈ InSEA World Congress
2011*, in Budapest, to revive its spirit. This collection of studies, presented at the "Research
Pre-Conference" of this event, intends to provide a critical overview of assessment of visual
skills and abilities of 6–18-year-old students as it is reflected in current international research.
The authors reconsider evaluation practices of art education as well as existing models for
the development of the visual skills and abilities of children and young adults and suggest
new approaches to better suit the paradigm change that global art education has experienced
recently.

The first group of studies discusses the history and current perspectives of assessment in
the visual arts, based on large-scale national investigations. Assessment of the outcomes of art
education has a long tradition: the first surveys were published in the 1930s. Stanley Madeja not
only summarizes the history of American art education assessment, but also provides a unique
overview of the evolution of evaluation instruments: from drawing tests to electronic portfolios;
from targeting visual skills to documenting the creative process. He outlines models of policy
making that shaped the past and influence the present and future of art education worldwide.
He reveals reasons why the arts have failed to assume the place in the school curriculum they
deserve. Lack of consensus with educational leadership and social stakeholders about what
should be taught, scarcity of reliable assessment procedures, and insufficient time and effort
dedicated to measuring and disseminating outcomes of art education at schools have largely
contributed to the current, unacceptably low status of our discipline.

Further in this chapter, national art-assessment studies introduce the interplay of educational and aesthetic, cultural and social trends that shape the contents and methodology of art education, resulting in more and more authentic documentation of its outcomes. For art educators, the quantitative nature of psychological measures of visual skills and abilities is inadequate, but to produce reliable information that convinces decision makers about the importance of the arts for human growth, "hard data" are needed. John Steers introduces a unique example of a synergy of formative and summative assessment practices. The system he significantly contributed to developing, the General Certificate of Secondary Education (GCSE) in the United Kingdom, is valid, reliable, flexible, and cost-effective, and builds on the expertise of art educators. This "teacher ownership" makes this system sustainable and influential for the practice of art education.

New media in "The Age of the Image" require a redefinition of the aims, objectives, and methodology of our discipline. In France, the modernization of educational content and the introduction of digital media in synergy with traditional ways of imaging seem to be the focus of attention both for researchers and practitioners. Bernard Darras gives a critical analysis of the path leading from cultural education to "the art of living", a model that is relevant for youth growing up digital and provides a synergy of values of "high" and "low" art through a semiotic and constructivist approach to visual culture and new forms of creativity.

Teaching content – the knowledge and skills of art that is selected for transmission at school – seems to be the most influential factor in evaluation design. From 1996, "Visual Culture" has been the name of the discipline of art and design education in Hungary to indicate the inclusion of issues of visual communication and environmental design and aesthetics in the national core curriculum. Assessment practices were soon harmonized with this model, and authentic assignments like the portfolio and the art and design project replaced traditional task-centred approaches. In 2009–2010, "Visual Culture" was among the basic disciplines selected for national assessment and a national survey of visual creation and perception in Grades 2, 4, and 6 (ages 8, 10 and 12) was executed. The chapter by Andrea Kárpáti and Emil Gaul gives an overview of the structure of visual skills and abilities that are important in many areas of studies and indicates how a system of tasks including expressive forms of youth subcultures, idioms of national minorities, and individual uses of visual language may result in a new, multimedia model of child art development.

Authentic assessment in the arts may only be performed by the teachers themselves, as a continuous effort to improve learning through a better understanding of creation and communication processes in the classroom. But are teachers willing and able to undertake this task? The study presented by Oğuz Dilmac assesses the competencies of Turkish visual arts teachers through performance evaluation methods. This research is not the usual questionnaire-based, critical overview; it is a vivid and realistic documentary of everyday assessment practices. Although they regularly engage in performance evaluation, primary school arts teachers often experience difficulties in finding time to prepare and evaluate development portfolios. Even the collection and storage of works is difficult where no art storeroom is available. "Rubrics" – assessment criteria developed by (inter)national experts – are available but not always understood because of their embeddedness in theory rather than school reality. The author suggests, as many others in this volume do, that mentoring by a professional well-versed in the evaluation of artistic practice is needed to reveal the multiple benefits and functional deficits of art education.

New assessment practices

The new generation of these art-assessment specialists who may alter the negative feelings of teachers about evaluation are practising artists, designers, and teachers, often working in teams with psychologists and sociologists. They revisit old methods of evaluating development in creation, perception, and criticism and develop new measures of assessment. Douglas G. Boughton shows how summative rather than formative assessment has the potential to improve the quality of student learning and thus gain respect for the discipline. Director of the International Baccalaureate in Art for many years, he proposes this model, flexibly adaptable to different cultural contexts, as a form of assessment that is authentic, educationally relevant, reliable, and politically correct at the same time. He contextualizes the model with basic issues of debate concerning evaluation in art education: major targets ("what"), evaluator roles ("who"), and exercise design issues ("how") evaluation needs to be undertaken. A comparative review of the International Baccalaureate (IB), GCSE, the Advanced Placement examinations, and the ARTS PROPEL Project show how the model works in an international perspective.

While the IB model is a summative procedure, a complimentary approach suggested by Diederik Schönau – developmental self-assessment – offers a formative path. After an overview of the needs and goals, standards and contents of arts assessment, the author shows how developmental assessment may become an integral part of the learning process through a joint ownership of students and teachers. The process involves repetitive feedback: reflection on the process and partial results of an assignment, not only its end product. This model is based on the Constructivist Learning Theory that emphasizes the role of student experiences in constructing new knowledge – a model with clear artistic implications and relevance for a discipline focusing on the individual creative endeavour.

However, in the 21st century, an age when all participants in the creation of visual language have been brought up within the practice of Information and Communication Technologies (ICTs), the meaning of "individual" versus collective, and "creation" versus adaptation, combination, and recontextualization has to be considered. Kerry Freedman, a leading protagonist of "Visual Culture", perhaps the leading contemporary paradigm in art education globally, discusses assessment issues based on such consideration. The practices that she suggests embrace both "high" and "low" art, "established" and "outsider" idioms of visual expression. She shows their role in the curriculum as they document student growth in the process of (re)constructing visual culture. New methods of assessment are imminent because the culture of ICT-based sharing implies the importance of group cognition assessed through group critique as opposed to traditional, individual processes of creation and criticism.

Individual assessment, however, will always be needed when policy makers have to be convinced about the importance of learning though art, or educational practices have to be evaluated in order to be modernized. In Finland, national assessment of skills and abilities from all disciplines are regularly carried out by the National Board of Education. New methods of assessment in this large scale evaluation context often mean the modernization of accepted formats and the adaptation of creative practices to mass examination requirements. Sirkka Laitinen reports on the 2010 national survey of visual skills and abilities of secondary school students assessed by two, interrelated methods: paper-and-pencil tests and creative tasks. Results showed what students know about techniques, how they process theoretical knowledge about art while putting procedures into practice, and how they respond to works of art. The major objective of the assessment exercise was to provide detailed feedback for teachers about the results of their strategies, in order to improve them. As Finland assumes a leading position in most knowledge areas in international assessment projects, experiences of this practice-oriented art education research may provide interesting insights into the whole system of educational improvement.

"Assignments touch the core of teaching more than any other issue." With this strong starting statement, Ernst Wagner indicate that assessment is strongly related to competence-oriented teaching and learning practice. Both teachers and evaluators are concerned about the skills and abilities that the arts – often only the arts – may successfully develop. Showing examples of German practice, the authors outline a new competence model that serves as a basis of assignment development. This model served as a basis for the work of a group of national evaluation experts, members of the Internationales Netzwerk Kompetenzorientierung in Kunst und Design (International Network for Competence Orientation in Art and Design) that hopes to provide both a research- and practice-based visual competence sturcture that may serve as a framework for further reserach. This framework is based on previous national studies of the members from Austria, France, Germany, Hungary, the Netherlands, and Switzerland and will contribute to the discussions about the value and relevance of national evaluation results to defining what can, may, and must be assessed in art-related skills and abilities. The group intends to propose a common "European Framework of Visual Competences" for discussion in the near future.

Research paradigms on evaluation and assessment at schools and beyond

As with the previously mentioned international project, research on assessment in art education often starts with the reconsideration of well-established models that have been guiding our thinking about the role and content of evaluation endeavours. Folkert Haanstra, Marie-Louise Damen, and Marjo van Hoorn address one of the most disputed models, the *U-shaped curve* of graphic development by Howard Gardner and members of the Harvard

Project Zero research group. This model suggests a decline in aesthetic production in middle childhood, implying the negative effects of art education in early and later adolescence and ultimately negates or minimizes the role of school in fostering development in the visual arts. The authors performed a partial replication of previous research to challenge U-curve findings. To avoid the cultural bias of American studies employing only western judges, artists and art educators from different cultural backgrounds were invited to assess a cross-cultural collection of works. Results indicate that developmental patterns in art education are strongly related to the cultural background of the evaluators.

Are there any skills and abilities that escape judgmental biases and are important enough to inspire continuous and successful assessment efforts? Spatial abilities are certainly among these unquestionably vital visual skills. Edith Glaser-Henzer reports on a Swiss research project on spatio-visual competencies that form the basis for the development of perceptive, processing, and creative capacities in children and teenagers. The "raviko" research project resulted in a redefinition of spatial abilities through an assessment of the "processing competency" that forms the basis of children's spatial representations. This project provides reliable tasks for detecting the individual strength and weaknesses of representing and perceiving space and promotes better targeted developmental strategies. Through a shift from cognitivist-stage models to subject- and process-oriented competencies, this research project provides a much-needed catalyst for discourse among artists, educators, and around competence models and educational standards.

Another area where psychologists and educators have to come to terms in order to develop more profound methods of creativity development is metacognition. Kazuhiro Ishizaki and Wenchun Wang, two scholars from Japan, discuss the relationship between metacognition and appreciation skills through introducing a study on the effects of metacognition in the process of writing about art. In an educational experiment, the group that received instructions about how to improve intuitive appreciation skills through metacognitive processes provided richer and more focused analyses of artworks. This project is an excellent example of evaluation of competences with direct relevance to improving teaching practice.

The documentation of cognitive and metacognitive processes activated in the course of artistic creation is a related research problem. Ricardo Reis presents a Portuguese research project on the content of visual literacy as perceived by students and teachers. Narratives about creation and perception of art are analysed to show the relevance of the role of schools in the development and social appreciation of visual literacy. The author also discusses methodological and ethical issues arising from the use of narrative discourse for gathering data. This research points out the need and difficulties of documenting and assessing not only the tangible results, but also the ideas and plans, and expressions of emotions and moods evoked by the creative process.

The aim of this collection of studies is to inspire those who believe that assessment based on international standards contributes to our knowledge about visual skills and their development, and convince those still in doubt. If properly contextualized to ensure cultural validity, regular assessment improves art education and its chances to survive the 21st century as a respected and relevant school discipline. In order to conceive new models that better accommodate emerging educational paradigms and well-established practices of "child" and "youth" multimedia art, a critical look at current research seems to be useful. However, to quote Jerry Hausman, "We were Modernists. We were interested in research because we thought that there was truth at the end of the road. Today I am a Post-Modernist, and believe in multiple truths."

Acknowledgement

The publication of this volume of studies was supported by the "Development of Diagnostic Assessment Project, co-ordinated by the Research Group on the Theory of Education of Szeged University. (Phase 1: Project No. TÁMOP-3.1.9-08/1-2009-0001 and Phase 2: Project No. TÁMOP-3.1.9-11/1-2012-0001)

PART I

History and current perspectives of assessment in the visual arts:
National studies

Chapter 1

The status of assessment in the visual arts in the United States

Stanley S. Madeja, Northern Illinois University, Dekalb, Illinois, USA

Abstract

The author gives an overview of the history of assessment in art education in the United States, intending to improve assessment in art education through a rigorous review of current practices. The evaluation of results in art education is discussed within the context of assessment practices in other disciplines. The work of institutions and organizations as well as individual experts influencing education in and through the arts is critically reviewed and consequences of policies are reviewed in the context of international research. The historical overview concludes with an introduction to current good practices and suggestions about the improvement of assessment in art education to strengthen the position of this important area of human experience in education.

Introduction

I am celebrating my 53rd year as an arts education professional by reviewing a century of developments in assessment methodology for visual arts education. This chapter is a review and documentation of the ebb and flow of evaluation and assessment projects and programs in the visual arts in the United States and of the positioning of visual arts within that enterprise. To borrow a metaphor from the distinguished philosopher Mortimer Adler biography I am taking "A Look in the Rearview Mirror". During the past half century I was directly or indirectly involved in the research, design, implementation, and evaluation of visual art assessment strategies and curriculum design. I have been fortunate in my career to have a strong teaching background at all levels of instruction. My teaching experience has been coupled with administrative appointments in the arts at the university level as a dean of visual and performing arts college. I have represented our federal government as the Visual Arts Research Specialist with the US Office of Education, and served as a vice president of an educational research and development laboratory and as chairman of the boards of directors of visual and performing arts non-profit organizations. I have been a teacher in the public schools, a college professor of art, as well as, a working artist. Thus, my "rearview" reflections of the initiatives in research and development that are described in this chapter come from a long and varied journey.

The data that I acquired from those experiences are used to make recommendations and generalizations about the status of visual arts assessment in the United States and to make recommendations and suggestions as how we can assess the visual arts education of every child. The opinions and recommendations presented here are my own.

Testing and evaluation in American public schools and in higher education have become a major public issue in the United States. State legislatures and Congress are being held accountable for the condition and quality of American education at every level. The public sector in every state is committed to support education through taxes, which continue to increase. Hence, the demand for accountability has increased in order to answer the following two questions: what are our students learning? Moreover: are the high costs of education justified? Measurement and assessment programs in education are now being developed to answer these questions and to justify the investment of public and private monies in education at an ever increasing rate. Further they are being developed to answer these questions and warrant that the investment of public and private monies in education, at an ever increasing rate, is justified.

Assessment in education at all levels, including the universities, is a unique problem in the United States. The accountability for education is not mandated at the national level. The Congress of the United States and the executive branch of the government headed by the president has no constitutional authority to regulate education. The constitution clearly defines and limits the powers of the federal government. The education of the populace in the fifty states of the Republic is not mentioned. By this constitutional omission the states inherit responsibility for the education of the citizens within their boundaries. Consequently, there is a great deal of variance in the design and make-up of the public and private educational systems in each of the states.

Independent and often autonomous school districts also influence the diverse nature of the American education system. Such districts are the governmental units that control the local educational mission, policies, and resource allocation. School districts vary in size and geographic areas. The United States has 98,000 public schools and 14,000 school districts. All school districts within each state's boundaries are responsible to a state department of education for standards, curriculum, assessment design, and fiscal responsibility. The state provides monies to support the school districts. Each school district, in turn, has responsibility for providing additional funds for the education of the students within their boundaries. The rationale for this was the rejection of national educational initiatives that would infringe on the local control of the school districts. The relevance of this structure of government to assessment is that each state has control of divisions within the various state departments of education that administer testing programs assessing the effectiveness of public-school districts. This state-based structure poses a significant problem for standardizing curricula in academic areas. It also accounts for tremendous variance in the quality of education delivered by the individual school districts. Given the structural constraints of the American educational system, it is very difficult to develop visual arts instrumentation addressing the diverse populations and ideologies represented in American schools.

The National Art Education Association and a number of State Departments of Education have established standards and defined outcomes for art programs. Furthermore, artists, art teachers, college instructors, district and state arts administrators differ in their interpretations of available guidelines and content models. The body politic in each state or district defines the content for the art curriculum. This variance in each state is the greatest deterrent to developing effective national assessment instruments in the visual arts.

Visual arts as general education

Providing a liberal education in and about the visual arts for every American child seems to be of secondary importance to the public. There are a number of advocacy groups working for parity of the arts in general education. At the state level, the Illinois Arts Alliance is a very powerful and active advocacy group for the arts and arts education. In 2005, the Alliance conducted a survey of administrators, principals, and superintendents in the state about the status of the arts in their curriculums. The study reinforced that parents, the corporate community, governing agencies, and school administrators do not advocate for the arts. Conversely, at the national level, Americans for the Arts is very active in arts advocacy. The National Art Education Association (NAEA), under new dynamic leadership, is dedicated to making a strong case for high-quality arts education for all American children. NAEA has joined with other arts organizations to craft unified policy recommendations for pending federal legislation. This consortium of organizations is also crafting a skills map in aligning the arts with broader challenges in education.

Since the 1980s, art programs in America have been significantly diminished. During these 30 years, schools have gone through economic crises which haves culminated in our current, major economic downturn. There has also been a shift in the organization of elementary and secondary education with a movement away from junior high schools towards the formation of middle schools. For most of the last century, the visual arts, music, home economics, and industrial arts were still a significant part of junior high school in the seventh, eighth, and ninth grades. During the last three decades, however, under the middle school model, instructional time has been significantly reduced in the visual arts and music. Home economics and industrial arts have been eliminated entirely. In 1956, I started my art-teaching career in the Minneapolis Public Schools in a junior high school. At that time, the seventh and eighth grade students received one semester of instruction (18 weeks) in art. For ninth grade students, visual art was an elective course of study. A student could, therefore, enroll for the entire 36-week school year in a visual arts class. Currently, in middle schools, art has either been eliminated from the curriculum, or reduced to six to eight weeks of instruction in the sixth or seventh grade. There are no elective courses offered in the eighth grade in most middle school programs. The instructional time a student spends in the visual arts in school has been tragically diminished. This contributes to excluding the visual arts from state required courses and, consequently, in state assessment programs.

School districts are competing with one another for monies from federal, state, and local governmental agencies. Like the old city-states of Europe, the school district is an island unto itself but remains subject to dictates from the local, state, and federal level for funding. Each school district is in a public relations race to become the best school system in its region, state, or the nation. Schools are measured by their performance on standardized tests. The number one ranking goes to the system with the highest test scores. School report cards are commonplace. Test scores are TV specials, front-page newspaper articles, and the subjects of blog postings on the Internet. The testing race has accelerated in the last decade; unfortunately, the visual arts, for the most part, have been left out. Only about 20% of the states are actively participating in the arts assessment program of the federal government's No Child Left Behind programs. The other states have no visual arts assessment program.

What follows is a review of attempts to gain content consensus for the arts in our schools' curricula and strategies for strengthening the positioning of the arts curriculum in general education. In the last century, there have been a number of programs, projects, advocacy groups, and foundations that have attempted to correct the imbalance and benign neglect of the arts in the curriculum.

The arts and humanities as general education

In 1960, the John F. Kennedy administration recognized the arts as being a significant part of American life by appointing August Heckscher to the first federal, high-level arts post – Special Council on the Arts to the President. Unlike European countries, which have a Minister of Culture, the arts have no representation within the president's cabinet. In 1963, the US Office of Education, now the Department of Education, established the Arts and Humanities Program. Around the same time, private foundations began advocating for the inclusions of the arts in the education of every child. The US Congress, with the leadership of Connecticut Senator Claiborne Pell created the National Endowment for the Arts (NEA). The agency is responsible for the national welfare of arts and culture, but does not have the resources or status of European ministries of culture. The National Endowment for the Arts cooperated with the Office of Education's Arts and Humanities Program in funding various programs for research and development in the visual arts. The Arts and Humanities Program concentrated primarily on educational research grants in arts and humanities education. The NEA focused on supporting state arts councils, arts organizations, and the artistic community. Their major educational program was to establish the Artist in Schools program. The private foundations, such as the Rockefeller Foundation, Rockefeller Brothers Fund, The Ford Foundation, and the JDR 3rd Fund also invested significant resources towards grants for arts education programs.

Arts and humanities program of the US Office of Education

President John F. Kennedy, in 1960, appointed Francis Keppel as Commissioner of the Office of Education. This was the agency that controlled federal programs in education. Keppel used the recommendations of the Heckscher Report to establish a new arts and humanities unit in the Division of Educational Research by allocating $700,000 in funds for the fiscal year 1964. Kathryn Bloom was appointed director and played a major role in the success of the Arts and Humanities Program over the next several years. Harland Hoffa provided a summary in 1992 of the accomplishments of this investment in arts education programs. He wrote:

> Jones and Murphy compiled a list of the titles of 185 research projects that were completed between 1961 and 1972, the overwhelming majority of which are dated between 1964 and 1968. Almost two-thirds of those projects were in art education and music education, with 61 in each discipline, and the remaining 63 were divided between other categories, which ranged from architectural education (1) to aesthetic education and interdisciplinary projects (14 between them) to humanities (17) and theatre education (19). The roster of those conducting that research is, however, even more impressive than the number of projects that were involved. It includes *Nelson Goodman (Harvard), Frank Barron (California), Irvin Child (Yale), Jacob Getzels (Chicago)* and *Rudolf Arnheim (Harvard)*, to name only a few of the scholars from fields other than arts education, plus a real Who's Who of researchers from within the arts education disciplines themselves. In addition, AHP was directly or indirectly involved in several long-term research programs, most of which outlived it by a considerable period. These included *CEMREL's Aesthetic Education Program, ETS's Advanced Placement Testing in Art and Music, Project Zero at Harvard,* and the *IMPACT Project* which tested an arts based curriculum in school settings ranging from rural Alabama to suburban Los Angeles to inner-city Philadelphia and demonstrated its effectiveness by improved learning in all subjects. Murphy and Jones estimated that no more than fifteen to twenty percent of the research AHP supported could be called "basic research" though, clearly, the work of those behavioral scientists who are noted above fall readily into that category. Developmental activities such as conferences that identified critical research issues accounted for about one-third of the total and the remainder, were "curriculum development" or "applied research" projects of one sort or another. (Hoffa, 1992, p. 62)[1]

The aesthetic education program

The largest investment the Office of Education made was a curriculum effort including all the arts called the Aesthetic Education Program. The Arts and Humanities programs supported a conference at the Pennsylvania State University (Mattil, 1966) initiated by Harlan Hoffa, the art specialist in 1965 for the A&H program. Because of that activity Jerome Hausman, Manual Barken, and Laura Chapman offered a proposal for a major research effort that included all the arts. The initial proposal was for two universities in the Midwest – the University of Illinois and Ohio State University – for a research and development Center for the Arts. This proposal was rejected but the initiators were asked to submit a second proposal for a curriculum development program that included all the arts and which would assist schools in providing a liberal arts education in aesthetic education for the elementary and secondary schools. The Aesthetic Education Program (AEP) emerged from that request and A&H funded Phase I for any three-year period starting in 1967 to develop the Guidelines for Aesthetic Education (Barkan, Chapman, and Kerns, 1970). The project was supported by The Ohio State University and the Arts and Humanities Program of the US Office of Education. The contracting agency for the project was Central Midwest Educational Laboratory (CEMREL, Inc.), a federally funded educational laboratory in St Louis, Missouri which is also supported by the Divisions of Laboratory of the US Office of Education. Phase II of the program concentrated on designing a curriculum with electronic media-based educational materials that represented all of the arts: visual arts, music, theatre, dance, and literature (Madeja and Onuska, 1978).

The Arts and Humanities Program of the US Office of Education encouraged the development of interdisciplinary arts programs. The office established a policy that favoured grants integrating one or more of the arts. The Aesthetic Education Program promoted the idea of the arts as an area of study. That concept was similar when the social sciences combined American and world history, government studies, geography, and (sometimes) economics into what we now call Social Studies. In the same way, I advocated integrating the arts into a singular curriculum, and encouraged schools to consider the arts as a core area of study. I also recommended introductory, arts integrated courses at the university level. My ideas, however, were not well received by the individual arts disciplines. Perhaps, historic territorial dogmatism prevailed. Undaunted, I continued to focus on the mutual benefits of integrated disciplines. I believed linking all the arts together was a strategy that was more likely to be adopted as part of a basic curriculum. Furthermore, the arts, as a whole, were stronger together when advocating for their position in the liberal arts curriculum. I also believed and demonstrated within the aesthetic education curriculum that the arts could integrate the disciplines easily in the early grades, K-3. Students would become aware of their differences in the intermediate grades, and the various disciplines would emerge with their own identities in the middle school and high school programs (Madeja and Onuska, 1978). In conjunction with designing integrated curricula, the AEP program also conducted significant studies and implemented pioneering authentic assessment techniques in classroom settings. They are described later in this chapter.

Arts in education program of JDR 3rd

John D. Rockefeller III, initiated a campaign comparable to the Arts and Humanities Program. His, and other large private foundations, had a sincere interest in bringing the arts into liberal education. He also had an interest in Asian arts and endowed the Asian

Cultural Program as part of the JDR 3rd Fund. The two programs were a personal interest to Mr Rockefeller, but had no formal connection to the Rockefeller Foundation, which he also chaired. It is the mission of the JDR 3rd Fund that is most relevant to this chapter. Katherine Bloom, Director, describes the purposes and activities of the Fund:

In 1963, the Rockefeller Brothers Fund, a non-profit foundation, asked the group of prominent citizens from all parts of the country to join in this study of the future development and support of the performing arts in the United States. The study was conducted as a panel report on the future of this theater, dance, and music in America under the chairmanship of John D. Rockefeller 3rd. The report that resulted, "The Performing Arts: Problems and Prospects", was published in 1965. The purpose of the study was to present a thoughtful assessment of the place of the performing arts in our national life and to identify the impediments to their greater welfare and to their wider enjoyment. As such, it was not intended to address specifically the issue of the arts in education. However, as testimony was presented, education and its role in making the arts central to American life were emphasized time after time. As a result, the report contained a chapter regarding the importance, families, and arts institutions in helping young people develop an understanding and enjoyment of the arts. A remark made by one panel member caught Mr. Rockefeller's attention. It was that perhaps no more than one or two percent of the total population nationally was actively involved and interested in the arts.

During 1966, following the publication of "The Panel Report", John D. Rockefeller 3rd convened three exploratory meetings to discuss the feasibility of establishing several pilot projects to determine whether or not the arts could be made a part of the education of every child in entire school systems. The number of participants attending each meeting was not large, but they represented a wide range of interests, experience, and commitment of school administrators and teachers, concerned citizens, persons associated with public and private agencies, and representatives of professional organizations. (Bloom, 1980, pp. 3–5)

The report noted that the arts are not considered as part of liberal education in the elementary and secondary schools and that they play only a secondary role in liberal arts education at the college level. The report advocated that our schools make comprehensive arts programs available to every student. Many schools at that time had excellent art and music programs but did not make available subjects such as dance, theatre, poetry, film study, architecture, and literary criticism. It also advocated utilizing the services of arts organizations as primary resources for the arts in general education. Relationships between artists' organizations and school systems to promote a comprehensive arts program are encouraged. The first arts in education program was introduced in the University City Schools, Missouri in 1968 (Madeja 1973).

Gaining national consensus in the arts

The Aspen Institute Conferences

However cogent were the arguments and rationale for integrating the arts they were not readily accepted by the field. With the support of the National Institute of Education CEMREL sponsored four major conferences at the Aspen Institute in the 1970s on various issues relating to arts education. The first conference was in 1976, titled *Arts and Aesthetics: An Agenda for the Future* (Madeja, 1977). The purpose of the conference was to address two major national issues in the arts and aesthetics education in the United States:

1. To create and recommend a national research and development agenda for arts and aesthetic education.
2. To consider how a national research and development centre in the arts might be configured and the type of research that would be conducted.

At that time, the federal government was supporting the development of subject area research centres. The centres were discipline oriented in the sciences, psychology, mathematics, reading, and literature. The response of the conference participants was a negative reaction to the policies established by the Arts and Humanities Program favouring interdisciplinary programs. The national arts organizations, such as the National Art Education Association and the Music Educators Association, were opposed to these ideas because they thought it would harm and minimize their positioning in the public schools. This was especially true of the music ensemble directors who were interested in engaging students at early ages into chorale groups and with musical instruments for bands or orchestras. Theatre, dance, and literature were in favour of integrating curriculum at all levels of instruction with the other art forms. This discourse continued throughout most of the 1970s and was not a positive influence on the field itself. It was most evident when the publication entitled *Coming to Your Senses* (Hanks and Quinn, 1977) was launched by a nonpartisan cadre of influential artists, community leaders, and philanthropic groups. David Rockefeller Jr was the convener and director of the project. He and a distinguished group of scholars in the arts and humanities conducted hearings throughout the United States about the role of the arts in education. How, they asked, could the arts be better served and how could they become an integral part of the liberal education of every student? Because of the rejection of these efforts, mainly from people in the visual arts and music, Mr Rockefeller lost interest and assumed his uncle's role as head of the Rockefeller Foundation: an ally lost.

Further conferences were held at the Aspen Institute: *The Arts, Cognition, and Basic Skills* (Madeja, 1978) and *The Teaching Process and the Arts and Aesthetics* (Kneiter and Stallings, 1979). The fourth conference was entitled *Curriculum and Instruction: The Arts and Aesthetics* (Engel and Hausman, 1981).[2]

Gaining consensus in the Congress of the United States and from the arts associations

A negative attitude towards federal monies supporting the arts in education is another example of resistance to bringing the arts together in a curriculum. John Bradamis was an influential Speaker of the House from Indiana in the Congress of the United States and an advocate for the arts in that body. There was a great deal of interest in the arts community to gain federal financial support of an agency such as the National Science Foundation, which promoted research and development in science and mathematics. The arts community was asked to submit a proposal for this type of governmental unit. Bradamis became frustrated with the program because the arts could not come together as an area of study and articulate programs that the federal government would support to improve arts education in the schools and universities. He was interested in legislation similar to the National Science Foundation support for the sciences and mathematics programs in the public schools until he left office.[3]

The arts associations changed their minds about interdisciplinary programs and formed, in 1994, a consortium of visual arts, music, and dance and issued a report titled *National Standards for Arts Education*. The project was commissioned by the Department of Education, a federal agency, to define what every young American should know and be able to do in the arts. The final report defines the standards, outcomes, and content for each of the arts disciplines. Current practice by the associations now supports national standards for arts education (National Standards for Arts Education, 1994).

However federal support for education had a negative effect on the organizational structure of the various state departments of education. The Arts and Humanities Program within the Office of Education, which represented the arts disciplines at the federal level, no longer exists. The Office of Education also had subject area specialists in other disciplines as well and they have been eliminated. The states followed the federal staffing pattern for state departments of education and eliminated state directors in the visual arts, music, and literary arts. In the 1980s the state subject area positions were eliminated and replaced with positions that related to federal initiatives, such as early childhood education. The arts have suffered dearly because of this reorganization and re-ordering of priorities of federal funding. In the opinion of the author, this change in staffing pattern has had a devastating effect at the state level on art curriculum development and arts assessment.

National assessment of educational progress

Currently, there are two initiatives supported by federal monies in assessment of the arts: the National Assessment of Educational Progress and the No Child Left Behind Act (NCLB, 2001). Commissioner Francis Keppel was interested in the larger issue of developing instrumentation that maintains assessment of what America's students know and can do in various subject areas. In 1969, he established the National Assessment of Educational Progress (NAEP) with the following mandate:

The National Assessment of Educational Progress is the only nationally representative and continuing assessment of what America's students know and can do in various subject areas. A report card was first initiated as a testing program to the nation's schools in 1969. Since then, assessments have been conducted periodically in reading, mathematics, science, writing, history, geography and other fields. The arts music and the visual arts are considered to be part of "other fields". The testing in this area is performed every 10 years. In 1988, Congress established a national assessment governing board to formulate policy guidelines for the program. The board defines appropriate student performance levels for developing assessment objectives and test specifications through a national consensus approach for designing the assessment methodology. It also develops guidelines for disseminating the NAEP results and for developing standards and procedures for interstate, regional and national comparisons determining the appropriateness of the test items and ensure that they are free from bias and for taking actions to improve the form and use of national conducted. (Askew, Persky and Sandene, 1999)

It was the first time that the federal government attempted to assess the conditions of American education and it was the first time that the arts were included. The NAEP engaged Brent Wilson (1972) as their national assessment director. The Educational Testing Service was the contracting corporation to administer the project. In 1971, they reported the following art objectives defined by 12 distingished art educators who made up the advisory committee to the project committee:

- To perceive and respond to elements of art.
- To recognize and accept art as an important realm of experience and participate in activties related to art.
- To know about art.
- To form reasoned, critical judgments about the significance and qualiity of works of art. (Wilson, 1972)

These four objectives were defined in more detail in the report and became the content for the development by Wilson and the advisory committee for the NAPE instrumentation. The arts have been included in each phases of the assessment. David Burton, Read Dicket and Robert Sabol (1997) have conducted analyses of each of the NAEP's visual arts testing efforts. The most recent assessment analysis was conducted in 2009 (Arts Partnership, 2009).

No Child Left Behind Act (NCLB) of 2001

On 8 January 2002, President George W. Bush signed the No Child Left Behind Act of 2001, pre-authorizing the elementary and secondary education act of 1965 and modifying the 1994 re-authorization known as the No Child Left Behind Act (NCLB) of 2001.

The legislation has four basic principles: (1) stronger accountability for results; (2) increased flexibility and local control; (3) expanded options for parents; and (4) emphasis on methods that have proven to work.

Laura Chapman (2005) reviewed the legislation and enlisted its implications for arts education in the United States. She states:

> The arts were initially included in NCLB. In 2003 earmarked funds were cut on the grounds that the Bush administration had a policy of terminating small category programs with limited impact in order to fund higher priorities. [...] Funds were limited to $30 million and focused on programs that integrate the parts into the curriculum; one of the several acknowledgements that the arts are not really part of the regular core program curriculum. The law also authorizes arts education activities in research; model school based arts education programs; development of statewide tests; in-service programs; and unspecified collaborations among federal agencies of arts and arts education. (Chapman, 2005, pp. 6–16)

Laura Chapman's article was accurate in its predictions that legislation would have a negative effect on positioning the visual arts in public education. Robert Sabol (2010) of Purdue University has conducted the most recent study of the effects of this legislation on the visual arts. He surveyed a random sample of 3,000 art educators from elementary, middle, and secondary schools, from supervision and administration in higher education, and from museum education. All 50 states and the District of Colombia were represented. The data was released in February 2010. In the area of teaching loads, there were limited negative consequences because of the legislation. However, the legislation also created a number of negative effects on art education programs in the area of scheduling, increased workflow, funding, and the work environment for art teachers.

The general response participants had about the overall affect of NCLB on their programs was not positive. Art educators in this study, as a group, have negative attitudes about the impact NCLB has had on a number of essential aspects of their programs. Collectively, these negative effects have damaged the scope and quality of art education in the United States. Moreover, they appear to be widespread and present to varying degrees, at all instructional levels, within public schools. Many respondents suggested that instead of improving the status of art education, NCLB has contributed to furthering its marginalization and diminishing the status of art education.

Sabol's survey did report some positive impact of the legislation, which may assist art education in improving on the problem of gaining consensus about what-should be taught. He states:

The No Child Left Behind legislation emphasized national and state standards in the curriculum. 43% of states reported spending increased time on building or revising a curriculum. 38% increased emphasis on higher order thinking skills. A bothering finding was that 5% reported a decrease in studio art time and CLE content in their art classes. Only 19% of the sample population reported no changes in curriculum. (Sabol, 2010).

Robert Sabol also comments on the overall effects and challenges that the No Child Left Behind legislation poses for art education in the United States:

> NCLB has caused the American public to focus its attention on the purposes of education in the United States and its expectations for the education systems in the nation. As the era of NCLB comes to a close with the reauthorization of the Elementary and Secondary Education Act, the continued inclusion of the arts as one of the core subjects is more important than ever to have in the legislation as the nation moves forward on a renewed agenda for improving America's schools. While the arts have been included among the core subjects in this important legislation, they have yet to realize parity in the curriculum with other core subjects. It is hoped that the next reauthorization will not only affirm the importance of the arts as a core subject, but will find ways to support the allocation of federal, state, and local resources to fully realize this important vision for all students. (Sabol, 2010, p. 6.)

In summary, the major problems facing arts educators in their attempt to address the marginalization of their disciplines are:

- The responsibility for education is not mandated at the national level.
- The lack of an accepted curriculum structure, which may guide us in the development of a qualitative art curriculum and evaluation instruments.
- An intellectual community who is not willing to become arts advocates and validate programs.
- Currently, programs are teacher-centred, while institutionally-based efforts have proven more effective.
- Today, individual school districts maintain control of program standards and the design/content of assessment instruments; thus, neglecting that state standards, assessment models, and state administered tests give relevance to programs and influence decision makers.

It is evident that in the United States if we are to be successful in an advocacy effort and assessment of visual learning, we must first define what we are teaching, i.e. the content of the curriculum. Further, it is imperative that we have support and consensuses by art educators on the content taught, K-12. The current initiatives by the National Art Education Association are promising first steps uniting the leadership in the field on these issues. Although, from the above, it would appear that assessment in the visual arts is a contemporary dilemma, arts educators have periodically attacked the same problems in the past. In fact, there is a long history of the arts contributing to assessment initiatives in American schooling.

What follows is a chronicle of these assessment projects and test designs in the visual arts in the United States. A review at this point reminds the reader that there was, indeed, a rich body of research in assessment of the visual arts in the last century; however, it has, for the most part, disappeared. Therefore, it behooves us to look to the past to be ready for the future.

Standardized tests in the visual arts: A historical review

Research and development in evaluation in the visual arts in United States is not solely a current event. Surprisingly, we can trace the development of tests in the visual arts over 100-year development cycles. During the early part of the 20th century, the emphasis on scientific methods and research became very influential in many areas of education, and the visual arts were no exception. In general, standardized testing was motivated by the economic and social needs of the country. In the 19th century, the increasing industrialization of the country resulted in the need for an educated workforce. The visual arts were introduced as part of school programs in the eastern schools to address industrial needs. Student interest in art schools was impressive. *The American Art Annual* listed 318 art schools in 46 states. Thirty-three of the schools were in New York City. Total national enrollment in art schools was 25,123. (Levy, 1901)

Principally, mechanical drawing and freehand drawing were introduced as part of the elementary schooling in the latter years and in the junior high school. Later, elective programs at the secondary level were initiated in commercial art, anticipating the needs of designers, illustrators, draftsmen, and photographers. Separate vocational schools were oriented towards vocational preparation of students for the work force.

Standardized tests in the measurement of artistic abilities

In 1933, Madeline Kinter conducted a survey of scientific studies in the graphic arts of existing art measurement devices and instrumentation in the visual arts in the United States. In her introduction to the study she states:

> To some, attempt to measure artistic ability may seem incongruous, or a creative spark at the core of such ability may or forever elude the approach of solid scientific devices seeking to measure it. [...] Admittedly, there may be certain attributes of artistic ability that can be measured. There is no question, however, that individuals differ to produce and to appreciate works of artistic merit, and you will agree that those who are talented should receive suitable training. In so far as education fails to discover and to develop the greatest gifts in the possession of its pupils it falls short of its possible contributions to society. (Kinter, 1933, pp. 6–7)

She goes on to pose questions defining traditional beliefs in 1933.

- To what extent are people artistic or not artistic by nature?
- Are there any basic principles of artistic merit, and if so what are they?
- Is artistic appreciation esoteric and confined to few, or is it the faculty which many can acquire?
- Can the teaching of art be standardized?
- What is the psychological validity represented by the phrase "artistic temperament"?
- Is artistic aptitude relatively fixed and stable or can it be altered by intensive training?
- Is the concept of fixed talent, based perhaps erroneously on the scriptural parable, correct?
- To what extent is artistic production emotional and to what extent intellectual?

But she goes on to note that questions like this cannot be decided on the basis of personal or prolonged speculative discussions. They will be decided only on the basis described in her survey (Kinter, 1933 pp. 6–7).

The tests in the survey are divided into three categories: art appreciation, art aptitude, and drawing abilities. The survey is a comprehensive documentation of research and the development of assessment instrumentation in the first 33 years of the 20th century.[4]

The sections in the report for collateral literature and further experiments addressed ongoing projects or programs, which use the test or conducted experiments about the test. The distinction in both surveys between published and unpublished tests, now called fugitive documents, is important to note. Publishers specializing in test development disseminated published tests along with research information about the tests, such as normative data. They also distributed use patterns by professionals in the field in educational institutions, corporations, and governmental agencies. The mass distribution of published tests reached larger audiences and provided larger samples and normative data. Kinter lists 75 entries in her annotated bibliography of related subjects and visual art tests. What follows is a description of the type of tests in each of three categories: drawing scales, tests of art appreciation, and art aptitude tests. Included are descriptions of the type of studies that were conducted during that time frame. Madeja (1959) updated Kinter's study, which contained descriptions of 15 art tests. Using the same format, Madeja identified 12 additional tests developed after 1933. The 27 tests are listed in Table 1.

The arts are suitably concerned about how we develop artistically and aesthetically. Each of the art fields has taken the most obvious and observable phenomenon within them to study and categorize. In the visual arts, the visual statement by the child, the painting, or drawing, has been the most researched area. Numerous scholars have all created, in one form or another, developmental levels or categories for children's artwork. Notably included are: Betty Lark-Horowitz, Hilda Present Lewis, and Mark Luca in 1967, and Victor Lowenfeld in 1955. The stages of drawing categorized by Lowenfeld – scribbling, pre-schematic, schematic, realism, and pseudo-naturalistic – still predominated the literature. While Lowenfeld

Table 1: Art Test Reviewed in the Kinter and Madeja Studies

Tests	Year	Published	Type of test
Bully-Burt	1933	Yes	Appreciation
Bully-Burt Picture Post Card Test	1936	Yes	Appreciation
Christian- Korwoski Art Appreciation Test	1929	Yes	Appreciation
Graves Design Judgment Test	1946	Yes	Appreciation
Goublomme Scale	1935	No	Scale
Drawing Aptitude Tests	1940	Yes	Aptitude
Horn Art Aptitude Inventory	1944	No	Aptitude
Kelly-Lemos, Art Appreciation Test	1929	No	Appreciation
Kerrs Scale	1933	No	Scale
Kline Carey Scale Part 1	1922	Yes	Scale
Kline Carey Scale Part 11	1933	Yes	Scale
Knauber Art Vocabulary Test	1932	Yes	Appreciation
Knauber- Pressy Art Ability Test	1927	Yes	Aptitude
Lowerenz Test of Fundamental Ability in Art	1927	Yes	Aptitude
McAdory Art Test	1929	Yes	Appreciation
McCarthy Drawing Ocala	1942	Yes	Scale
Meier Art Judgment Test	1940	Yes	Appreciation
Meier-Seashore, Art Judgment Test	1929	Yes	Appreciation
Paulson, Test of Artistic Ability	1932	NO	Aptitude
Pecks Scale	1936	NO	Scale
Providence Drawing Scale	1928	NO	Scale
Seven Modern Paintings	1939	NO	Appreciation
Smith-Fyler Tests of Sensitivity to Art Values	1940	NO	Appreciation
Tiebout Scale	1936	NO	Scale
Thorndike Drawing Scale	1913	Yes	Scale
Whitfords Drawing Test	1920	No	Scale
Varnum Selective Art Aptitude Test	1940	Yes	Aptitude

Sources: Kinter (1933, p. 117), Madeja (1959, p. 100).

and others addressed children making art, comparatively few studies were available on categorizing children's responses to art. David Ecker, David Perkins, Ralph Smith and Brent Wilson have, to some extent, started to categorize the student's verbal response to an art object or event, but any developmental schema for verbal response to the work was still forthcoming in the late 1970s. The need for better understanding of the total process of artistic development was one of the needs at that time, which would contribute to the larger domain of human development.

The question was: how might we go about gaining this understanding in the arts and what areas of study should be developed to broaden our knowledge base and make the linkages to the broader domain of human development? We propose that there are three generalized areas be studied that contribute to methodology for describing aesthetic and artistic development, and further relate these categories to human development. They are: aesthetic perception, the critical process, and knowledge about the arts. All contribute to the creative or artistic process and are essential to human development. An initial inquiry into this domain of aesthetic responses to artworks led to a description of the end state of the able responder.

Authentic (non-standardized) evaluation methods

Authentic evaluation methods, such as observation techniques as a research methodology, have some distinct advantages for evaluation in the arts: they are characteristic of a more humanistic and less mechanistic approach to describing the phenomena; they are compatible with the diversity of the arts experience (which tends to be non-linear). Because observation reports are more descriptive of a non-linear process or event they are based on primary data – student work – rather than on secondary data – student performance on a test. Thus, they provide concrete examples of the actual experience while taking a neutral stance as to the worth or value of the experience. On the other hand, there are some distinct disadvantages and shortcomings to the techniques of descriptive evaluation: the methods are non-standardized, therefore subject to the criticism of bias and non-objectivity; they are subject to personal interpretation, so observers have to be trained; and generalizing the data is potentially suspect because of the collection methods. In our work in the Aesthetic Education Program, during classroom observations and through the evaluation of the instructional materials, we were able to develop methodologies and systematic approaches, which resulted in quantitative data.

The most important objective for future development of classroom observation is to be able to provide convincing evidence that learning is taking place. Therefore, *controlled observation techniques that result in quantifiable evidence* will be the paradigm shift necessary to make these techniques applicable to current demands for hard data. The future provides opportunities to comfortably live in both worlds – authentic assessment and standardized testing. We need standardized measurements in the visual arts that measure content of curriculum and assess student progress over time. The scholars in art education should conduct research on the qualitative aspects of the instruments used in standardized testing. Alternative assessment devices, such as portfolios as described in the last section of this chapter, should be integrated with standardized measures in order to gain a comprehensive view of students' capabilities and achievements.

Studies in alternatives to standardized tests

Portfolio assessment has been used as an exit evaluation strategy at Northern Illinois University (NIU) for a number of years. "Portfolio" has been traditionally used in drawing and design studios and as a criterion for graduation in art education. At NIU, we have been conducting electronic applications of portfolios as primal assessment devices that complement testing programs. They provide additional information on student capabilities and interests. Our research has demonstrated that elementary and secondary students are also capable of designing and recording their academic performance utilizing existing software programs; thus, enhancing their portfolios. Student participation in the evaluation process is a positive step forward, and the use of electronic portfolios has reinforced the history, accuracy, relevance, and validity of student achievement, from the college applicant to the doctoral candidate.

In the visual arts, we can reproduce images at the same resolution as the original works; thus, creating an authentic technological alternative to standardized test scores when determining academic standing and student competencies. The wedding of traditional assessments and technology reveal a more accurate image of a student's longitudinal progress and knowledge in visualization. The International Baccalaureate Program has, for a number of decades, used portfolios to track student proficiencies in visual arts courses and is an excellent model for the E-portfolio concept. Douglas Boughton has done pioneering work in the United States with the International Baccalaureate Programs in the use of portfolios in high school art programs.

Assessing the Expressive Learning Project

The most recent effort I have been involved in has been developing alternative assessment strategies that provide authentic assessment programs from preschool to the Ph.D. level. My recent work in collaboration with Charles Dorn and Robert Sabol in a joint program of Northern Illinois University, Purdue University, and Florida State University also explores these strategies. It defines the direction that I support and advocate for assessment in the visual arts. The research project which was supported by the National Endowment for the Arts for a three-year period concluded with the publication, *Assessing Expressive Learning: A practical guide for teacher directed authentic assessment in K-12 visual arts education* (Dorn, Madeja, and Sabol, 2004). It expounds upon a number of findings that relate to the use of electronic portfolios as a methodology and instrumentation for documenting a student's progress over time. The quantum leaps that the technology has taken in just the last five years further enhance the possibilities for future research and development in this area. The study tested the feasibility of using different electronic formats for the development of portfolios at the elementary, secondary, undergraduate, and graduate college levels. The study suggested a number of generalizations about using electronic data collection methods, including existing software programs. All of which to collect, organize, analyse, interpret, and assess student performance in the visual arts, especially in the studio areas. The results suggest the following:

- Student at all levels are able to organize and collect data electronically
- Electronic case studies presented in our research project further demonstrate that expressive learning can be measured in ways other than used in traditional testing programs.
- Expressive learning can be quantified.

Our research project presented a number of electronic case studies and suggested several generalizations about using electronic data collection methods, using existing software programs. As part of a case study in the Expressive Learning Project, Karen Popovich demonstrates how e-portfolios can be used in the classroom. The following are her reflections on using electronic portfolios in art classes at the elementary and secondary level:

- Assessment is a natural and integral component to the teaching and learning process.
- Critical thinking and reflection are vital components in integrating curriculum and assessment.
- It is imperative that students have time and opportunities to reflect on content and processes.
- Electronic portfolios and process journals are a key element of my middle school program.
- I have had many opportunities to share this experience with many of my colleagues.
- The more meaningful the projects, the stronger the reflective writing statements.
- Provide authentic assessment of student learning. (Popovich, 2006, p. 36)

Popovich's research validates that electronic portfolios can be used at any level of instruction, starting in the lower elementary grades and continuing through graduate education. Portfolio assessment activities can be designed so that each student's artistic development can be measured over time and can be compared with other students in the class or the school. This provides the possibility for normative hard data that can describe a student's performance in specific areas such as drawing ability Popovich (2006).

The work of Shei-chau Wang illustrates the importance of program evaluation at all levels of learning in the field of visual arts. As a graduate student at the University of Northern Illinois, his research was included in the authentic assessment project by Dorn, Madeja, and Sabol (2004). Wang proposed the integration of electronic evaluation strategies into courses in drawing and art education. Today, Wang teaches courses in drawing and in the evaluation of student art. He has incorporated innovative ideas for electronic portfolios and assessment using imaging technologies. Originally, because of the limitations of the technology, he used websites for storage of digital images. In the 1990s, he pioneered creating websites for each student so they could save their images and PowerPoint presentations. A decade later, we now have less cumbersome methods to store the images. Wang provides a structure in which the student can visually model information into a product that can be stored in portable hard drives and can be transmitted worldwide. This enabled him (and the student) to track improvements in visualization and drawing skills from the beginning of the class to the end. He can also quantify the visual artefact, thus translate an assessment of performance and an evaluation of product into a valid grade. Additional benefits of Wang's electronic documentation of student progress are that it aids in his self-evaluation of program effectiveness, and it provides relevant evidence for evaluation from regional accrediting associations, a periodic mandate for all state institutions of higher learning. I, too, have implemented e-portfolios into courses in art and art education.

Measurement of the aesthetic response

In the 1970s, the Department of Education created the National Institute of Education. This became the research and development arm of the Office of Education in our federal government. The two research groups within the United States that were obtaining funds from the National Institute of Education were the Aesthetic Education Program of CEMREL Inc. and Projects Zero at Harvard University, College of Education. David Perkins and Howard Gardner were co-directors of the project, and Stanley Madeja was director of the Aesthetic Education Program. There had been a six-year period of exchange of ideas between these two programs. Perkins and Gardner were presenters at the Aspen research conferences in the 1970s. In 1979, Madeja and Perkins initiated a joint project that would develop a model for aesthetic responses to art forms. The project was conceived to answer a key question about how to sensitively, insightfully, and appreciatively perceive works of art.

Our review of the contemporary psychology of visual perception quickly disclosed that to "see", to perceive, even ordinary and mundane objects is an awesomely complex achievement of the human organism. One of the most rich and subtle episodes of perception to be found by any reasonably sophisticated observer is to encounter a visual, literary, musical, or other work of art. The project goal was to develop a phenomenological account of perceiving the arts, an account that captures something of the character of that experience. The results of the project were reported in a monograph. What follows is a description of the visual arts component of the project (Madeja and Perkins, 1982). Analysis, of course, is closely related to decryption, but implies a number of different ways of responding to the work itself, i.e. a higher order of descriptive discourse. It implies that the sophisticated responder is able to analyse the relationships between the parts of the work and describe their characteristics, and then is able to relate these parts to the characteristics of the whole work. This ability to describe the interaction between the parts and the whole is significant to the end state. The less sophisticated or naive observer or responder might only pay attention to the parts themselves and never discern the total effect or impact of the work. Describing the interrelationships between elements or aesthetic features of the work is a key to the end state.

Aesthetic response theories

These questions would be keystones for the process of analysing the work and would include questions about individual aesthetic features of the work, such as motion, or questions for how the responder might compare this work to other works of art, and what perceptual clues are important for comparative purposes. Further, there would be questions about how one might generalize about the work in the context of other works and draw implications as to its artistic intent, aesthetic significance, and historical relevance. Smith (1968) has characterized analysis as a close look at the details or elements of the components that make up a work. The larger groups are complexes into which they are composed and sustain relationships. "Analysis in art is not a mere enumeration or cataloging of components; it cannot be done in meaningful ways, it seems, without at the same time describing or often characterizing what is singled out for inspection". Thus, Smith has elicited other criteria for the end state, and that is to be able, within analysis, to isolate those key characteristics that may bear further description and, as he terms it, characterization. Smith makes the distinction between description and characterization, using *characterization* whenever aesthetic qualities are pointed out, and *description* to indicate the more literal properties of the objects. Thus, the ability to select those properties of the work that are the key aesthetic features would be essential in the definition of the end state. Smith states that interpretation should be distinguished from analysis. He sees description and analysis being supportive of interpretations of the work itself. He considers interpretation of the work a higher order of analysis and in our definition of the end state, we see the sophisticated viewer as being able to interpret either the whole work or part of it in a variety of ways.

Smith goes on in his article to say

> The connection between interpretation and analysis is often ambiguous and the relationship between the subject matter of representational work and its message or content is even more so. It is probably a good rule to say that a critical response is inadequate if it offers as an interpretation merely a description of subject matter. (Smith, 1968, p. 25)

Thus, we can conclude that in our end state analysis is a higher order of description and it contains interpretive dimensions. Perception, description, and analysis are pre-requisites to judgment, a fourth step in the process of responding. Judgment relates most closely to Perkins's third theme, "accounting for excellence" (Madeja and Perkins, 1982). Probably the most complex part of the end state will be to determine the quality and level of the sophistication of the judgments or evaluations that the sophisticated viewer makes. There is no doubt that judgment is part of each of the other categories. It is sometimes difficult to describe a work without making some sorts of judgment about its content or its aesthetic worth. It is also difficult to exclude judgments from perceptions if we accept them as part of the cognitive process. There are some judgments made in the beginning of perceiving a work as to what it is that you are noticing or choosing to notice. Consequently, rather than simply saying that judgment is a category by itself, we can make distinctions between the types of judgments that would be made, and between what might be considered a simple response versus a more complex response. "I like it" or, "I don't like it" is a simple psychological response. However, characterizing the work as good or bad is more complex. Declaring a work's aesthetic merit or cultural significance requires justification of the first two categories of response and is the most complex cognitive process. If we are dealing with the first category only, liking or disliking a work, it is a judgment of sorts, but, if no reasons are given, it remains nothing more than a psychological report. Thus, there are different levels of sophistication in aesthetic judgments, and one can analyse and even categorize them.

Brent Wilson (1972) in a study of high school students developed a set of categories that he contends distinguishes between adequate and less adequate aesthetic judgmental criteria. He used a review of the literature to develop the criteria, which he applied to the judgments of high school students about works of art. He listed the following categories as criteria:

- Organize – the criteria of unity, coherence, cohesiveness, and complexity.
- Contextualize – the criteria of intensity and vividness.
- Hedonism   the criterion of affective pleasure.
- Communication – the criterion of expressive ability.
- Moral Worth – the criterion of desirable content.
- Originality – the criterion of uniqueness.
- Mimesis – the criterion of correspondence to reality.
- Technical Achievement – the criterion of skill.
- Narrow a Priori – the criterion of intrinsic formal value.
- I Like It – the criterion of personal preference.
- Broom Closet – a category of statements containing no judgmental criteria.

Defining the end state: The performance of the sophisticated responder

The implication for end state would be that the sophisticated viewer would perform in a number of these categories and make arguments and evaluations of the work itself. It would imply some kind of summation of the work in terms of its aesthetic merit. Again, the part/whole relationship becomes a factor in the making of aesthetic judgments. That is, the work could achieve aesthetic merit through its technical competency but be very weak in its expressive characteristics.

Thus, the criteria by which we would judge the sophisticated responder's ability to compare the different features of the work for its aesthetic merits and give adequate reasons for them in defense of their position would be: the discourse itself, how the language is used, how the arguments are presented, the logic or quality of the arguments, and the rationale. End state criteria are established through: the discourse itself, how the language is used, how the arguments are presented, the logic or quality of the arguments, the rationale for the arguments, and other features of aesthetic reasoning.

Ecker (1967), Smith (1967), and Wilson (1972) all agree that judgment is related to the ability to give reasons for opinions, and these reasoned opinions become the criteria for judging the quality and worth of the rudiments that are made. This is probably the least definitive of the categories that one could develop and remains ambiguous for an important reason. In judging works of art, there is no right or wrong answer, and it is difficult and probably unwise to give absolute criteria in talking about the end state for the sophisticated responder. His or her ability to draw upon description, analysis, and interpretation to support aesthetic judgment of the work becomes the overall criterion by which we would want to assess the judgmental aspects. If the first three components of a personal critique are present, usually the fourth, that is, judgment, will logically proceed. If the student is able to perceive those parts which are important, is able to describe them with some sophistication, and is able to develop some analysis of their content, s/he has reached the state of making a judgment by doing a thorough job of the first three categories. The result of the study was a definition of the able responder. The following is a summary of end state characteristics of the able responder:

- The ability to locate and to recognize aesthetic clues through visual and aural perception.
- The ability to pick out the dominant characteristics of the work and establish a relationship between the perceptual clues, the whole work, and its meaning or expressive content.
- The ability to describe a work with depth and breadth of knowledge about the art form.
- The assimilation of different modes in which description can take place (modes here are referential in definition to our model).
- The ability to describe the work in different contexts – a cultural context, historical context, and so on.
- The ability to write a qualitative discourse about a work.
- The ability to analyse relationships between the parts and whole of a given work of art.
- The ability to formulate questions about the work, which elicit discourse, and further, to know a set of questions to ask about a given work.
- The ability to analyse a work and include interpretive dimensions as well as literal properties.

The importance of the study, *A Model for Aesthetic Response in the Arts* (Madeja and Perkins, 1982) is the time and effort devoted to the definition and testing of the end state as a first step in the development of instrumentation. By that, we meant that we should be able to describe categories of performance and development in aesthetic inquiry of the student before we develop a test. This was established by engaging the student in the classroom in aesthetic discourse and analysis which gave us a roadmap and the content to develop instrumentation for assessing outcomes of instruction in arts criticism. Unfortunately, we are unable to gain support for the next phase of this program, however, the study is a research model for what needs to be accomplished before we develop standardized measures.

Evaluation progress in the United States: A summary and prognosis

The international economic downturn has not excluded the United States. There is a great deal of public discontent with American education, especially in the larger urban areas. There have been numerous attempts to correct the imbalance of school districts in various states. The unfortunate result of this dilemma as far as assessment of student progress is concerned, has been the desire on the part of many pressure groups to tie teacher and administrator performance to the testing programs at the state level.

This means, because of low test scores, the federal government, for the first time in history, can directly influence the education of children in each of the states by withholding federal funds. This type of federal intervention in American schooling is a new phenomenon. The early results are frightening. It is common practice for teachers, administrators, and parents to support the idea of teaching subject matter that improves the student's capability to perform well on the state's testing programs. It is common practice for teachers, administrators, and parents to "teach to the test"; that is: support content and instruction that improves student performance on the state's testing programs. The instructional goal is limited to improving student performance on the states' standardized tests. The danger is that it diminishes content, abridges subject matter, and demeans the historical concept of a liberal education. Defending curricula that includes the arts is very difficult when public media report test scores. Newspapers and television news celebrate or chastise local and state results. Many teachers, and most professionals in education today, are opposed to this type of injunction.

Future direction: A wedding of electronic media and assessment

The importance of the visual arts has been enhanced in the last fifty years by new technology, which provides the infrastructure and a growing audience to create, transmit, and read images in digital formats. As described earlier, the role of visualization has dramatically changed, becoming a major domain of study in today's technological society and in art education.

Art education programs should emphasize how the visual arts relate to other domains of inquiry, such as information technology, imaging technology, educational delivery systems, and visual culture. The greatest paradigm shift in education and communication since the inventions of the alphabet and the printing press is the sophistication of the multimedia wireless digital transmission systems, and their capacity to access and deliver high-resolution images to any part of the planet with sound and text. The multimedia popular culture now dominates the world we live in, and students are well versed in receiving and decoding multisensory information. The natural need and capability of humankind is to record events, ideas, concepts, and data about multi-sensory modalities. It is now a reality. Today, the data generated in each of the sense modalities – verbal, visual, auditory, kinetic, and olfactory – interact and overlap in interfluent ways. Our exposure to the translation, synthesis, juxtaposition, and combining of sense modalities, such as language and image, is an everyday occurrence. The last two generations of students in our schools and universities are wizards with multimedia presentations and multitasking. They are embraced by them every day in games, cell phones, CDs, television, and films. All of us have the capabilities to collect data and develop multimedia formats for presenting information. Research is showing us how to strengthen these capabilities through art education. We need to understand how images are used and their relationship to other sensory data in the process of cognition. It is imperative that art programs, in school and non-school settings, implement multimedia formats for delivering, assessing, and evaluating information (Madeja, 2003a).

Art programs and assessment in the arts should be defining the new role for the study of visual culture. This concept frames the question facing art education today: "Can the visual culture we have created enhance and complement the natural environment and order, or will it conflict, distort, and/or destroy the natural order?" (Madeja, 1997, pp. 147–154). Art education must work toward, and be about, establishing and promoting harmony and order between the natural, technological, and constructed environment, educating the public to be visually literate in a society that is dominated by visual imagery; and to understand that imagery has an impact on every facet of our existence and on how and what we know about it. Art education must work toward, and be about:

- Establishing and promoting harmony and order between the natural, technological, and constructed environment.
- Educating the public to be visually literate in a society that is dominated by visual imagery.
- Understanding that imagery has an impact on every facet of our existence and on how and what we know about human kind.

An agenda for future developments in advocacy and assessment in the visual arts

Advocacy is not a part-time job! It is full-time all of the time. It must be: active and not passive, forward looking not reactionary, collaborative not a cause célèbre. It should relate to larger issues, i.e. economic growth, critical skills, cultural development, quality of life, and creative thinking. The advocacy effort must continue beyond the schools. In Illinois, there is a close working relationship between art educators, professional artists, and arts organizations. Together, they address problems in a holistic context. If we are to advocate art education for school programs, then we must tie those efforts to the larger advocacy efforts at the community, city, state, national, and international levels. The following are starting points for improving evaluation of art programs and student achievement in the visual arts in the United States. This field of study, must take the responsibility for the development of instrumentation, the tests, in the visual arts. This implies that our professional associations, such as the National Art Education Association, National Association of Schools of Art, National Endowment for the Arts and their state affiliates, need to actively participate in developing evaluation strategies and instrumentation in the visual arts. Further they should become advocates and take a proactive role in supporting tests they initiated and the content areas defined in collaboration with scholars and practitioners in the field, e.g. exemplary programs which integrate evaluation instrumentation with curriculum development.

This would emulate the other national models of associations in English and Mathematics. Further, they should assist in:

- Gaining consensus from the professionals in the field and the body politic, which includes the general public on basic curriculum content and standards for the schools K-12.
- Defining the content or subject matter that the students will be tested on and hold them responsible for a common curriculum based upon the agreed content and standards and conducting research programs in evaluation methodology and the development of instruments for assessing the visual arts at every level. This would consist of creating and testing evaluation instruments that could be developed in cooperation with universities and school systems. The visual arts must develop a sound research data base to support their inclusion as part of the general education of every student resulting in hard data. In conjunction, research universities should develop a visual arts strand congruent with the text-based curriculum dominating education, but emphasizing *visualization*. They should make it available to K-12 schools and to museums through teacher education and in-service training. This interactive and parallel visualization curriculum should reflect a strong content foundation in visual art. It should be based not only upon artists and great works of art, but also on the products and processes of our media-oriented visual culture. The new direction for evaluation by visual artists and educators is to utilize the new technologies for the development of relevant and valid instrumentation.

References

Arts Partnership (2009). *The Nation's Arts Report Card*, http://nces.ed.gov/nationsreportcard/arts/interpret_results.asp. Accessed 18 February 2013.

Askew J. W., Persky H. R., Sandene B. A. (1999). *The NAPE 1997 Arts Report Card*. U. S. Department of Education, Office Of Educational Research And Improvement, NCES.

Barkan, M., Chapman, L. H., Kerns, R. D. (1970). *Guidelines: Curriculum Development for Aesthetic Education*. St Louis, MO: Cemrel Inc.

Bloom, K. (1980). Defining A Task. In Foweler, Charles (Ed.). *Arts Education Source Book: A View from the JDR Third Fund*. New York: The Fund. 3–5.

Burton, D., Diket, Read M., Sabol, R. (1997). *Implications of the 1997* NAEP *Visual Arts Data or Policies Concerning Artistic Development in American Schools And Communities*, CFDA number 84. 902B. Hattiesburg, MS: William Carey College. 1–111.

Chapman, L. H. (2005). No Child Left Behind In Art. *Art Education*, January. 6–16

Davis, D. J. (1966). *The Effects of Two Methods of Teaching Art Upon Creative Thinking, Arc Attitudes, and Aesthetic Quality of Art Products in Beginning College Arc Students* (Doctoral dissertation, University of Minnesota, 1966). Dissertation Abstracts International 1427, 2272.

———— (1970). Evaluation and Curriculum Development in the Arts. *Toward an Aesthetic Education*. Washington, DC: Music Educators National Conference. 117–128.

Dorn, C., Madeja, S., Sabol, R. (2004). *Assessing Expressive Learning: A practical guide for teacher directed authentic assessment in K-12 visual arts education*. Mahwah, NJ: Lawrence Erlbaum and Associates. 201.

Ecker, D. (1967). Justifying Aesthetic Judgments, *Art Education*, Vol. 20, No. 5 (May, 1967). 5–8.

Engel, M., Hausman, J. J. (Eds.) (1978/1981). The Fourth Yearbook, *Curriculum and Instruction in Arts and Aesthetic Education Research in Arts*. St.Louis, MO: CEMREL, Inc.

Freeman F. S. (1950). *Theory and Practice: All Psychological Testing*. New York: Holt & Co.

Hanks C., Quinn T. (Eds.) (1977). *Coming To Your Senses*. New York: McGraw-Hill Book Co. 334.

Harris D. R. (1963). *Children's Drawings as Measures of Intellectual Maturity*. New York: Harcourt Brace and World Inc.

Hastie, W. R., Schmidt, C. (1969). *Encounter with art*. New York: McGraw-Hill Book Company.

Hausman, J. J. (1973). *Evaluating Total School Art Program*. New York: JDR third Fund. 61.

Horovitz, B. L., Lewis, H. L., Luca, M. (1967). *Understanding Children's Art For Better Teaching*. Columbus, OH: Charles E. Merrill Inc.

Hoffa, H. (1992). Through the Washington Looking Glass, in Madeja, S.S. (Ed.). *Kathryn Bloom Innovations In Art Educatin*. Dekalb, IL: Northern Illinois Art Museum. 59–87.

Hurwitz, A., Madeja, S. S. (1977). *Joyous Vision:* An Art *Appreciation* Text for *Art Teachers*. Englewood Cliffs, NJ: Prentice Hall.

Hurwitz, A., Madeja, S. S., Katter, E. (2003). *Pathways to Art Appreciation*. Reston, VA: National Art Education Association. 124.

Johnson, T. J., Hess R. J. (1971). *Test in the arts*. St. Louis, MO: CEMREL Inc. 1–158.

Kinter M. (1933). *The Measurement of Artistic Abilities: A Survey of Scientific Studies in the Field of Graphic Arts*. Prepared for the Carnegie Corporation, Psychological Corporation, New York. 1–117.

Kneiter J., Stallings, G. (1979). *The Teaching Process and Arts and Aesthetics*, 3rd Yearbook on Research in Arts and Aesthetic Education. St. Louis, MO: CEMREL, Inc. 263.

Levy, F. N. (Ed.) (1901). American Art Annual 1900–1901, (III.) Boston: Noyes, Platt & Company.

Lewerenz, A. S. (1927). *Tests In Fundamental Abilities Visual Arts.* Los Angeles: Los Angeles Research Service.

Lowenfeld, V. (1955). *Create A Mental Growth.* New York: The MacMillan Company. 408.

Madeja, S.S. (1959). A Survey of Existing Art Measurement Devices. (Master's degree plan B paper, University of Minnesota, 1–100.)

———— (1964). *Comparison of Two Methods of Teaching Art to Students of High and Low Art Ability.* (Doctoral dissertation, University of Minnesota, 1965). Dissertation Abstracts International, 26, 5297.

———— (1973). *All The Arts for Every* Child. JDR 3rd Fund Inc. New York, NY: The Fund

———— (1974). Aesthetics an Area of Study. *Art Education, 24* (8). 16–19.

———— (Ed.) (1977). Arts and Aesthetics: An Agenda for the Future. *First Yearbook on Research in Arts and Aesthetic Education.* St. Louis, MO: CEMREL, Inc. 430.

———— (Ed.) (1978). The Arts, Cognition and Basic Skills. *Second Yearbook on Research in Arts and Aesthetic Education,* St. Louis, MO: CEMREL, Inc.

———— (1992). Implanting the Arts into the Liberal Arts. *Kathryn Bloom: Innovation in Arts Education,* DeKalb, IL: NIU Art Museum. 88–105.

———— (1992). Kathryn Bloom and Genius of the Arts in Education Movement, *Art Education,* vol. 45 No. 4 July, 45.

———— (1997). Images and Language in an Electronic Age. *New Technologies in Art Education: Implications for Theory, Research, and Practice.* Reston, VA: National Art Education Association. 147–54.

———— (2003a). Spaces for Learning and Creating in a Cyber World. *In-Sight: Yearbook.* Charleston, WV: The Institute for Advancement of Emerging Technology in Education. (3), 65–87.

———— (2003b). In Sync with Visual Culture, *School Arts, 102* (5), 22–24.

Madeja, S. S., Perkins, D. N. (Ed.) (1982). *A Model for Aesthetic Response in the Arts,* Joint Research Project, CEMREL, Inc. and Harvard University monograph, St. Louis, MO: CEMREL, Inc. 169–207.

Madeja, S. S., Onuska, S. (1978). *Through the Arts to the Aesthetic,* St. Louis, MO: CEMREL, Inc.

Mattil, E. L. (1966). A Seminar in Art Education or Research and Curriculum Development. Research Project V-002, Pennsylvania State University, University Park, PA.

Levy, F. N. Ed. (1901). The American Art Annual 1900 – 1901, (III.) Boston: Noyes, Platt & Company.

National Standards for Arts Education (1994). The National Arts Education Associations. Reston, Virginia: Music Educators National Conference.

Principles And Standards For Art Programs (1999). The National Art Education Association: Reston, Virginia.

Popovich, K. (2006). Designing and Implementing: Exemplary Content, Curriculum and Assessment In Our Education, *Art Education,* (59), 11, 33–39.

Smith, R. A. (1967). *An Exemplar Approach to Aesthetic Education.* Bureau of Educational Research, College of Education, University of Illinois, U.S.ED project, no. 636–06122.

———— (1968). Aesthetic Criticism: The Method of Aesthetic Education. *Studies in Art Education* Spring (3), 22, 12–31

Sabol, F. R. (2010). *NCLB: A study of its impact on our education program.* Reston, Virginia: The National Art Education Association.

Stake, R. (1975). *Evaluating Arts in Education: A Response Approach.* Columbus Ohio: Charles E Merrill publishing company. IV–14.

Torrance, E. P. (1962). *Guiding creative talent.* Englewood Cliffs, NJ: Prentice-Hall. 278.

Wilson, B. (1971). *Procedures For Developing Art Objectives.* National Assessment of Educational Progress; Art objectives, Ann Arbor, MI: National Assessment of Educational Progress. Revised 06. May. 2011.

——— (1972). A Relationship between Years of Our Training and the Use of Aesthetic Judgmental Criteria Among High Schools Students, *Studies in Art education, 13* (2), 335–338.

Notes

1   A surprising $11,000,400 was invested in arts education research between 1964 and 1970 in amounts ranging from less than $2,000 to $2,300,000 for a massive theatre education project. About a third of the approved proposals had budgets of $10,000 or less and, though the number of projects that were supported in art education and music education were identical, music educators managed to outspend their colleagues in visual arts by two to one, $3,000,000 to $1,700,000 (Hoffa, 1992, pp. 59–87).

2   I was the convening chair of the conferences and series editor of the yearbooks. Guest editors were selected for the last two publications. NAEA and MENC assisted in the dissemination of the publications.

3   John Bradamis later became one of the most successful college presidents of New York University and raised billions of dollars for the institution and improved the quality and reputation of the NYU arts programs. Thus, art education in public schools lost one of our most powerful advocates.

4   Kinter created an outline for the review of each of the tests (Kinter, 1933, p. 7):
- Name of the Test
- Author and Publisher and Date of Publication
- Nature of the Test
- Content, Administration, Standardization, Scoring,
- Collateral Literature Relating to the Test
- Further Experiments

Chapter 2

Assessment of art and design in England: A focus on the GCSE Examination

John Steers, National Society for Education in Art and Design

Abstract

This chapter is concerned specifically with assessment in England and in particular the General Certificate of Secondary Education (GCSE) examination principally taken by students at age sixteen. A brief history of art examinations and a description of the current (2011) assessment instrument are provided and these are followed by a critique of practice and procedures. (It is important to note that assessment procedures in the other countries of the United Kingdom vary – increasingly so now that education policy is devolved to the Scottish Parliament, and the Northern Ireland and Welsh Assemblies.)

Brief history

A problem with any attempt to provide a history of public examinations in England is to know where to begin. Art and design examinations, particularly drawing examinations, date back at least to the early 19th century. The first examination boards (today they are called awarding bodies) were the Oxford Delegacy of Local Examinations established in 1857 and the University of Cambridge Local Examinations Syndicate that followed the year after. However, for the purposes of this account, the modern era started with the introduction of the General Certificate of Education (GCE) in 1951. GCE "O"level (i.e. ordinary level) was taken by school students aged 16+ and "A"level (i.e. advanced level) by those aged 18+. A further GCE examination for those aged 17+ called Advanced Supplementary (AS level) was first examined in 1989. The GCE O level was aimed originally at students in the top 20 percentile while the Certificate of Secondary Education (CSE), introduced in 1965, was aimed at the middle 60 percentile. The CSE was a school leaving qualification taken at age 16+ that was introduced to provide a school-leaving qualification available to all schoolchildren distinct from the GCE, which was aimed at the more able students mostly those aiming for places at a university. Before the introduction of the CSE the majority of school students did not take O-level examinations and so left school without any formal qualifications.

In 1965 the government required local education authorities to devise schemes for "comprehensive reorganization" – that is to end a two-tier system of Secondary Modern Schools and "elite" Grammar Schools and to create Comprehensive Schools. A year later a new examination to replace GCE and the CSE was proposed but it was not until the late 1970s that proposals for a new examination system (N and F) were developed only to be rejected subsequently by the government. After further delays the General Certificate of Secondary Education (GCSE) was eventually introduced in 1986 – it was hardly a rushed affair. The new GCSE examination was aimed originally at the top 60 percentile of the 16+ ability range although, in the case of art and design, from the start the range was often much wider than this. Today virtually all secondary school students are expected to take a broad range of GCSE examinations at 16+.

The GCSE and GCE examinations have been subject to constant revision and particular syllabuses (more recently entitled "specifications") seldom remain unchanged for more than a year or two. Since the election of a coalition government in May 2010 the whole education system in England is in an extreme state of flux with many government agencies such as the Qualifications and Curriculum Development Agency (QCDA) being swept away. A comprehensive review of the national curriculum is yet again underway and another major "reform" of the examination system is in progress.

Description of current system

This chapter focuses on the biggest art and design examination, the GCSE – a complex enough subject without the complication of trying to describe the GCE and the range of other art and design qualifications available to students in schools and colleges.

The GCSE is a qualification awarded in a specified subject and most students take between eight and ten subjects. The examination is available in slightly different versions in England, Wales, and Northern Ireland but there is a common code of practice for GCSE and GCE in all three countries. The examination is administered to a common specification by three awarding bodies in England and one in each of Wales and Northern Ireland.[1] (In Scotland the nearest equivalent to GCSE is the "Standard Grade" examination.) Candidates for the GCSE examination, including adults, may enter at any point either internally through an institution or externally.

The education systems of some other countries also use the qualification and there is an international version, the IGCSE, which can be taken anywhere in the world. When GCSEs are taken by students in secondary education, they can often be combined with other qualifications, such as those offered by the Business and Technology Education Council (BTEC) and 14–19 Diplomas.[2] All these qualifications, and many others, form part of the National Qualifications and Credit Framework (QCF). Education to GCSE level is often required of students who study for the International Baccalaureate or to GCE Advanced Level (A-level). In 2010, 188,193 candidates (36.5% male; 63.5% female) sat the full GCSE examination in art and design.[3] (This marks a decline of some 25,000 candidates in the last ten years.)

The majority of candidates follow an "unendorsed" (i.e. general) art, craft, and design course that explores practical and critical/contextual work through a range of two- and/or three-dimensional processes and new media and technologies. However awarding bodies may also offer a number of alternative specifications that are taken by relatively small numbers of candidates in schools aged 16 (proportionally more older candidates opt for these). The endorsed options are:

- *Applied* – a course that is explicitly vocational in nature and content, requiring a broad understanding, knowledge, and skills of art, craft, and design applied within a work-related, client-orientated context. Learners explore the application of techniques and processes of art, craft, and design based on professional practice.
- *Fine art* – a course that offers a range of approaches, including painting, drawing, mixed-media sculpture, installation, printmaking, lens and light-based media, and new media.
- *Critical and contextual studies* – this includes areas of study across art, craft, and design.
- *Textile design* – this includes fashion, printed and/or dyed fabrics, constructed textiles, and installed textiles.
- *Graphic communication* – this includes illustration, web design, advertising, packaging, design for print, multimedia, and animation.
- *Three-dimensional design* – this includes jewellery, body ornament, theatre design, exhibition design, film-set design, interior design, product and/or environmental design, and architectural design.
- Photography – Lens and light-based media –this includes traditional and digital photography, documentary, photojournalism, experimental imagery, photographic or digital installation, animation, video, and film.[4]

The QCDA and its predecessors[5] was responsible for the development of the current overall specification for each GCSE examination although the coalition government scrapped this "quasi-autonomous non-governmental organisation" (Quango) with effect from March 2012. Its role has been subsumed into the central control of the Department for Education (DfE). All qualifications are overseen by the Office of the Qualifications and Examinations Regulator (Ofqual) which answers to the DfE.

GCSE format, assessment criteria, and methodology

Since the early 1980s syllabuses have provided more and more detailed guidance. Typically, in the earlier generic GCE or CSE syllabuses, a few paragraphs sufficed to outline the content of an art and design examination course, but by 1999 separate art and design syllabuses of 20–40 pages were the norm. Twenty years ago syllabuses rarely contained specific aims, objectives, subject content, or mark schemes – principally because the GCE "O" level examinations generally were externally marked and it was not thought necessary to provide such information for teachers or candidates. There were distinct differences between syllabuses but over time an ever-greater conformity between examinations boards/awarding bodies has developed, as a consequence of requirements to comply with the increasingly rigid examination specifications of the QCDA.

The development of the most recent specifications for art and design started in 2005 and was carried out by a working party convened by the then QCA comprising practising teachers, academics, representatives of subject associations such as the National Society for Education in Art and Design (NSEAD), representatives of the awarding bodies, and QCA staff. The final criteria were signed off by QCA in 2006, subsequently, awarding body specifications were accredited the following year and the new courses were taught in schools from September 2008 and first examined in July 2010.

The specifications set out the knowledge, understanding, skills, and assessment objectives common to all GCSE specifications in art and design. They provide the framework within which individual awarding bodies create the detail of the specification. Subject criteria are intended to:

- Help ensure consistent and comparable standards in the same subject across the awarding bodies;
- Ensure that the rigour of GCSE is maintained;
- Ensure that specifications build on the knowledge, understanding, and skills established by the national curricula for England, Northern Ireland, and Wales, and facilitate progression to higher-level general or vocational qualifications in art and design, applied art and design, or related sectors of employment;
- Help higher education institutions, employers, and other stakeholders such as learners and parents/guardians know what has been studied and assessed. (QCA, 2007)

The specification includes sections on the expected "Aims and learning outcomes", "Subject content", "Assessment objectives", the "Scheme of assessment" and "Grade descriptions".

The four interrelated and connected assessment objectives are as follows and require candidates for the examination to demonstrate their ability to:

- *AO1*: Develop their ideas through investigations informed by contextual and other sources, demonstrating analytical and cultural understanding.
- *AO2*: Refine their ideas through experimenting and selecting appropriate resources, media, materials, techniques, and processes.
- *AO3*: Record ideas, observations, and insights relevant to their intentions in visual and/ or other forms.
- *AO4*: Present a personal, informed, and meaningful response demonstrating analytical and critical understanding, realizing intentions and, where appropriate, making connections between visual, written, oral, or other elements. (QCA, 2007)

These assessment objectives need not be equally weighted and awarding bodies have the leeway to weight each one at between 20 and 30%. Nevertheless most choose to weight them equally (25% each). The awarding bodies develop mark schemes and assessment criteria (grade descriptors) based on the assessment objectives. In 2005–2006 the assessment criteria for art and design were developed in cognisance of the new secondary curriculum being introduced at the same time. Consequently, and for the first time, it was possible to chart expected progression from age 7–18 by relating the curriculum attainment targets to GCSE and GCE assessment objectives. Examples of awarding body specifications including mark schemes and grade criteria can be found on the Internet.[6]

There are two examination components and GCSE specifications in art and design: (1) a candidate portfolio, and (2) an externally set task to elicit a personal response. Awarding bodies must allocate a weighting of 60% to the candidate's portfolio and a weighting of 40% to an externally set task in their overall scheme of assessment.

The examination process

Candidate portfolios have traditionally consisted of a portfolio of selected work ("Coursework") produced during a two-year course by students aged 14–16. With effect from 2009 "controlled assessment" was introduced ostensibly to ensure the reliability and authenticity of candidates' work. Like coursework this is designed to allow candidates to produce an extended personal response to an area of the specification. It may include work carried out both in and outside the classroom/studio. Teachers may offer guidance but they are required to ensure and authenticate that the work is the candidate's own.

The externally set task is set by the awarding body. The question papers are sent out each January and number of "starting points" are provided on each paper. Candidates choose one starting point or a more open-ended theme in their chosen option and they usually have about a four-week preparatory period prior to the supervised "test". During this period teachers may discuss approaches, materials, processes, and research methods and candidates may make their preparations in school, home, or elsewhere.

For the "test" itself candidates are allowed ten hours of supervised time in which to produce a final piece(s) of work in response to the starting point they have chosen. The test takes place in school and a reasonable block of time must be allowed – often two whole days are timetabled but the first supervised session must be at least two hours' duration. Candidates may continue to produce preparatory studies between sessions if they wish to do so before submitting for assessment both the preparatory work and the supervised work done during the controlled test.

Assessment procedures

The awarding bodies appoint Chief Examiners, Principal Examiners (specialists in endorsed options), and Moderators for each subject. Moderators also work in teams with Team Leaders to help them with their work. They also appoint a Chair of Examiners whose role is crucial to the awarding process. They may have an advisory panel for each subject drawn from experienced teachers, academics, and others. Teams of moderators are appointed and trained and annual standardizing meetings take place at which point common agreed standards are set. "Centres" (i.e. schools, colleges, etc.) that enter candidates for the examinations are expected to attend regional standardizing meetings (attendance is mandatory for new teachers and Centres where problems have been encountered previously). These meetings also have a limited professional development function: examples of work are provided and discussed which illustrate the expected standards and information is provided on interpretation of the assessment objectives and mark schemes.

The examination is internally assessed and externally moderated. That is to say the candidates' own teachers first mark the work and, in a school where there are a large number of candidates taught by different teachers, internally moderated to arrive at an overall "rank order" of candidates' marks. The marks are then checked by an awarding-body-appointed moderator visiting the Centre who will inspect a sample of candidates' work or in some instances a sample of work is sent to a moderation Centre for inspection. Some awarding bodies offer area moderations where work is taken to a centre and teachers cross-moderate each others' work supported by an awarding body moderator. In either case the moderator appointed by the awardingbody is required to standardize the Centres' marks to ensure they are aligned with the common standard. In cases of disagreement at this stage an appeals system exists and a team leader or chief moderator may be sent to Centres to resolve problems.

The final process before examination results are published is the awarding meeting. For each subject specification, an awarding committee is appointed which is presided over by the chair of examiners. The committee is responsible for ensuring that the required standards are brought to bear and for assisting the chair of examiners in arriving at recommended grade boundary marks for each externally and internally assessed unit/component. The chair of examiners' recommendations must be reviewed by an appropriate senior officer of the awarding body to ensure that grades awarded represent continuity and parity of standards over time and across specifications. In this review, the officer must consider the committee's recommendations, evidence of awarders' professional judgements on the quality of candidates' work and, significantly, the technical and statistical evidence available before confirming the grade boundaries.

The grades awarded are from A* or A–G with the addition of an unclassified or "U" grade. Grades A*–C are often required for progression to a GCE A-level course. In 2010 66.5% of those entered were awarded grades A*–C.

The entire examination process is governed by a detailed Code of Practice[7] published by the government's regulatory body, Ofqual. The awarding bodies must strictly adhere to this code.

Issues and concerns

The reader will conclude that national examinations in art and design in England are long-established, have been subject to constant revision and reform, are strictly regulated and therefore have the necessary validity, reliability, and utility for students, teachers, parents, higher education institutions, and employers to have full confidence in them. However this is not necessarily the reality and some significant issues and concerns can be identified. These include the impact of an exceptionally "high stakes" examination system, the "washback" or influence of the examination on classroom practice, the utility, validity, and reliability of the examination, bias, and teacher autonomy and "ownership". Each of these issues will be discussed in turn.

"High stakes"

It is beyond doubt that in today's schools assessment and examination pressures in secondary schools are overwhelming. It is said that children in English schools are tested more than in any other country and the results of tests and examinations are used relentlessly to make judgements about pupil progress, the quality and effectiveness of individual teachers, schools, and the education system itself. Teachers are under unremitting scrutiny by their colleagues, consultants, inspectors, politicians, and the media, and under unrealistic pressure to constantly improve test and examination results and to compile data showing steady progress for every child.[8] The GCSE is just one element of this regime where children in extreme cases may be tested almost weekly in every subject against the national curriculum attainment targets (levels). England provides a classic example of a "high stakes" education system. Mary James, from Cambridge University and a member of the Assessment Reform Group, describes the problems that come with this:

> Assessments that were originally designed to indicate what a student knows and understands of a subject have now become proxy measures of the quality of teachers, heads, schools, support services, local authorities, the Government and the nation. With stakes this high, no wonder results are represented in dubious ways and the means of achieving them are subject to games-playing. If a school takes actions designed to improve its performance, such as drilling to earn marks at the expense of teaching for deeper understanding, the consequences for students are often against their long-term educational interests. (James, 2009)

An even more radical view is expressed by John White from the Institute of Education, London University:

> Imagine [students] freed, post-14, from the shackles of public examination! So much less reason for good teachers to prostitute themselves by teaching candidates how to play the system. So much more scope for students to throw themselves into studies and practical activities that grab them. (White, 2010, p. 25)

Washback

The question here is whether "washback" from tests and examinations overtly influences classroom practice. James for one appears to be in no doubt but it would be wrong to think this is an entirely new phenomena. In 1895 the *Journal of Education* complained:

"a competitive examination […] is absolutely indefensible […] [as] it encourages masters and mistresses to teach not the best gymnastic for their students but those which will obtain, at least cost, the greatest number of distinctions for their schools" (Attwood, 2010).

In 2006 Rachel Mason and I published a summary of a systematic survey of research concerned with the "washback" of examination practices on the curriculum – issues such as "teaching to the test" and "assessment leading the curriculum" (Mason and Steers, 2006, pp. 119–127). Despite much anecdotal evidence about the impact of examinations on classroom practice and the orthodoxy of much studio practice there was little hard evidence to be found in the research literature – not, we concluded, because the problem does not exist, but because it has not been properly investigated.

At one time examination board syllabuses included a wide range of optional papers with a focus in particular on fine art, design, and craft skills, for example, lettering, photography, printmaking, pottery, theatre design, and mural design. The number of students opting to pursue specialisms such as these in-depth appears in general to have diminished, partly as a consequence of the decision to introduce the "unendorsed" art and design examination and partly by the "rationalization" of standard titles for endorsed papers.

By the end of 20th century the overwhelming majority of art and design candidates were entered for unendorsed papers although much of the work submitted took the relatively narrow form of drawing and painting (Downing and Watson, 2004; Ofsted, 2009). It is clear that one consequence of the changes that have taken place has been that specialisms have been lost in many schools along with the real choice between studying a particular art and design discipline in-depth and following a more general course of study.

The Office for Standards in Education (Ofsted, 2005) previously noted the danger, evident in some schools, of the curriculum for 11–14-year-olds being little more than a preparation for the examinations at age 16. Inspectors noted the limitations placed on the breadth of study required by the national curriculum in order to perfect a particular style of work associated with examination success.

Utility

From their first days at school to GCE A-level at age 18, students in England experience a massive burden of formal assessment. It needs to be questioned what exactly this is all for and whether the substantial investment is worthwhile. The *utility* of an assessment instrument is its convenience, flexibility, and cost-effectiveness; all assessment procedures have to operate within the time and resources available.

The possible functions of assessment are both varied and can often appear to be in conflict:

- Providing feedback for the student or teacher (formative or "Assessment for Learning"[AfL]);
- Diagnosing the student's future needs or direction (diagnostic);

- Providing motivation for the student or teacher (formative);
- Providing a means of licensing or qualification (summative);
- Providing a basis for selection (e.g. for higher education or employment) (summative).

Assessment can also be used for:

- Ensuring accountability by monitoring national, local, or individual teachers' standards;
- Controlling the curriculum. (Steers, 2007, p. 167)

This is complicated by institutional misunderstandings and tensions where government and teachers tend to assign different priorities and understandings to each assessment function. For example, the General Teaching Council for England (GTC, 2004) recommended that "the summative assessment of individual students is separated from the collection of summative data to be used for national monitoring" and that a rolling programme of sampling pupil cohorts could accomplish the latter. I concur: it does seem unlikely that a wholly effective assessment system could be designed and implemented that is both formative and summative in nature – which manages to provide students with feedback about their future learning needs whilst at the same time effectively monitoring national standards.

Reliability

As far as possible assessments should be designed and operated so that they give a similar result when taken by students of similar ability under similar conditions – this is *reliability*. A perfectly reliable assessment is probably impossible to achieve because unreliability may be a consequence of differences in the conditions for, or the context of, the assessment judgements of examiners and moderators, or bias of one kind or another.

Most of the change that has taken place over the years has ostensibly been in the interests of increasing GCSE examination reliability. However in art and design it remains an issue, particularly given the size of entry for GCSE art and design examinations (± 200,000 each year). In the past, smaller examination boards with relatively small entries employed small teams of examiners. These boards were not dependent on formal mark schemes or assessment criteria, but I can personally confirm that a good level of consensus used to be reached on standards, especially as one examiner often assessed all the work for a particular component. On the other hand small teams may sometimes have limited the nature of the work submitted because of a narrower range of expertise. Today one awarding body employs over 200 moderators and it is obvious that reliability must be dependent entirely on highly effective standardization procedures.[9]

In reality achieving accurate standardization presents a considerable challenge to the awarding bodies and the ever-tighter drafting and specification of assessment criteria and their rigid application may not be the answer. Boughton succinctly identified the inherent problem:

> [A]ny attempt to use written statements intended to describe the range of complex and subtle characteristics of visual expressive work at any level of schooling will be less than adequate. [...] The qualitative nature of the arts [...] cannot be effectively captured in words alone. Linguistic representation of the arts is at best reductionist, and at worst misleading. (Boughton, 1995, p. 146.)

Common criteria do have value in helping to focus the assessors' attention on particular concerns but they do not provide absolute measurement standards – assessment of the arts in schools still requires aesthetic judgement and connoisseurship based on experience of what students of a particular age can achieve.

Validity

The *validity* of an assessment is the extent to which it serves its purpose, employing methods that reflect the aims and objectives of courses and educational programmes. The Assessment Reform Group questions the validity of much assessment practice:

> Yet there is now a great volume of material cataloguing the educational side-effects of a structure which is too focused on performance indicators. These include the often excessive and inequitable focus of many schools on students whose results may be key to a school hitting particular achievement targets; the repetition involved in months of focusing on what is tested and on test practice, which also serves to narrow the curriculum; and the consequent undermining of professional autonomy and morale among teachers.
>
> The impact on pupil motivation to learn is an area of particular interest. If one of the central aims of assessment for learning is to encourage independent motivation to understand among students, findings from research that learners in high-stakes testing systems can become dependent on their teacher to guide them towards answers should be taken seriously. (Mansell and James, 2009, p. 25)

The past 20 years have seen a trend away from holistic assessment with no published criteria or mark schemes to a process of aggregation of component marks, based on mark schemes closely related to the published assessment objectives; as a consequence examinations often determine the taught curriculum. It is becoming evident that this leads to fragmentation and to teachers teaching to specific assessment criteria in the knowledge that so long as students provide clear evidence of some engagement with the ideas and practices embedded in the criteria they are rewarded, almost regardless of the actual quality of their work. Out of necessity, assessment criteria are drafted so as to be generally applicable to a wide range of specialisms and activities. As a consequence they can be difficult to apply to some of the more unusual outcomes and inhibit some of the more creative responses to new media and technologies that, for example, reflect contemporary practice in art and design. In effect, when there is over-reliance on criteria they act as a regulatory device through which both teaching and learning practices tend towards the orthodox and are risk averse.

There is another important issue – one that is not generally acknowledged – that some might think undermines the validity of the examinations. The GCSE is said to be "criterion referenced". That is to say that the published assessment criteria are applied throughout internal assessment and external moderation to arrive at a mark which is translated into a grade only at the final awarding meeting. However, at this stage, the grade borderlines may be adjusted to ensure that the overall results are closely comparable from year to year.

Why does this norm-referencing happen? The argument is that given the size of the cohort entered for the examination there should be little deviance from the bell-curve distribution of grades from year to year. For many years there has been a tendency for grades to rise across all subjects each year. The press immediately respond with accusations that the examinations have been "dumbed down" while government ministers claim the improvements are due to their policies. The reality is probably that teachers just get better and better at teaching the test and it may be equally true that candidates are getting better at passing examinations but, nevertheless, there is no guarantee that all candidates receive the grade that is justified by the criteria alone.

Of particular significance is the marked trend away from an optional, formal art and design history element towards a general requirement for a "critical and contextual studies" component or the endorsed paper.[10] This shift has been largely non-contentious but is not unproblematic. Pragmatism has played a part in the widespread acceptance of critical studies in secondary schools because the "old" art history was very demanding of teaching time and the way it was taught made it only suited to reasonably academically-minded students. In contrast, critical studies at examination level are often dependent on students researching the "personal study" component of the examination in their own time.[11] The outcomes of this approach are varied with some exceptional projects in evidence. More generally, however, "descriptive and non-contextual studies" might be a more apt title. It is questionable whether or not students gain a coherent knowledge of art and design history from independent "research" that often has a narrow focus and possibly encourages plagiarism accompanied by unproblematic pastiches of style. There is a continuing need to develop a clear rationale and assessment principles for the critical and contextual studies component in the GCSE and GCE examinations.

Bias

Examination bias may be defined as unfair opportunity, partiality, favouritism, or influence within the examination procedures and practices – anything that places a candidate or groups of candidates at an advantage. Sources of bias include cultural background, ethnicity, age, gender, native language, and socio-economic standing.

While, undoubtedly, the awarding bodies work hard to avoid problems of bias in art and design, as in other examinations, this has not been entirely eliminated. For example, according to some research the apparent under-achievement of boys can be attributed to a feminized examination system and a higher number of boys suffering behavioural problems (Blair, 2007). Bowden (2000) suggests that in schools where boys' achievement is comparable to girls' the factors include the majority of students coming from middle-class backgrounds, three-dimensional work and graphic activities as a significant component, and critical studies do not feature significantly as a written or theoretical component of the examination course.

There has been some evidence of cultural background and ethnicity affecting examination results, for example, in schools with a very high proportion of students from anIslamic background or recently arrived immigrants with little or no knowledge of English. However in my experience awarding bodies have tended to deal with such cases sympathetically on appeal.

Resources for both the examination course and the "terminal test" are not the same in every school. For example, some schools may offer no opportunities for working in clay or textiles while others have excellent facilities. And, of course, teachers have their own preferences, strengths, and weaknesses with regard to what they choose to teach and this may place limitations on students' experiences and opportunities. Further more some parents will buy additional or better quality materials than those generally available in a particular school and, of course, some candidates have access to more sound advice than others both in and out of school.

More recently new generic regulations have been introduced by the JCQ[12] for the conduct of all examinations and "Controlled Assessments" have also been instigated designed to deal with a supposed problem of plagiarism. It is evident thatschools' examination officers are applying these regulations for the conduct of examinations conducted at desks in examination halls, to art and design final assessments traditionally conducted in art rooms. This creates a number of problems including, the exclusion of art and design teachers from invigilation of art and design examinations – despite the need for a level of technical support that can only be provided by such staff. This has resulted in some cases in candidates being prevented from using some materials (e.g. ceramics and photography). Some schools remove or cover all wall displays, despite the need for candidates to respond to external stimuli and the work of others, the use of cameras is banned during the examination period (even for photography candidates!), Internet access is denied, and candidates are prevented from working beyond the examination space or moving work from that space – despite the fact that the overall examination includes long unsupervised periods.

As noted above, 'Controlled Assessments' for art and design were introduced in 2009 and have proved problematic from the outset. Art and design examinations already had the requirement for teachers to ensure and to confirm that the work presented by candidates was their own independent work, both in their portfolios and for the externally-set task. Additionally the externally-set task had the requirement for a period of sustained work to be conducted under art and design examination conditions. This simply duplicated existing controls and served only to confuse schools about the need for two distinctive experiences within the art and design examination. This confusion impacts negatively and unfairly on candidates who again face a range of interpretations from both examination centres and awarding bodies.

In any circumstances these regulations would be inappropriate for a practical art and design examination but the problem is compounded by the disparate interpretation of the rules by schools and so a lack of consistency across the country for candidates. Some schools clearly apply the letter of the law whilst others use their common sense and simply ignore the JCQ guidance thus introducing a wholly unnecessary element of bias.

Teacher autonomy and teacher control

On the positive side art and design teachers undoubtedly have a high degree of autonomy in what they choose to teach and how to go about it. Neither the national curriculum nor examination specifications define curriculum content in any detail. The best teachers exploit this freedom to devise courses that are inclusive, motivate their students, offer a wide range of options for personal learning, and encourage the genuine creativity of individuals.

However the extraordinary pressures created by the high-stakes education system often leads to the production of "safe" work, which teachers can rely on for the award of those vital A*–C grades. Teachers become adept at finding an effective prescription for their students to follow that satisfies the various demands not only of the awarding bodies, but in turn school league tables, inspection, and promotion. When work of a particular kind is rewarded by the system, it is rapidly imitated and what was a genuinely innovative or creative approach is reduced in no time at all to a cliché or mere pastiche resulting in the dreary orthodoxy of "school art" with which the history of art education in schools is littered. Too often students' work has little relationship to contemporary activity in the world of art and design beyond the school art room and has no real relevance to the students' own interests and concerns (Binch, 1994; Downing and Watson, 2004; Hughes, 1998; Steers, 2009). There is also a tendency for teachers to concentrate attention on students likely to be at or around the C/D grade borderline to try to increase the number achieving grades A*–C. This does not necessarily result in the most able students being challenged to achieve more while the less able may be neglected.

It is also clear that while initial teacher education courses encourage new teachers to think creatively for themselves, the ethos and pressures within some schools can result in younger teachers simply reverting to the ways in which they were taught themselves rather than developing a more challenging vision.

Creativity

In the 1960s when the examination system was extended there were some art teachers who declared that this would lead to the inevitable death of creativity and imagination in students' art and design work. Ross (1993, p. 92) summarized this view when he wrote: "The status system embodied in the mundane curriculum stresses impartiality, inequality, secularity, acquisitiveness, discrimination, epicureanism. All these are anathema to the arts and to the true artist."

Has this prophecy been borne out in reality? Yes and no. There is little that is intrinsic to the examination system that is consciously intended to discourage creativity. Indeed the importance of creativity is made very explicit in the GCSE assessment objectives and in the English National Curriculum programme of study for art and design. In practice there are some restraints such as those imposed by "controlled assessment", but it is evident from the best work in the best art and design departments that creativity can and does flourish. The real barriers seem to be in those teachers' mind sets where they feel under enormous pressure to guarantee good results and are consequently reluctant to encourage the "risky thinking" that is an integral element of creativity.

Many of the changes over the years have had a positive impact. These include more guidance for students and teachers and more examination time. There has been a move away from question papers offering little more than one-word "starting points" or instructions to examination supervisors about how to set up a still-life group or pose a model. Instead question papers favour formats that offer more support for candidates, for example, a detailed design brief. One awarding body provides a "question paper" with a single common theme covering a wide range of art, craft, and design activities that includes long, discursive discussion of ideas candidates might wish to develop. Clearly, the intention is to motivate students to respond as creatively as possible to the required "terminal test".[13] Thirty years ago the time allocated for a terminal examination was often short, typically two to three hours in which to produce a drawing or composition. The time for all the examining groups is now around ten hours, excluding the three of four weeks allowed for candidates to research and plan their work.

More fundamental issues need to be addressed. As I have written elsewhere (Steers, 2009), creativity in the art and design classroom can be in conflict with the ethos of many schools – social institutions that often place a high value on some degree of conformity – and teachers often unwittingly stifle students' creativity. It will only flourish in an ethos where there is mutual trust and where experiment is positively encouraged.

Unresolved questions and tentative conclusions

The principal question is: Are art and design public examinations needed at all and what purpose do they serve? Ross identified one key dilemma for arts teachers:

> If teachers do participate in public examinations they run the risk of allowing their work to be wrestled from its legitimate roots, yet if they do not they seem to push the arts further out along the educational limb, accepting the more the arts become exceptions to the rules of schooling the less relevant they are likely to appear. (Ross, 1993, p. 92)

In England art and design teachers seem resigned to the reality of examinations such as the GCSE and recognize that the results are used not only to assess their students' achievements but their own teaching ability, the success of their department, and ultimately the success of the school. It could be said that the functions of the GCSE include all those listed earlier from providing pupil feedback to monitoring national standards. But what are we really trying to assess? Pupil capability? Pupil potential? Pupil attainment and/or achievement? "Effective" teaching?

Nevertheless there are those who question increasingly whether the GCSE is either fit for purpose or indeed has a purpose. When the examination was introduced the school leaving age was 16 and so for many it provided a final summation of their achievement in school. Now virtually all young people remain in one form or another of formal education until age 18 and GCE A-Level, amongst a range of other qualifications, has the function of the pre-university examinations that are common in other countries or qualifications leading more directly to the world of work. In these circumstances some have argued that the GCSE has no useful function other than, perhaps, as an interim litmus test of progress, in which case they seem over elaborate. In today's straitened circumstances their cost-effectiveness is also called into question.

Others question the validity and reliability of the whole examinations system. Mick Waters, a former director of curriculum at the QCA has called it "diseased, almost corrupt" (Bangs et al., 2011. p. 105). Waters is also quoted in the same book as saying,

We've got a set of awarding bodies who are in a market place. [...] In previous jobs I had seen people from awarding bodies talk to head teachers implying that their examinations are easier. Not only that [...] [the awarding bodies] provide the textbook to help you through it (Bangs et al., 2011. p. 105).

It is certainly true that over the years the awarding bodies have published or supported publication of books, often written by chief examiners, which exemplify the work expected for the examinations (for example, Edexcel, 2000; Read,1988/1994). More recently websites with similar content have arrived such as BBC Bitesize[14] which boasts "Everything you need to succeed". Such publications in part are designed to reinforce systems of standardization by providing exemplars of "good practice". But it must be questioned whether they affect course content and teaching and learning styles for better or for worse.

Do prescribed criteria tend to fragment knowledge, skills, and understanding and does a more holistic approach to teaching and learning suffer as a result? Boughton (1995) questions whether the language of criteria can ever be sophisticated enough to encompass all the possible outcomes. Much earlier, before standard draft-grade criteria had been drafted for the first time, Price (1982) prophesized problems with such assessment criteria:

The existing relationship between curriculum and examination syllabuses is a "dog and tail" affair. The influence of external examinations has, to some extent, bred a species within the genus of "School Art". [...] The question of whether the "tail wagging the dog" is a satisfactory state of affairs must be linked with the possibility that the existing dog is a mongrel that defies simple definition. This is not to say that some mongrels are not more healthy than some more easily categorised pedigrees, but it does make the establishment of national criteria guidelines more difficult – more difficult in the sense that criteria will necessarily be based upon generalisation of a plethora of objectives and practices – generalisation which will undoubtedly influence the future of art education. (Price, 1982, p. 399)

Swift and Steers (1999) and Atkinson (2001) warned of the importance of avoiding "hidden" criteria preferences such as "accuracy", "likeness", "in perspective", "expressive", unless they are clearly stated and explained in their various meanings. As I have written elsewhere (Steers, 2007) notions of objective judgement are largely spurious since in reality any claim to objectivity in art judgements is based on the amount of comparative, experiential knowledge the teacher or examiner possesses and can apply. The reality is that differences of opinion and interpretation are axiomatic: for example, consider the concept of "originality" as applied to children's art.

Should assessment be more holistic, authentic, negotiated? Is a "terminal test" or "controlled assessment" really necessary? What does an "examination" assess that cannot be equally well assessed through a coursework portfolio? *Authentic assessment* strategies reject examinations and testing in favour of procedures which require students to engage in long-term, complex, and challenging projects reflecting real life situations. For art and design a structured *portfolio*may prove to be a particularly authentic assessment instrument.

Torres Pereira de Eça (2005) has proposed that such a portfolio could take the form of a folder, exhibition, work journal, CD-ROM, web page, etc., and that the data for assessment might include:

- Reports or notes, either visual or written, of previous experiences, interests, etc.
- Final visual products such as paintings, drawings, sculptures, prints, graphic design, product design, multimedia, photographs, films, video records of performances, installations, exhibitions, etc.
- Visual or written preliminary studies, developmental records.
- Investigation reports and data, critical inquiry (written and visual).
- A self-assessment report that might include interviews – tape, video, digital records of the students' intentions, progress, investigations, achievements, presentations, self-assessment and "crits". (Torres Pereira de Eça, 2005, p. 211)

In our review of the research literature for the Evidence-based Policy and Practice Initiative (EPPI) Mason and I concluded:

It is clear that more reliable and valid studies of assessment are required. As a matter of some urgency, systematic investigations should be designed and undertaken of the impact of art and design examinations on curricula and, in particular, the extent to which external assessment dictates classroom practice. This concern has been discussed for far too long in the absence of any empirical evidence. It seems quite extraordinary that there appears to be no research in the public domain (if it exists at all) into the impact of examinations on the curriculum by any of the awarding bodies or by government agencies such as the QCA. Arguably such research should be undertaken by an independent body, such as the National Foundation for Educational Research (NFER), rather than QCA, and could include a comparison between assessment and classroom practices in each of England, Scotland, Northern Ireland and Wales. Important foci of such research would be to examine:

- The extent to which art teachers' pedagogical styles are test or examination-driven;
- How the resources available to art teachers influence what is taught and assessed;
- How different examination options influence teaching and assessment. (Mason and Steers, 2010, pp. 129–130)

To date this call for action has gone unheeded.

As for the GCSE, there is no doubt that art and design examinations have improved over time: perhaps achieving a Grade B with the comment "Still room for improvement".

The future

At the time of writing in March 2012 the future direction of education and assessment in England is uncertain. There has been an avalanche of highly experimental and ideological initiatives driven by Michael Gove, the current Secretary of State for Education in England. There are plans the make the GCSE "more rigorous", by eliminating modular approaches and not allowing candidates multiple re-sits to improve their grades as they do at present in some subjects. This measure will not have a significant effect on art and design The debate may intensify about whether the 16+ GCSE examination is necessary when 18+ now marks the end of some form of compulsory education for all but the very few. There are calls for the GCE A-level-examination development to be more directly controlled by academics from the leading universities. In future the role of Ofqual may be to regulate the awarding bodies rather than the detail of individual examination specifications.

More generally it is expected that the "new" secondary curriculum will be slimmed down with the principal emphasis on the so-called STEM subjects (Science, Technology, English, and Mathematics). It is unclear to what extent this may affect art and design. A vigorous debate is emerging (Bangs et al., 2011; Aynsley Green, 2010) about the proposed changes with some critics describing the government as vandals. It does seem that the government is driven more by right wing ideology than empirical evidence. It does not seem to be in a listening mode but rather on a mission. The principal driver of the new policies appears to the concept of a "knowledge-based curriculum" such as that set out in the ideas of E. D. Hirsch and his "Core Knowledge Foundation"[15] concerning "What every child needs to know".

Without doubt a period of mainly very positive developments backed by considerable consensus came to an abrupt end in May 2010. The question now is whether the promised "reforms" will take education generally – and art and design in particular – forwards or set things back half a century or more. The change of government has rapidly changed my mood of growing optimism into a rather more familiar pessimistic mindset.

Plus ça change, plus c'est la même chose...

References

Atkinson, D (2001). Assessment in Educational Practice: Forming Padagogised Identities in the Art Curriculum, *International Journal of Art & Design Education, 20* (1), 96–108.

Attwood, R. (2010). Making the A level work a little harder. *Times Higher Education,* 4 November. 34–39. http://www.timeshighereducation.co.uk/story.asp?storycode=414077. Accessed 10 November 2010.

Aynsley Green, A. et al (Ed.) (2010).*Take Heed, Mr Gove.* Prestwood, UK: Iris Press.

Bangs, J., Galton, M., Macbeath, J. (2011). *Reinventing Schools, Reforming Teaching: From Political Visions to Classroom Reality.* Abingdon, UK: Taylor and Francis.

Binch, N. (1994).The Implications of the National Curriculum Orders for Art, *Journal of Art & Design Education, 13.2,* 117–132.

Blair, A. (2007). Exam bias' makes the boys look like failures. *The Times (Education Section),* 24 April.

Boughton, D. (1995). Six Myths of National Curriculum Reforms in Art Education, *Journal of Art & Design Education, 14* (2), 139–152.

Bowden, J. (2000). Art & Design: The Rhetoric and the Practice, *Journal of Art & Design Education, 19* (1), 20–36.

Downing, D., Watson, R. (2004). *School Art: What's in it?* Slough, UK: NFER.

Edexcel (2000). *GCE A level Art & Design: Guide for Teachers and Moderators.* London: Edexcel

Eisner, E. (2004). What Can Education Learn from the Arts about the Practice of Education?, *International Journal of Education & the Arts, 5* (4), http://ijea.asu.edu/v5n4/. Accessed 20 October 2010.

General Teaching Council [GTC] (2004). Internal and External Assessment: What is the Right Balance for the Future? Advice to the Secretary of State for Education and Others, http://www.gtce.org.uk/publications/assess_advice1004/. Accessed 20 October 2010.

Hickman, R. (Ed.) (2005). *Critical Studies in Art Education.* Bristol, UK: Intellect.

Hirsch, E. (1996).*The schools we need and why we don't have them.* New York: Doubleday.

Hughes, A. (1998). Reconceptualising the Art Curriculum, *Journal of Art & Design Education, 17* (1), 41–50.

James, M. (2009). Tailors of assessment must find a better fit. *TES,* 21 August, http://www.tes.co.uk/article.aspx?storycode=6020977. Accessed 20 October 2010.

Mansell, W., James, M., the Assessment Reform Group (2009). *Assessment in schools: Fit for purpose? A Commentary by the Teaching and Learning Research Programme.*London: Economic and Social Research Council, Teaching and Learning Research Programme, http://www.assessment-reform-group.org/assessment_in_schools-fit-for-purpose.pdf. Accessed 24 September 2010.

Mason, R., Steers, J. (2006). The impact of formal assessment procedures on teaching and learning in art and design in secondary schools, *International Journal of Art & Design Education, 25* (2), 119–133.

Ofsted (2005). *Ofsted subject reports 2003/04: Art & design in secondary schools*, http://www.ofsted.gov.uk/publications/annualreport0304/subject_report. Accessed 14 April 2005.

——— (2009). *Drawing together: Art, craft and design in schools.* London: Ofsted.

Price, E. (1982). National Criteria for 16+ Examinations, *Journal of Art & Design Education, 1* (3), 397–408.

QCA (2007). GCSE subject criteria for art and design, http://www.ofqual.gov.uk/files/qca-07-3441_gcsecriteriaartanddesign.pdf. Accessed 19 October 2010.

QCDA (2010). Qualifications and Credit Framework (QCF), http://www.qcda.gov.uk/qualifications/60.aspx. Accessed 13 September 2010.

Read, W. (1988/1994). *GCSE Art and* Design (2nd ed.). Harlow: Longman.

Ross, M. (1993). *Assessing Achievement in the Arts.* Milton Keynes, UK: Open University Press.

Steers, J. (2007). Reconsidering Assessment for Learning in Art and Design. In Addison, N., Burgess, L. (Eds.). *Learning to Teach Art and Design in the Secondary School.* Abingdon, UK: Routledge. 165–175.

——— (2009). Creativity: Delusions, Reality, Opportunities and Challenges, *International Journal of Art of Art & Design Education, 28* (2), 126–138.

Swift, J., Steers, J. (1999). A Manifesto for Art in Schools, *Journal of Art of Art & Design Education, 18* (1), 7–14.

Torres Pereira de Eça, M. (2005). Using portfolios for external assessment: an experiment in Portugal, *International Journal of Art of Art & Design Education, 24* (2), 209–218.

White, J. (2010). The escalator taking teens straight from school to university is a crazy way to proceed. *TES*, 22 October. 25.

Notes

1 In England these are Oxford Cambridge and RSA Examinations (OCR) – www.ocr.org.uk; the Assessment and Qualifications Alliance (AQA) – www.aqa.org.uk; and Edexcel – www.edexcel.org.uk. The WJEC, previously the Welsh Joint Education Committee, is the awarding body in Wales – www.wjec.org.uk; while Northern Ireland has the Council for Curriculum, Examinations and Assessment (CCEA) – www.ccea.org.uk.

2 For more information go to: www.ofqual.gov.uk/diplomaguide.

3 Data from the Joint Council Qualifications: www.jcq.org.uk.

4 www.ofqual.gov.uk/files/qca-07-3441_gcsecriteriaartanddesign.pdf.

5 These include the Schools' Council, the School Examinations and Assessment Council (SEAC), the School Curriculum and Assessment Authority (SCAA), and the Qualifications and Curriculum Authority (QCA).

6 See for example: http://www.edexcel.com/migrationdocuments/GCSE%20New%20GCSE/Specification-art.pdf.

7   The GCSE Code of Practice for 2010 may be downloaded at: http://www.ofqual.gov.uk/for-awarding-organisations/96-articles/247-codes-of-practice-2010.

8   A series of working papers on assessment on the NSEAD website address these issues. See: http://www.nsead.org/publications/papers.aspx.

9   The "GCSE, GCE, principal learning and project code of practice" (April 2010) which may be retrieved from: http://www.ofqual.gov.uk/files/code-of-practice-2010.pdf. Accessed 19 October 2010.

10   Examination specifications usually include a number of units and/or components – units are the smallest part of an examination or qualification that can be separately assessed; components are discrete assessable elements within a specification butwhich are not separately certificated.

11   Current specifications for GCSE art and design examinations in England and Wales can be accessed at: http://www.ofqual.gov.uk/files/qca-07-3441_gcsecriteriaartanddesign.pdf.

12   The JCQ (formerly the Joint Council for General Qualifications) was established on 1 January 2004 and represents the major awarding bodies that serve England, Wales, and Northern Ireland: AQA, CCEA (the Northern Ireland Council for the Curriculum, Examinations and Assessment), City and Guilds, Edexcel, OCR, and WJEC.

13   Terminal test – in art and design this is not a test in the usual sense but normally the final, summative or confirmatory examination unit. Often takes the form of an extended assignment that is externally set, internally assessed, and externally moderated. Several weeks may be allowed for research and preparation but the "test" consists of a defined period (e.g. ten hours) for the candidate to work unaided under examination like conditions.

14   GCSE Bitesize: Art & Design: http://www.bbc.co.uk/schools/gcsebitesize/art/. Accessed 4 November 2010.

15   See: www.coreknowledge.org.

Chapter 3

From artistic and cultural education to the art of living: Evaluation of the French situation in 2010

Bernard Darras, Université Paris 1 Panthéon-Sorbonne, France

Abstract

The fever of evaluation has gripped the world and France has not been spared the virus. A whole culture has emerged and is spreading, its protocols are more or less accepted and implemented, experts have appeared, and evaluation is becoming institutionalized and bureaucratized. In France at least, the evaluation culture is still often a culture derived from hierarchical top-down management, and is often seen as a strategy of control more than a policy of support, reward, and commitment.

Although they may be inefficient or diverted from their intended uses, these tools can allow us to correct certain defects and to anticipate certain risks while creating an environment preparing for adaptation and change, but also to promote competition among systems and among human beings.

In this chapter, we will summarize the results of the symposium, which assessed the impact of art education in Paris in 2007, and then we will present the French system of art and cultural education and its recent changes. We will then utilize two major national surveys, which will allow us to assess and anticipate the impact of these recent changes. We shall show that the true beneficiaries of the export and expand of the elite's cultural capital to the entire population, are children and youth who already belong to the "creative class". To go beyond, art and cultural education clearly must become cultural before being artistic.

On evaluation

In recent years, my career, my publications, the training and the research centre I direct have been evaluated several times. I now devote a significant amount of my time to anticipate these assessments and to some extent I feel that I conform to their requirements, both explicit and implicit. In general, my results have been very good ... except once. Then I felt a deep sense of incomprehension and injustice, then a real revolt against a one way system that has never explained to me its evaluation methods or the reasons for this underachievement.

In France at least, the evaluation culture is still often a culture derived from hierarchical *top-down* management, and is often seen as a strategy of control and punishment more than a policy of support, reward, and commitment.[1]

Although they may be inefficient or diverted from their intended uses, these tools can allow us to correct certain defects and to anticipate certain risks while creating an environment preparing for adaptation and change. But make no mistake, this trend in evaluation and change is also used to promote competition among systems and among human beings.[2]

In this chapter, we will summarize the results of the symposium which assessed the impact of artistic education in Paris in 2007, then we will present the French system of artistic and cultural education and its recent changes, we will then utilize two major national surveys, which will allow us to assess and anticipate their impact.

Evaluating the impact of artistic and cultural education: A European and international research symposium

The school, which has always been a centre for the evaluation of learning, has been for some time encouraged to use on itself the tools it had so far reserved for its students. It is in this context of evaluation and preparation for change that, in January 2007, the French state organized an international symposium on the evaluation of the effects of artistic and cultural education. As a member of the scientific committee of this event, I was in the perfect position to observe this scientific event.[3]

The scientific committee had carefully avoided inviting institutions accustomed to generous pleas regarding the benefits of artistic education, but too general to assist in steering education policies. Instead, invited researchers had to provide precise, empirical and experimental results on the effects of artistic education. The well-documented and discerning presentation of Anne Bamford on the global evaluation of the quality and major defects of artistic education conducted for UNESCO (Bamford, 2007, pp. 21–30; Bamford, 2006a and 2006b) opened the symposium. The majority of the conferences that followed tried to highlight a particular benefit or absence of benefit in the following areas: emotional impact, such as pleasure, pride, a sense of success, self-esteem and confidence, but also the benefits in focus and attention, the acquired general knowledge regarding heritage, arts and cultural identity, but also regarding the ability to analyse, criticize, innovate, and the ability to collaborate with and respect others, etc. (e.g. Lord, 2007)

Contrary to the expectations of the organizers, the quantitative or qualitative research presented was not able to demonstrate in a decisive and convincing way the positive effects of art education. As no economist or social economist has responded to the call for contributions, it was impossible to assess the impact of school art education on the citizens' cultural practices and preferences according to their gender, class, or education.[4] This data is of course generally available, and that is what we will try to show in this chapter, but nothing really helps us discover where the interest in art and culture is formed outside the family environment. Similarly, no study has managed to highlight the chain of cause and effect between compulsory art education and the improvement of individuals' well-being. At most could we verify that a quality art education contributed to improving students' self-esteem and that the artistic practices undertaken in class had a slight positive impact on their learning or behaviour in other disciplines. The cognitivist and comparative research of musicologists have appeared far more advanced than those of other art forms. But, as shown by France Rauscher, musical education has as much impact on the learning of other disciplines as a mental management session or an IT course (Rauscher, 2007). All of these barely positive results were not really favourable to the defenders of the teaching of these disciplines at school.

It therefore seemed reassuring to claim that traditional evaluation methods were not very suitable in the area of education, which is probably true; and that the effects of art education might be found outside the school, which is also probably true (e.g. O'Farrell, 2007). As for me, I was surprised to see that all these researchers from around the world were not dismayed by this irrelevant and barely favourable outcome.

As I tried to show in a critical and prospective article published in *The International Journal of Art Education*, the research presented did not seem to take the proper distance, either with the challenges or with what is really relevant to assess. Until such assessments are implemented, let's focus on those available in France (Darras, 2009).[5]

Where does the French system stand?

Because of their history and methods of government, all education systems are complex and therefore somewhat difficult to explain as they result from multiple agencies and more or less successful adjustments.

The French education system is probably no more complicated than others, but insofar as it results from the more or less efficient collaboration of two key ministries – the Ministry of Education and the Ministry of Culture – it is not easy to describe its operation without simplifying a complexity that can be considered as an asset or a lack of organization. In recent years, this system has undergone profound restructuring and diversification. That's what we will try to describe after making some semantic clarification on key concepts.

Two semantic preliminaries

Art

In French and English, the word "art" is rooted in the same ancient Latin world in which the semantic space of *ars* derived from the Greek concept of *teckne*. But over the centuries, the semantic space of "art" took different turns in the Latin and Anglo-American worlds. If the latter kept the two meanings of "art" as a cultural practice of liberal elites on the one hand, and as a set of techniques, skills, and mastered practices on the other, the Latin world favoured the liberal version: the scholarly culture of the elite.

The consequences of these two approaches are numerous and have an impact on the terms *"éducation artistique"* and "art education". The first is mainly devoted to high culture, while the second has a much broader spectrum. Somehow, the new term "artistic and cultural education" that has been used in France since 2001, is closer to the semantic and practical space of "Art Education" and even has a broader spectrum (see Darras, 2009).

Visual Arts

In France and some other Latin countries, the term *"Arts Plastiques"* was preferred to *"Arts Visuels"*. This difference is not insignificant. On the one hand, the object and the product are valued as well as one of their intrinsic properties: the shape and hence the plasticity, and on the other hand, the extrinsic process of receiving, i.e. the vision, is enhanced.

The distinction is subtle, but in one case as in the other, the approach is not the same. The preference for the term "Arts Plastiques" explains in part why French teachers are more focused on the artworks than on the students' concerns. However, in both cases, the designations are simplistic and not appropriate to name the composite reality of experience and creation in the very open field of communication, design, and art.

The artistic and cultural education system

In France, the system of state schools is quantitatively much more important than the private system. But overwhelmingly, the latter follows the recommendations and programmes of the state with which it is contracted. One can therefore speak of a unified system. In both cases, the quality of schools varies from excellent to poor, but overall the French education system has a good reputation and the performance of its students is situated in the average band of European nations. (See the results of the Programme for International of Student Assessment PISA surveys within the OECD[6] countries and the critical study on French Republican elitism by the educational sociologists C. Baudelot and R. Establet [2009].)

Initial training

Artistic and cultural education is compulsory from primary school (which starts at the age of three) and until the end of the first cycle of secondary education. In primary schools, artistic and cultural education includes visual arts (*arts plastiques*) and music. Both courses are taught by generalist teachers who on the whole have received only a very brief training in this area. But, in big cities, these courses are provided by specialist teachers.

However, in the first cycle of secondary education, lessons of 55 minutes each are provided by specialist teachers. In the second cycle of secondary education, art is also taught by specialist teachers but is no longer mandatory but voluntary or optional.[7] When voluntary, pupils receive three hours of instruction per week and five hours if it is optional (specialized discipline). Both methods can be combined. In both cases, pupils' performance is evaluated for the *baccalauréat* which concludes secondary education and marks the entry into higher education, which we will not discuss here. From 2010, this teaching has changed its name into "Création et activités artistiques" (Creation and artistic activities). As everywhere in the world, one is witnessing a major resurgence of creativity (see Darras, 2011).

All schools in the second cycle of secondary education do not provide artistic education and if they do, the schools can choose their specialty. In general, most teach music or visual arts, but there is also teaching in film, theatre, etc. We will return to this later.

One must also note that in the second cycle of secondary school, pupils who want to specialize can access extensive technical training in various areas of applied arts and crafts.

Two important new developments

To this basic architecture were recently added two additional mandatory subjects for all pupils.

They cover on the one hand, image education, for one hour per week in all classes of lower secondary school.[8] On the other hand, since 2009, a weekly hour of history of the arts at all levels of the first cycle of secondary education.[9] Officially,

> this teaching aims at offering all students opportunities to discover directly and personally artworks of reference within different artistic fields, from different eras and civilizations; to give them the ability to envisage these works, through a familiarity with them, from a more knowledgeable and sensitive point of view; the ability to acquire personal culture with a universal value; the means to obtain information on professions related to art and to culture. [...] The works studied belong to six major artistic fields: The arts of space: architecture, landscape design; The arts of language: literature (narrative, poetry); The arts of daily life: design, art objects; The arts of sound: music (instrumental, vocal); Performing arts: theatre, dance, circus, puppetry; Visual arts: "arts plastiques", cinema, photography. These artworks are historical and contemporary as well as scholarly and popular, national and international. They are chosen from a reference list for primary school and from lists of topics for secondary school.[10]

One should note the absence of digital culture, especially video games and multimedia. This historical focus prevents the system from adjusting to the real experience of its pupils and to the most promising technologies. We will return to this point.

When they are really and actually applied and when they work well, artistic education, image education and history of the arts constitute a relatively complete cultural foundation, which provides good education to students throughout their school careers.

A rich diversity

To this common foundation is added a large variety of voluntary or optional teaching impetus, which come in various cultural forms: workshops, immersion classes, visit programmes, projects of cultural activity, artists in residence at the school, etc.

This proliferation of initiatives results from collaborations and partnerships between the Ministry of Education and the Ministry of Culture at both national and regional level. Without prejudging the benefits of these improvements, it is obvious to those who are well informed or not fooled that the combination of formal education provided by educationalists and artistic and cultural awareness provided by artists or players who surround the art world is the result of a commitment of the state, which is motivated by at least three reasons. The first concerns the enrichment of the artistic career of pupils who wish to increase their cultural capital; the second is related to the first and aims at fostering partnerships with the rich network of French cultural institutions and facilities. The third reason is related to both the previous ones and aims at giving employment to many artists lacking financial and social stability.

This is how the art world enters the school where it contributes to the cultural and artistic training demanded by educated upper-middle classes as well as by members of the "Creative Class" (Florida, 2002). Incidentally, some pupils provided with less cultural capital from their families benefit from this situation and thus access cultural experiences that may promote their upward social mobility, and in particular to enter the creative class.

Issues of evaluation

Each level and each teaching method creates its own system for the assessment of pupils' skills and acquired knowledge. Teachers also benefit from great flexibility. The evaluation of compulsory education is both formative and summative, but teachers still have to mark each pupil. The performance of pupils is generally assessed from their answers to tasks set by the teacher or when participating in joint projects.

During the second cycle of secondary school, the method is more complex. In the case of visual arts (*arts plastiques*), for example, thematic programmes are set nationally for several years (e.g. for voluntary teaching: "The Polyptych", "Three-dimensional work and the public space". For specialty teaching: "Museum Architecture in the 20th century", "The Representation of the human face", "Innovation and tradition in photography from 1980 to the present day".)

For the *baccalauréat*, applicants must provide a portfolio of personal work and orally defend it by linking it to the national programme. The evaluation focuses on the artistic, technical, cultural and methodological skills expected, which are evaluated by a jury on four qualitative aspects estimating if the competence is: absent, present at a minimum, seriously demonstrated or demonstrated with great command.

For the specialty test, the candidate must also address artistic issues in writing. Throughout the year, pupils are evaluated on their progress, in line with official recommendations, but they are also assessed on their results regarding objectives. They must also answer written questions in a limited time on a certain subject. Another impetus of artistic and cultural education results in projects which are presented at exhibitions, concerts, theatres, etc.

Issues of national evaluation: 2008–2009 survey on artistic and cultural education[11]

As we have already mentioned, in addition to the basic artistic and cultural teaching, school education is enriched by a variety of cultural activities that pupils can attend at their school, provided that these opportunities are available. These cultural activities are part of various measures sponsored by the state to promote access to culture.[12] They are therefore subject to regulations that reorganize and enrich the existing system and receive direct or indirect funds from the state, regions and cities, which are the main financial providers of these activities.

In reality, the creation of a cultural activity depends on the initiative of the local teaching staff, that is to say the willingness of the teachers concerned and the head of the school. In 2008–2009, the Ministry of Education launched an extensive internal quantitative survey to assess the implementation of these activities. This survey led by the General Directorate of School education concerned every public or private school in contract with the state, from primary to secondary education.

The first observation of the final report concerned the difficulty of implementing such a national survey, as the different institutional levels are too often approached by such requests, although they do not have the staff, the adapted tools and the common classifications necessary to collect, collate, process and disseminate in a regular and reliable manner all the information that usually stays with the staff in the field. The culture of information, especially that of its transformation into knowledge, is not as widespread as one might think.

The many schools that responded to this survey have made available information on 2,912,379 pupils participating in these activities. But this survey which is focused on the activities and not the pupils, did not take into account children who practise one or more cultural activity. Consequently, one can never know the number of children involved in these activities, nor the proportion they represent in relation to the overall pupil population.

It remains that among a little over 12 million pupils enrolled during the survey period, almost 3 million participated in cultural activities and it is therefore not unreasonable to consider that about 20% of pupils were involved in the identified cultural activities.[13] The survey also shows that if all schools can legally create any type of cultural activity, it is not necessary the case. Despite the potential diversity of activities on offer, one can observe a kind of co-determination effect of supply and demand that benefits the most popular disciplines (drama, visual arts, and music), thus strengthening their position.

Furthermore, one can classify these activities into three groups: (1) those for pupils who have an individual project or an artistic career or a "talent" to develop; (2) activities dedicated to pupils who have a taste for art whether acquired through the family or personally, and (3) the activities of schools which collectively engage pupils in cultural practices. Let's examine these activities:

Group 1: Classes with flexible hours

These classes with flexible teaching hours arranged to allow intensive practice of an art are reserved for talented pupils who are keen on a professional artistic career. This applies to music in which 18,257 pupils are enrolled, and to dance (653). Along with their general education, these pupils attend classes at a conservatory of music or dance, as is the case for example for the Paris Opera, which is the most prestigious school of dance in France. This system of classes with flexible hours has been recently extended to theatre and visual arts.

Group 2: Educational support[14]

Since 2007, the state has reorganized and expanded after-school activities for voluntary pupils, which are mainly supervised by teachers or other approved staff, including artists. Primary schools and the first cycle of secondary education that have adopted this system offer pupils the five types of activities previously mentioned. The most attended activities are homework assistance,[15] sport, languages, IT, multimedia/documentary activities and artistic and cultural practices.

In 2009, the artistic and cultural practices accounted for just over a quarter (26.2%) of all hours of educational support. As all the disciplines are not offered by all the schools, the choice of pupils depends on availability. As a whole, artistic and cultural activities have attracted 155,000 participants.[16] In descending order of what is available/attended, it is theatre (14%), music (13%), science (11%), visual arts (11%), literature and poetry (7%) that attracts the highest number of students. Other disciplines such as film and dance are offered and/or chosen less frequently, they both attract only 4% of participating pupils. Photography, heritage, applied arts, culinary arts (cooking), architecture, circus, and landscape design are offered here and there thanks to local initiatives and attract a few hundred or a few thousand participants.

Moreover, the survey reveals that 34,144 pupils (22% of the participants) took part in diverse activities, which were so rare that they were grouped under the label "others" by the survey analysts. This number is a good indicator of the originality behind nearly a quarter of the projects in this sector. These figures alone justify the term "cultural" used by this system.

Group 3: Artistic workshops[17] and school choirs

These workshops dedicated to practice and criticism account for 4% of what artistic and cultural education has to offer. They are open to the cultural environment with which partnerships are established. The support of the state has helped to boost school choirs, which represent 21% of the activities offered by artistic and cultural education.

Group 4: Collective practices

The activities of image education in cinema attracted 1,163,015 pupils in 2008 and 2009, representing 40% of the activities offered by artistic and cultural education. The second project involves a joint action plan between the Ministry of Education and the Ministry of Culture and Communication.[18] Established in 2001, the *artistic and cultural project classes*[19] represent 18% of the activities on offer and mainly focus on music, visual arts, and theatre.

The survey thus shows that the initiatives of the state are actually implemented in schools and allow millions of pupils to benefit from in-depth or enriched artistic and cultural education in addition to the mandatory or optional training in their curriculum. The culture represented and valued depends inevitably on the legitimate and legitimizing structures and institutions that are in place. Classical or traditional areas are also overrepresented compared to more "unusual" disciplines such as circus, chess or culinary arts.

As this survey is primarily an inventory of the various activities and an evaluation of enrolment, one does not learn anything about the pupils, their social origin, their motivations, their aspirations, their aptitudes, or their skills. Such a survey still has to be undertaken as it would allow us to discover if the efforts of the state meet its mission in expanding cultural practices that is often mistakenly called "democratization of culture", or if these efforts only strengthen the cultural practices of segments of the population who already have a high cultural or creative capital (Darras, 2004, 2008a, 2008b). We believe that the latter is more likely. As we cannot confirm it through direct information, we will therefore use another series of national surveys to try to confirm our hypothesis.

Survey on French cultural participation in the digital age

Since 1973, the Ministry of Culture and Communication regularly questions people residing in France on their cultural practices and attitudes. These surveys were conducted in 1973, 1981, 1988, 1997, and 2008 and supported the policies for the democratization of culture. Since 1997, they have allowed to put into perspective the impact of these actions by showing that the cultural public was sociologically very homogeneous and concentrated in the most educated segments of the population. They also showed that these individuals were multi-practising and the major users of the activities for the mediation and dissemination of culture. However, when studying the data from these surveys from an individual point of view, the sociologist Bernard Lahire (2004) showed that the population's behaviour was changing and that people were developing more personal, diverse and open cultural strategies than their social class would have assigned to them. Somehow, people now tend to overcome the cultural obligations and assignments of class that Pierre Bourdieu documented so well during the 1960s and 1970s (see Bourdieu and Passeron, 1964; Bourdieu and Darbel, 1969; Bourdieu, 1979).

The 2008 survey was conducted in the homes of respondents from a representative sample of 5,004 residents of France of 15 years of age or older.[20] Answering the questionnaire took approximately 50 minutes and addressed all the contemporary practices of free time and "lifestyle". The survey focused on leisure and holidays as well as evenings out, social life, home appliances, video games, computers, media: television, video/DVD, radio, press, listening to music, reading, performing arts, cinema, visits to museums and heritage sites, but also pastimes, hobbies, and passions.[21] When exploring the results of this vast and complete survey, we were particularly interested in the responses from young people aged 15–17 and 18–24 (respectively 213 and 528 respondents).

To answer our initial questions, we focused our attention on two areas: video games that do not yet appear in the activities provided by artistic and cultural education, and pastimes and hobbies that may be good indicators of the impact of academic learning and scholarly activities on life outside school.[22]

Video games

Founded in the 1980s, the video game industry has radically changed cultural industries. This sector, which has taken over every screen, has become among the most popular cultural practices of today. Originally reserved for young males in developed countries, these games are globally expanding in terms of gender and age thanks to the ingenuity of scriptwriters, designers, and developers.

The development and practice of interactive scenarios and interacted images is undoubtedly one of the major cultural changes of the last 30 years. However, the presence of the video game in the education system remains marginal, if not banned. Parents and educationalists are constantly complaining about the perverse effects of interactive entertainment on youth, but few decide to integrate it into a real educational process, both aesthetic, narrative, strategic, logical, etc. (see Darras, 2003).

In the wake of edutainment, the recent development of "serious" games shows a new momentum in the sector. This suggests that if the management and personnel of large companies are discovering the virtues of scripted, interactive learning for vocational training, it is not impossible that such methods will gradually take hold in the school where gaming experts are already very numerous among pupils of all ages, young teachers and even their elders. Byron Reeves and J. Leighton Read (2009) pertinently observe: "One hundred million Americans, and many more around the world, played a computer or video game last week with levels of engagement and focus rarely seen at work. [...] For anyone convinced that *engagement* is a key ingredient of the future of work, games are the definitive model" (p. 4).

If the revolution of interactive edutainment has not taken hold in artistic and cultural education, or does not appear in the survey of the Ministry of Education, it nevertheless plays an important role in the survey undertaken by the Ministry of Culture and Communication. Unsurprisingly, it appears that pupils and students aged 15–19 are more likely to declare themselves as daily gamers (21%) and weekly gamers (35%). These figures decline with age but 11% of 20–24-year-olds admit to gaming every day and 28% play once or several times a week. 39% of men from 15 to 30 years of age play video games, compared to 16% of women of the same age. They prefer playing action and sports games (62%) but also strategy games (39%). Far from these results, only 7% of 15–30-year-old men play edutainment games, versus 13% of women of a similar age. As we see from the results of the survey, digital cultural practices are intense; the school should not ignore or despise them any longer.

Pastime practices

As we shall show in conclusion, we are convinced that one of the major goals of artistic and cultural education should involve the development of the "art of living". As such, we are particularly interested in pastime practices that reflect the ability of the individual to cultivate creative and expressive practices for individual and social purposes.

The survey shows that 74% of men and 67% of women of all ages have no pastime activity. They do not practice creative writing, they do not dance, and they do not act or practise visual arts. And 82% of them do not practise music.

The survey data also show a general decline in all pastime activities with age, but they confirm a greater interest in these practices in the most educated categories of the population. The closer you are to leaving school and the longer you remained at school, the more you will tend to cultivate your cultural capital.

In this area, this study does confirm all those that preceded it. Among the available data, we were particularly interested in the practices of photography and digital video on the one hand and, on the other, on more traditional graphic and visual arts.[23]

Photography and video

Among each group of 100 people who used a digital camera in the past 12 months, 72% of 15–30-year-old women and 64% of men of the same age have created a photo album on their PC and respectively 35% and 30% have retouched their photographs, while 56% and 52% have sent or uploaded their photographs using the Internet. These are massively popular practices of fixed image technology. Video is used a little less. In this case, in the same age group, 48% of men store videos on their PC, versus 43% of women. But 17% of men and 12% of women have retouched and edited their videos and respectively 20% and 16% have sent or uploaded their videos using the Internet.

All the reported activities are actually widely practised and almost by the entire population as even 40% of 63+ men and women take photos and keep them on their PC (38% for video for men and 21% for women).

When one addresses more technical activities such as retouching and editing, the practice rate decreases with age but it remains a common practice in the population. These two techniques are indeed part of the life of the population, they are certainly more practised by young people than by their elders and more by managers and the higher intellectual professions than by employees and workers, but these "middle-brow arts" such as Bourdieu (1965) called them are popular pastime practices, including the technical and aesthetic interventions that accompany them.

In this area, image education clearly has an important role to play in helping the development of technical, communication and aesthetic practices.

Painting and drawing

Compared to the very popular use of technological images, the more traditional "arts" of painting, engraving, sculpture and drawing seem less attractive. But fortunately they have not disappeared. 19% of women and 10% of men from 15–30 years of age claimed to practise at least one of these visual arts, and 30% of women and men of this age say they practise drawing. In both cases, these practices fall after the age of 30 and become rarer with age, reaching 5% of the population after the age of 63.

The intensity of professional and family activities is probably responsible for this decline in practices that affects all segments of the population. Even if 10–15% of members of the most educated segments claim having practised such activities, versus 5–10% among workers.

In the case of drawing, the results obtained are even more interesting as teaching drawing as a specific discipline has virtually disappeared from artistic and cultural education. It would therefore be interesting to know to which practices these statements refer to. Do the respondents mean communication graphics or do they mean creative or artistic practices? (Darras, 1996)

Further investigations on the follow-up of actual practices would be welcome to better assess the sustainability of school learning. However, it appears that although carried out by a minority of the population, these "traditional" practices remain stable through the different surveys and are undertaken by approximately 10% of the population. These results are well below those obtained by photography and video which are practised by four times as many people. On this point, the differences are very relevant and reflect the impact of digital technology on the practices.

Although it is difficult to establish a direct cause–effect relationship between artistic and cultural education and pastime practices, it is likely that a well managed education has a sustainable effect on these practices. Educational policies should take into account this information that should be better assessed by major decennial surveys.

Conclusion and redefinition of objectives

Does this survey on cultural practices make the debate between the expansion of culture or the reinforcement of cultural divisions by artistic and cultural education move forward? While there is a persistent gap between the practices of social groups of the same age, it is mainly the variables in gender and age that are most meaningful in relation to the practices studied.

As noted by Olivier Donnat (2009) who wrote the summary of the survey,[24] 22% of the French population who benefit from all the social and cultural advantages have regular, diverse and intense cultural practices. But the major change in the last ten years is the irresistible rise of screen culture to which French people dedicate on average 31 hours of their free time per week. These screens

[…] increase the permeability between the world of art and that of entertainment and communication. […] With the digital technology and the versatility of the terminals available today, most cultural practices now converge towards the screen: viewing pictures and listening to music of course, but also reading texts or for pastime practices, not to mention the now commonplace presence of screens in libraries, exhibition spaces and even in some performing arts venues. Everything is now potentially viewable on a screen and accessible through the internet. (Donnat, 2009)

Children and young people are surrounded by screens, gaming consoles, DVDs, broadband Internet, mobile phones. They live intensely in a flow of content that is both interactive and dematerialized through communication machines, which have a profound and perhaps permanent impact on their relationship with the world (Darras and Belkhamsa, 2009). Can the school adapt to this change? In the area that concerns us, the school seems to develop, reform after reform, opening after opening, trying to follow (and sometimes to attenuate) the cultural and technological changes. Artistic and cultural education clearly tends to become cultural before being artistic. As such and to various degrees, we believe that this cultural education should place the preparation for the "art of living" at the heart of pupils' training. In most ancient cultures, this objective was clearly stated for the minority of the population who attended the "scholè" in the Greek world or who practised the "otium" in the Roman world for example.

Today, the education for the "art of living in the digital age" should contribute to a synthesis of practices, experiences and knowledge. It should therefore help cultivate, refine, share and discuss the experiences of the world in order to help pupils constitute an "art of living" today, for themselves and with others.

To do so, it should contribute to the knowledge of contemporary creation (in design as well as art) without neglecting the knowledge of regional, national and universal heritage. It should contribute to the development of creativity and the implementation of individual and collective projects while supporting and encouraging the development of skills in communication and expression in all media, above all contemporary media. Finally, it should assure the development of critical and aesthetic skills in all areas of the body, space, image, sound, audiovisual, and interactivity.

The more contemporary the area, the more frequent the practices in the population, the closer to technology and the more popular. The more practises are up to date, the more there is permeability between them. For the moment, the gap between scholarly culture and the cultures of everyday life seems very great. Is it widening or diminishing? What are the good or bad practices? To answer such questions, all the partners of the education system need surveys and global evaluations on the trends but also local surveys conducted preferably in the context of action research methodology. Integrated to practices and experience, they will be truly pertinent and will help understand and support the changes underway.

References

Bamford, A. (2006a). *The Wow Factor: The global research compendium on the impact of arts in education*. Berlin: Waxmann Münster.

———— (2006b). Building innovation: The impact of education in and through the arts. In Oakley, K. et al. (Eds.). *How are we going? Directions for the Arts in the Creative Age*. London: Cambridge Scholars Press.

———— (2008). Mesurer l'impact: Recherche(s) en éducation artistique et culturelle. *Evaluer les effets de l'éducation artistique et culturelle: Symposium européen et international de recherche.* (Measuring the impact: Research on art and culture education. Evaluating the effects of art and culture education: a European and international research symposium.) Paris: La Documentation française-Centre Pompidou. 21–30.

Baudelot, C., Establet, R. (2009). *L'Elitisme républicain: L'école française à l'épreuve des comparaisons internationales.* (The Republican elitism: French education as represented by international comparative studies.) Paris: Seuil Publishers.

Bourdieu, P., Passeron, J-C. (1964). *Les Héritiers: Les étudiants et la culture.* (The Inheritors: students and culture.) Paris: Editions de Minuit Publishers.

Bourdieu, P. (Ed.) (1965). *Un art moyen: Essai sur les usages sociaux de la photographie.* (A Middle-Brow Art; an essay about the social use of photography.) Paris: Editions de Minuit publishers.

Bourdieu, P., Darbel, A. (1969). *L'amour de l'art: Les musées d'art européens et leur public.* (The love of art: The European art museums and their public.) Paris: Editions de Minuit publishers.

Bourdieu, P. (1979). *La distinction: Critique sociale du jugement.* (The distinction: Social criticism of assessment.) Paris: Editions de Minuit Publishers.

——— (1992). *Les Règles de l'art.* (The rules of art.) Paris: Seuil Publishers.

Chervel, A. (1998). *La Culture scolaire: Une approche historique.* (School culture – a historic approach.) Paris: Belin Publishers.

Darras, B. (1996). *Au commencement était l'image: Du dessin de l'enfant à la communication de l'adulte.* (At the beginning, there was the image: from the drawing of the child to the communication of the adult.) Paris: ESF.

——— (Ed.) (2003). *Jeux, medias, savoirs: MEI 18.* (Games, media and knowledge: MEI 18.) Paris: L'Harmattan.

——— (2004). Etudes des Conceptions de la Culture et de la Médiation. (Studies on the conception of culture and mediation.) In Thonon, Marie (Ed.), *Médiation Médiateur.* (Mediation/Mediator) Paris: L'Harmattan/MEI. 61–85.

——— (2006). De l'éducation artistique à l'éducation culturelle. (From art education to cultural education.) Paper presented at *UNESCO Conférence Mondiale sur l'Education Artistique,* Paris, 2006. http://portal.unesco.org/culture/fr/ev.php-URL_ID=29289&URL_DO=DO_TOPIC&URL_SECTION=201.html. Accessed 12 February 2013.

——— (2008a). As varias concepções da cultura e seus efeitos sobre os processos de mediação cultural (On different conceptions of culture and their effects on the process of cultural mediation.) In Barboza, Ana Mae; Coutinho, Rejane Galvao (Eds.). *Arte/Educaçao como mediaçao cultural e social.* (Art/Education as mediation of culture and social values.) São Paulo: Editora UNESP. 23–52.

——— (2008b). Del patrimonio artístico a la ecología de las culturas: La cuestión de la cultura elitista en democracia. (From the artistic heritage to the ecology of cultures: the issue of elitist culture and democracy.) In Aguirre, I.; Fontal, O.; Darras, B.; Rickenmann, R. (Eds.). *El access al patrimonio cultural: Retos y debates: Del patrimonio artístico a la ecología de las culturas, La cuestión de la cultura elitista en democracia.* (Access to the artistic heritage: Issues and responses: From the artistic heritage to the ecology of cultures: the issue of elitist culture and democracy.) Pamplona, Spain: Cátedra Jorge Oteiza – Universidad Pública de Navarra. 119–165.

——— (2009). Art education, are we on the right path?, *The International Journal of Art Education, 12,* 67–81.

Darras, B., Belkhamsa S. (2009). Technology and post-human imaginary: Semiotic approach of adolescents' system of belief regarding mobile digital technology. *Technology Imagination Future – Journal for Transdisciplinary knowledge Design,* (3) 2, 13–30.

Darras, B. (2011). Creativity, creative class, smart power, reproduction and symbolic violence. In Sefton-Green, J.; Thomson, P.; Jones, K.; Bresler, L. (Eds.). *The Routledge International Handbook of Creative Learning.* Oxford: Routledge. 90–98.

Donnat, O. (2009). *French Cultural Participation in the Digital Age.* Summary 1997–2008. Paris: La Documentation française - Centre Pompidou.

Evaluating the impact of arts and cultural education: A European and International Research Symposium, Paris, (2009). http://www.ladocumentationfrancaise.fr/catalogue/9782110071576/index.shtml. Symposium videos, http://www.centrepompidou.fr/streaming/symposium/index.html. Accessed 12 December 2010.

Florida, R. (2002). *The Rise of the Creative Class: And How It's Transforming Work, Leisure and Everyday Life*. New York: *Basic Books*.

French Cultural Participation in the Digital Age, http://www.pratiquesculturelles.culture.gouv.fr/. Accessed 12 February 2013.

Genin, C. et al. (2009). *Juger l'art?*. (Assessing art?) Paris: Sorbonne Publications.

Lahire, B. (2004). La culture des individus: Dissonances culturelles et distinction de soi. (The culture of individuals: cultural dissonances and their distinction.) Paris: La Découverte Publishers.

Lord, P. (2007). Le projet "art and education interface" Effets sur les élèves et les jeunes. *Evaluer les effets de l'éducation artistique et culturelle: Symposium européen et international de recherche.* (The project « Art and education interface » and their effects on students and young people. European and international research symposium.) Paris: La Documentation française - Centre Pompidou. 81–89.

Miller, J-A., Milner, J-C. (2004). *Voulez-vous être évalué?* (Have you been evaluated?) Paris: Grasset publishers.

O'Farrell, L. (2008). Evaluating the impact of Arts education: Posing pertinent questions, employing suitable tools. *Evaluating the impact of art and cultural education.* Paris: La Documentation française – Centre Pompidou. 35–41.

Rauscher, F. H. (2008). An empirical investigation of the effects of music instruction on cognition. *Evaluating the impact of art and cultural education.* Paris: La Documentation française – Centre Pompidou. 303–310.

Reeves, B., Read J. L. (2009). *Total Engagement: Using Games and Virtual Worlds to Change the Way People Work and Businesses Compete.* Boston, MA: Harvard Business Press.

Societé Francaise de l'Évaluation, http://www.sfe-asso.fr/index.php. Accessed 12 February 2013.

Notes

1   Every year, all pupils are evaluated regarding their acquired knowledge, which provides a national overview. (For example, http://www.education.gouv.fr/cid262/evaluation-des-acquis-des-eleves-en-ce1-et-cm2.htm, accessed 12 February 2013)

2   In 2009, several protests were raised in French universities regarding the "harassment of evaluation" which teachers and researchers are subjected to. After a series of conflicts and social upheavals that have paralysed universities for more than four months, numerous contradictory criticisms of the methods and purposes of evaluation were published both in the general and specialized press. (See for example, in 2009, the article in the magazine *Sciences Humaines*, no. 208) or the numerous debates on the website: http://www.sauvonslarecherche.fr. Since, the European strategies and constraints imposed by the Lisbon Treaty have received numerous criticisms in France but also throughout Europe.

3   Information on the event: http://www.centrepompidou.fr/Pompidou/Pedagogie.nsf/Docs/IDD9E5FC50EAF95536C12570D7004A1A24?OpenDocument&L=1;   Program   booklet:

    http://www.centrepompidou.fr/divers/pdf/SymEducartprogrammecouleurs.pdf;Proceedings: Evaluer les effets… (2008).

4 This absence was all the more regrettable as this point is crucial. In general, education is rather recalcitrant to an evaluation of its "profitability" and its efficiency, while policies always require more assessment indicators. In this area, the values of the cultural capital represented by the world of art are always presented as opposed to the values of material capital, any evaluation and judgement (even aesthetic) are therefore even more suspect. (Bourdieu, 1992; Genin et al., 2009).

5 This journal invited me to report on the Paris symposium and to communicate the points of view of the major players in this domain. I invited Professor Pierre Baqué, advisor to several Ministers of Education, to give his opinion on the impact of evaluation on the governmental supervision of artistic and cultural education. According to him, for the political decision makers, the family environment is considered as the real place for the cultural education … of the elite. The school only plays a minor role. See Baqué, P. *40 ans de combat pour les arts et la culture à l'école: 1967–2007.* (40 years of struggle for the arts and culture at school: 1967–2007). Paris: L'Harmattan, 2011.

6 http://www.oecd.org/document/44/0,3343,en_2649_35845621_44455276_1_1_1_1,00.html. Accessed 12 February 2013.

7 According to the well-informed article on Wikipedia, on average, it is the choice of 7–8% of students (http://fr.wikipedia.org/wiki/Éducation_artistique_et_culturelle_en_France, accessed 12 February 2013).

8 This teaching has been entrusted to literature teachers [*sic*].

9 This course is taught by voluntary teachers, mainly history and art teachers.

10 http://eduscol.education.fr/cid45674/enseignement-de-l-histoire-des-arts-a-l-ecole-au-college-et-au-lycee.html.

11 This survey that was only available internally has been directly provided to us by the Ministry of Education.

12 This survey only takes into account curriculum activities and, except in the case of partnership, does not take into account public or private teaching, which takes place in conservatories or schools of music, dance, etc.

13 Some of these activities were not mentioned by the heads of school.

14 This support is organized throughout the year. In general two hours a week, at the end of the school day, four days a week (Cf. the information homepage of the French Ministry of Education, http://www.education.gouv.fr/cid5677/accompagnement-educatif.html#l-accompagnement-educatif-pour-qui. Accessed 12 February 2013.

15 After school, French pupils must undertake various tasks at home.

16 Once again, pupils can participate in several activities.

17 Cf. the online journal EDUSCOL, http://eduscol.education.fr/cid45602/les-ateliers-artistiques-en-college-et-en-lycee.html. Accessed 12 February 2013.

18 The Ministry of Culture separated from the Ministry of Education in 1959. Since then, these ministries jealously manage their responsibilities but also have to work together on certain projects.

19 See the description of the project on the homepage of the Ministry of Education: http://www.education.gouv.fr/botexte/bo010614/MENE0101242C.htm, and an article on the project in the online journal *EDUCSOL*: http://eduscol.education.fr/cid46779/presentation.html, accessed 12 February 2013.

20 The details of the methodology used are available on the website: http://www.pratiquesculturelles.culture.gouv.fr/08methodologie.php, accessed 12 February 2013.

21 The complete questionnaire can be downloaded at: http://www.pratiquesculturelles.culture.gouv.fr/08questionnaire.php, accessed 12 February 2013.

22 Although the information provided would have allowed it, we have not undertaken a comparison with previous surveys.

23 One must note that music practice is very popular and recognized among the youth (46% say they know how to play a musical instrument and 16% create music on their PC).

24 http://www.pratiquesculturelles.culture.gouv.fr/08synthese.php, accessed 12 February 2013.

Chapter 4

Hungarian studies in visual skills assessment

Andrea Kárpáti, ELTE University, Budapest, Hungary; Emil Gaul, Hungarian Art Teachers' Association of Hungary, Budapest, Hungary

Abstract

This study discusses assessment methods used in different phases of Hungarian art education, in response to its changing paradigms and cultural contexts. First, we give an overview of the social context of education through arts in a central European setting; then we describe the contents of the new study areas called Visual Culture and Culture of the Environment that replaced the traditional, fine arts-focused approach in Hungary in the 1980s. Structure and objectives of the Basic and Final Examination System and the Dutch-Hungarian Portfolio Assessment Study will give examples of different approaches of the evaluation of visual skills development in European art education. We discuss how new paradigms in teaching and assessment influenced the training of art teachers and show our new Framework of Visual Skills and Abilities that forms the basis of our current developmental efforts in education through art.

The educational context

From curricula to guidelines, from fine arts to visual culture. The evolution of a liberal framework for art education

Profound educational reforms in Hungary began in the late-1980s, and continued during the change of regime period, 1988–1989. The most important prerequisite for these reforms was the establishment of ideological pluralism through the elimination of subjects reflecting one-sided ideologies and including only general humanistic values in curricula. Through the replacement of centrally commissioned, uniform teaching aids with a free but quality-controlled textbook market, a wide variety of subject matter and teaching methodology was offered. In 1989, the elimination of state monopoly in schooling enabled both legal entities (including all churches) and independent bodies (private persons and associations) to establish and own educational institutions. Another important educational policy measure was the legalization of a multiplicity of school structures: primary schools of 4, 6, and 8 grades and matching secondary schools of 4, 6, and 8 grades were established.[1]

The new *Hungarian National Core Curriculum* (HNCC, 2007), first introduced in 1996, was a set of guidelines which replaced the detailed, centrally developed syllabus and called for major innovations. It is the centrally-issued set of goals and thematic guidelines that should act as a regulatory agent and assure that a national cultural minimum be taught in all Hungarian schools. The HNCC describes output attainment targets for up to 50% of teaching material only, while local adaptations and programs at school level may be developed. Contrary to all negative expectations of educational policy – makers who feared that after 40 years under central regulation, teachers would be unable to cope with the responsibilities of freedom – even decades of strict central regulation of teaching methods and contents could not terminate the innovative spirit of educators (Halász, 2010).

Many new curricula overarch several school disciplines as the HNCC favours the *integration of the arts* with other humanities as well as science areas. In the structure of the HNCC, art education is included, along with music and dance, in the section called "Aesthetic Education" – thus, not just the possibility but also the official encouragement was given for integrative efforts. Integration, however, did not mean a complete merger. The possibility of a unified discipline integration all the arts is an idea educational policy makers repeatedly brought forward and were faced with a unanimous refusal to give up individual teaching programmes by music educators (followers of the world famous Kodály Method), visual arts, dance, and drama educators alike. Teachers of the discipline called "Culture of the Moving Image and Media Theory" that became a compulsory element of primary school curricula for Grades 7 and 8, ages 13–14 in 2009, offered to harmonize their teaching programme with those of visual arts but also opted for staying separate as an area of study. Up till now, "arts disciplines" managed to retain their integrity (along with their programs of teacher education and in-service training). Schools have the freedom of choice between them when designing the learning program for the competence area "Aesthetic Education" (Kárpáti, 2009).

To assist with the development of curricula and the organization of in-service teacher training courses, regional educational centres were set up to provide supervision and counselling. The centres created their individual versions of the national guidelines for each discipline – a development that resulted in substantial differences in teaching content, and consequently, in student achievement. Up till now, skills assessment in the area of aesthetic education is a discipline-based issue. Leaders of some of the disciplinary areas consider assessment important for revealing developmental effects and thus improving social respect and prestige while others perceive measurement as alien to the nature of aesthetic education. Experts defining the content and methodology of visual arts education belong to those who value authentic assessment that documents achievement without endangering creativity development.

"Art and Visual Culture": A new discipline with a new methodology

In 1996 the content of the visual arts segment of the Hungarian Core Curriculum was profoundly changed to include two new content areas that were meant to broaden our professional perspective and enrich our traditionally fine arts-focused art education:

1. "Visual Communication" that includes photography, video, graphic design, computer art, and focuses on "real-life" tasks of visual language usage

2. "Culture of the Man-made Environment", incorporating traditional folk crafts, elements of industrial design, and highlighting important aspects of shaping the human environment, like fashion and interior design.

"Fine Arts", as a traditional element remained but was suggested to occupy only about 50% or less of the learning program. The central curriculum with fine arts focus was replaced by these three alternative approaches. Both "Visual communication" and "Culture of the Manmade Environment" soon developed into new disciplines and served as an alternative content for the discipline now called "Visual Culture". Curricula for "Visual Communication", for example, included, besides the history and aesthetics of fine arts, also methods of appreciating photography, video, computer art, multimedia, and many genres of applied graphic arts. While learning to shape the environment, students also learned about the history of lifestyles, fashion, furniture, and interior design.

The new teaching programmes put an *equal emphasis on* the development of *visual perception* and *creation*. The history and aesthetics of a wide range of genres in the visual arts (fine arts, folk crafts, applied arts, photography, filming, and video) are included in the development of critical skills. National guidelines also underline the importance of teaching children *to do research, experiment with materials,* and carefully *plan and document* their visual problem solving process. These activities have never been included in any of the central curricula on art education before the reforms of 1996. With this innovative framework, Hungarian art education became more diversified and flexible. A new methodology was also required in the area of assessment of school programmes and student achievement. The enrichment of the field of art education with the above outlined two new content areas and the modernization of the examination system in the arts were perhaps the biggest innovation in the 120-year-old history of this discipline (Kárpáti and Gaul, 1998).

Assessing design and construction skills

In 1985, after a half year of preparatory work, the Design Center in Budapest, along with the editorial office of School TV, a division of Hungarian Television, announced a national competition for children aged 9–18 entitled "Let's Design Objects!". The key phrases in the announcement were: "We look forward to receiving designs for personal objects. Entries should be innovative and show how the article is more easily usable, more attractive, cheaper, or better in any other way than objects currently available." Children eager to take part could enter in four different age groups. Every primary and secondary school in the country, one thousand cultural centres and the press all received an invitation to submit entries, and the competition was announced several times on television. Eight hundred and fifteen works were received by the after-Christmas deadline. The works were evaluated according to the following criteria: the importance of the problem addressed the ability to recognize the important issues; the originality of the idea; the completeness of the solution; the quality and depth of execution; and finally the clarity of presentation and the beauty of the object. The top entrants received awards, while the next ten best received certificates of appreciation. A television broadcast series and numerous newspaper articles helped to publicize the results to a far wider segment of the population than the 815 children who took part. Thus, thousands of young people were inspired every year. Encouraged by its success, the organizers of the competition decided to hold it annually.

An analysis of the nearly 6,000 designs entered during the nine years of the competition provides an adequate basis upon which several conclusions can be drawn, and allows for an illustration of the children's abilities, too (Carswell, 1987). A statistical survey and analysis of the young people's work was unfortunately not conducted; therefore we have summarized what we learned from a qualitative analysis of the main features of the submitted designs. The proportion of boys and girls, as well as residents of villages, town, and the capital corresponded to the general demographic distribution of Hungary. Most submissions came from 11- and 12-year-olds (nearly 50%), followed by 13- and 14-year-olds. Nine- and ten-year-olds and especially 15–18-year-olds showed an increasing disinclination to participate. The nature of the submitted designs provided a fairly uniform picture. Most of the entrants recognized the *human factor* – if someone had some kind of challenge: for example attention was paid to matters of loneliness, disability, and note was made of badly designed or poor quality products. The jury dubbed this phenomenon the "twisting off the cap effect", since the children tended not to question the nature of their environment. They were not angry, they did not chide anyone, nor did they consider that the bottling industry might be willing to fit the bottle with adequately perforated lids of an appropriate softness and thickness. The children instinctively knew they could not count on anyone except themselves! Other strengths were the ideas of

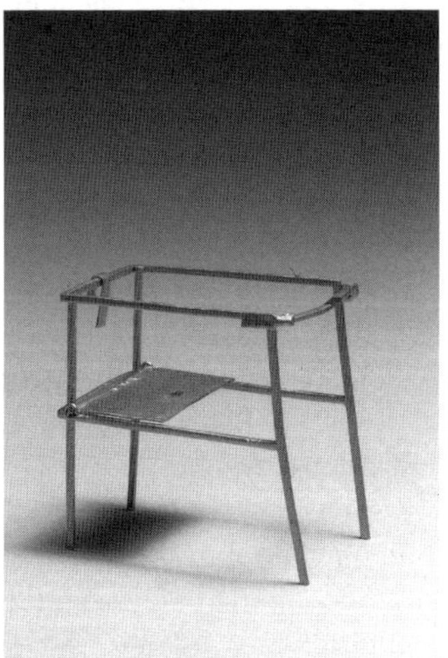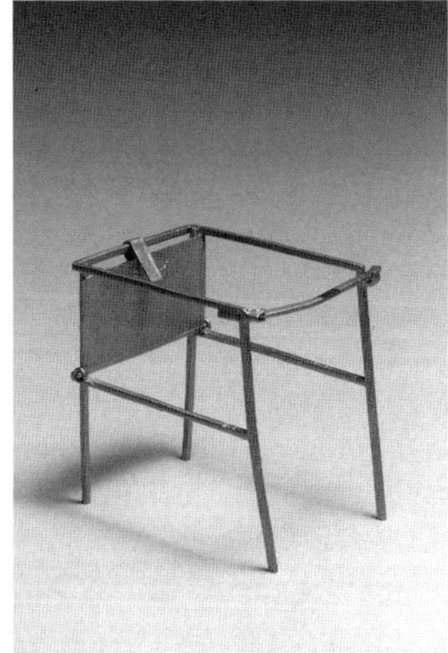

Figure 1: "Wire model of a walking frame with folding seat, for those people who are old, or have difficulties in moving around, and often get tired on the way". Andrea Fábián and Anikó Mazsárik, girls, aged 12. Size: 5.8 × 4.5 × 8 cm. Let's Design Objects! Competition, 1989.

the children, which, for the most part, were conceived with great pride. Very few children, however, were skilled in developing an imaginative idea, designing the article, and executing it. Here the assistance of a competent adult was clearly needed – whether a parent or teacher – in part to keep the child inspired and persistent, and also to ensure satisfactory workmanship. The most important result of the competition was the evaluation of Hungarian students' knowledge, attitude, and skills in the areas of design, problem solving, and construction.

The next important Hungarian research project examined children's abilities in technology. The starting point for this study was the British model of capabilities devised by Richard Kimbell (1991) and his team based on an analysis of the works of 8,000, 16-year-old students (Table 1).

Three hundred and thirty-three secondary school students between the ages of 12 and 16 participated in the 1996/97 Hungarian research project entitled "Survey of design skills in Practice". Students in ten schools, under the direction of ten teachers completed six construction tasks. A statistical and qualitative analysis of the results helped us to clearly identify and distinguish the capabilities required to solve each problem and thus characterize the students' operational skills (Table 2). Of the skill elements in the British construct of capabilities, we were only able to demonstrate the existence of one-third, presumably because Hungarian children did not study design and technology at the time of the survey. However, the skills that Hungarian students demonstrated were on the same level as their British counterparts; only factual knowledge of Hungarian children was smaller and less sophisticated.

Table 1:　The elements of design competence in Britain.

1. Holistic skills

Procedural skills
2. A grasp of the subject-matter, which leads to an elaboration and detailing of the task.
3. The ability to design and obtain sources of information.
4. The appropriate development of the product from the user's perspective.
5. The appropriate development of the product by the manufacturer.
6. Assessment of product development.

Communication skills
7. The complexity of communication.
8. The clarity of communication.
9. The security of communication.
10. Communication skills.

Conceptual skills
11. Knowledge and use of the material.
12. Knowledge and use of energy systems.
13. Knowledge and use of aesthetics.
14. Knowledge and understanding of the needs of customers.

Source: Kimbell et al. (1991).

Table 2: Construct of 15- and 16-year-old Hungarian students' design capabilities (Gaul, 2006).

1. Sensitivity to design problems

2. Orientation skills

3. Imagination

4. Judgment

5. Communication skills

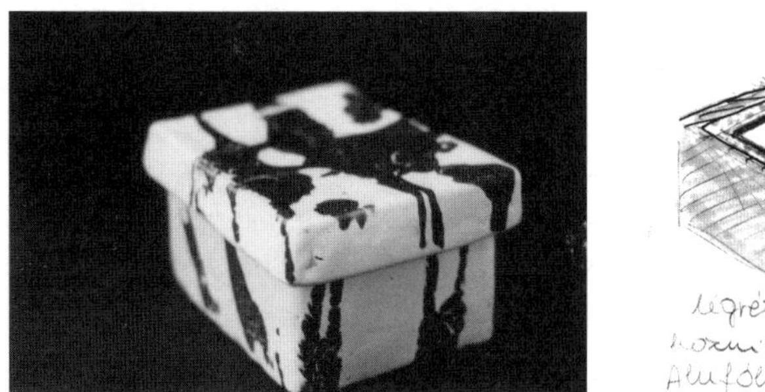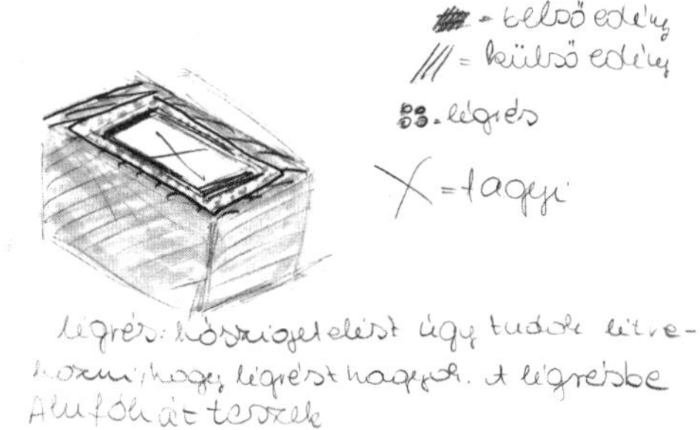

Figure 2: Ice-cream box. Borbála Sánta, girl, aged 12 years. Size: 15 × 13.5 × 8 cm. The outer part is made of clay, the inner is a plastic container, and the insulation is aluminium foil. Design Skills Research Project, 1996.

In a later study of 2010, we revisited design skills that have been developed, according to the Hungarian National Core Curriculum, through special programs since 1996. In the 6–12 age bracket, we chose to evaluate the skills that children under 12 generally use in the process of designing and making an object. Our model of design skills and abilities was further refined in the course of this study:

We tried to fit the set of skills children drew upon in designing and making an object, the necessary knowledge, and the related skills to the visual capabilities listed above. Finally, in carrying out the actual research, we used the list in the table below (Table 3) as a basis for evaluating the tests of the student's aptitude in object design and execution. We managed to take into consideration every element in the expanded list above by adjusting each one to the five degree scale of the evaluation criteria.

The skills identified by the design assessment projects were included in newer versions of the National Core Curriculum and consequently found their way into teaching programs. At Moholy-Nagy University of Arts, named after one of the distinguished professors of the German arts and crafts college, Bauhaus, pre- and in-service training in Art and Design Education for students with a degree in design was initiated in 1985. Till the present day, 2011, more than a thousand designer-teachers and more than 300 art teachers with a specialization in Design Education have been trained.

Table 3: The structure of design skills of Hungarian children aged 6–12.

Sensitivity to design problems

1. Intended function

2. Structural characteristics

3. Formal characteristics

Operational knowledge used in construction

1. Knowledge of the working process

2. Knowledge of structure

3. Use of tools

4. Knowledge of the material

5. Knowledge of form

Imagination

1. Quantity

2. Quality

Judgement: To what degree does the chosen solution suit …

1. the operation?

2. the material?

3. the structure?

4. the technology?

5. the form?

Communication skills

1. *Visual communication*

a. Depiction

b. Understanding a diagram

c. 3D modelling

d. Understanding models

2. *Verbal communication*

a. Speaking

b. Listening comprehension

c. Writing

d. Reading comprehension

3. Changing modalities2

Source: Pataky (2011).

Table 4: The list of skills adjusted to the given technology tasks. (The numbering in the left column refers to the list of visual skills evaluated.)

5. Creating 2D and 3D forms	Representation of observed and imagined forms.
10. Making and interpreting diagrams	10.1 Making diagrams: The ability to create assembly and procedural diagrams as well as drawings that are based on conventions, follow rules, have meaning, and communicate and explain the idea or concept; the ability to represent real or imagined relationships and connections.
10.	10.2 Interpreting diagrams: The ability to interpret explanatory drawings and assembly and procedural diagrams.
16. Construction	Object design, construction, creating structures from various materials and for various purposes.
17. Adequate use of visual tools that express or represent 2- and 3D forms.	Use of nuanced lines, tone, colour, form, etc. to adequately express or represent forms (which can involve anything from copying patterns to independent application).
18. Creativity	Imagination, divergent thinking, flexibility, and the ability to associate.
19. Shaping the material, use of tools	A knowledge of materials and procedures; use or choice of tools suited to the function of the object or the goals of expression.

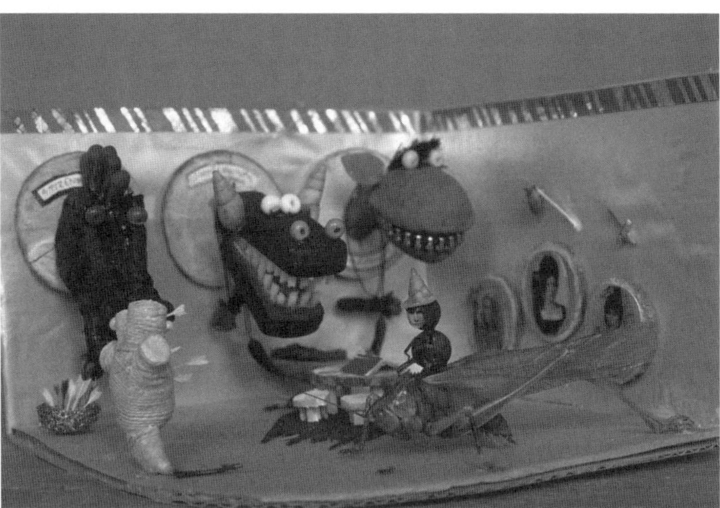

Figure 3: Tom Thumb's room. Model. Károly Csávási, boy, aged 10. Size: 12 × 8 × 9 cm. The body of Tom is made of pepper. He is riding on a grasshopper. The dragon teeth are made of a zipper, the portraits of captive princesses are cut-outs of a television programme. A brilliant example of miniaturization. Let's Design Objects! Competition, 1994.

Central assessment of art and design skills and abilities in Hungary

The National Basic Examination: An experiment in diagnostic assessment, 1992–1997

The first effort to introduce contemporary methods of assessment in the visual arts dates back to 1995, when a diagnostic assessment project, the National Basic Examination was introduced for those who intended to finish their studies at age 16, on completion of the compulsory primary school. This type of measurement of educational progress was offered as an elective for 16-year-old secondary school students to support their career choices. Progress in mathematics, Hungarian and world history, Hungarian literature, foreign languages, and disciplines in science was evaluated. The "Basic Examination in Visual Arts" included tasks to assess student achievement in theory and practice of fine arts, design, and visual communication/media. As this examination was *intended for those who have an interest in the history and practice of visual language* but not necessarily plan to embark on an arts-related career, content and methods of assessment did not resemble those employed at art colleges. Basic skills and abilities of perception and creation both had to be evaluated, so the *task structure* of this examination was as follows:

- *Art History Test* with multiple-choice and open-ended questions as well as matching and visual analysis tasks (the latter involved the production of structure and/or colour schemes for works of art).
- *Visual Language Tasks* that evaluated selected skills of design and creation. (In 1999, a spatial abilities test was employed as teaching methods in the area of spatial representation, a very important competence for many professions, were reported to be ineffective.)

Testing knowledge in art history – with a special emphasis on traditional and contemporary Hungarian art, local trends, and international influences – is highly relevant in a small country, the national identity of which resides mostly in its cultural values. Examinations, reflecting preferences of our educational policy makers, urged art teachers to enrich their curricula with the appreciation of historic and contemporary works of fine arts, design, and architecture. "Teaching for the exam" in this case actually served a very important cause: the preservation of our national cultural heritage.

Employing *spatial ability tests for art exams* may sound unfit for the purpose of assessing achievement in a school discipline traditionally cherished for its potentials for developing creativity. However, another, equally important aim for teaching the arts is the need of the acquisition of visual language for both expressive and utilitarian, everyday uses. Repeated surveys of spatial representation and perception skills of architecture, engineering, and medical students revealed severe problems in these areas. Future professionals whose jobs will routinely involve the application of spatial abilities were unable to solve even the simplest mental rotation and completion tasks. At the same time, the majority of art education curricula collected and analysed in the course of the National Basic Examination emphasized the development of spatial abilities through a variety of two-dimensional tasks. Teaching strategies in this area were unsuccessful and urgently needed reconsideration in the light of the findings of spatial tests. We decided to employ these as screening features that gave an orientation for both the student and the teacher, providing an objective assessment of the developmental level of basic visual skills.

Needless to say, high achievement in any ability test is no guarantee for creative excellence – but low scores may be a warning. Future engineers, or surgeons are not examined at university entrance on their visual skills – but in the course of their studies, their success will be largely dependent on them. If diagnosed early, preferably before adolescence, insufficient skills may be developed through focused remedial exercises. Art educators need to be constantly informed about the results of their work in order to reconsider teaching strategies and search for new, more effective ways. The National Basic Examination was an excellent *diagnostic tool* both for the student and his/her teacher.

Basic examination in visual arts, developed by a group of teachers and researchers, has proven to be a success. Many students elected to take it in order to receive information on the developmental level of their visual abilities and thus be assisted in choosing a future career. Parents often encouraged their children to opt for art education as an examination subject because they felt the need for a more profound, better organized knowledge in art history as a necessary component of erudition. The skills test in many cases revealed problems of vision and spatial orientation that needed medical care – in other cases they served as tools for the identification of a type of visual talent. This new assessment system was meant to contribute to the appreciation of art education as a discipline that develops important mental and psychomotor domains and transmits basic human values. The Basic Examinations were discontinued after 2002, but the results of the eight-year assessment effort that involved about 800 schools and more than 12,000 students were utilized later in the modernization of the final examination.

The final examination in visual culture and art history in Hungary

The first, centrally developed assessment system for art education in Hungary, the National Final Examination in Visual Arts was introduced in the 1970s.[3] Art is an elective discipline of the Final Examination, but those who opt for it are not only aspiring artists or art teachers. Many students choose art because of personal interest or lack of motivation or knowledge to take another science subject or a second foreign language. Thus, students with basic visual skills and those with excellent ones sat for the exams side by side until 2004, when Intermediate and Superior examination levels with different sets of tasks were introduced. In the first part of the 20th century, till the 1970s, final examinations closely resembled the fine arts academy entrance procedures of the 19th century. In the old system, students had three hours to complete one of the following task types specified by the examination committee whose "developmental" role is restricted to selecting of one of the tasks and giving some restrictive hints about size, lighting or the use of drapery:

1. Study drawing of geometric shapes.
2. Reconstruction of a given projection.
3. Still-life (using natural or artificial shapes).
4. Interior with figure – a model drawing.

The *oral questions* of the examination were selected by the examiners from a set of 20 topics developed by local art teachers. Students pulled a ticket, received visual materials (slides or prints) of their choice to illustrate their answers and, after 20–30 minutes of preparation, presented a short "lecture" on the three questions that every ticket contained:

1. Description of major art trends of an epoch in art history (all epochs must be represented, there are one or two 20th century art related topics out of 20).
2. Analysis of a work of art based on a reproduction.
3. Description of a technique (for painting, graphic arts, sculpture, or building).

This system has proved more and more unacceptable for both secondary school art educators and university and college staff responsible for entrance examinations of art-related careers. The centrally-set drawing task reflected the aesthetic ideal of the 19th century and revealed skills that were of minor relevance for the assessment of creativity or expressive abilities. Therefore, experiments to modernize assessment were carried out that led to the introduction of the portfolio method that is in the centre of evaluation efforts till the present day.

Portfolio assessment as a teaching method, national competition task, and examination format

The method

Assembling a *portfolio* of the output of one or more academic years has been a traditional method for the evaluation of visual skills and abilities in Hungary for more than a century. For (aspiring) artists, the compilation of a collection of excellent work means an overview of past endeavours and may inspire them to embark on new creative directions. The portfolio as assessment tool for the average student has an entirely different meaning. It helps to overview techniques and topics learned and identify strengths as well as weaknesses. With an oral commentary that involves knowledge about and usage of terms and concepts of art criticism, students also manifest their abilities to judge works of art and reflect on their own creative output. Taste and attitudes towards the visual arts are also revealed in the course of these, often very inspiring both for the examinee and examiners interviews.

Both the complex test/essay and the project proved to be an excellent measuring tool for the development of visual thinking, planning, and creation (Kárpáti and Schönau, 1997). *Projects* are "domain-specific" as they address problems related to a given domain of human experience. This examination task resembles *portfolio-based assessment* (a traditional method of judging artistic merit based on the examination of selected works from a certain period) but it is in many respects more diverse than that. First, a project task enables students to present their ideas in any medium or material they choose while the portfolio usually contains tasks set by the teachers with techniques assigned. A project documentation (also called *process folio*) contains varied and reliable data on the development of spatial ability, basic design skills, and the knowledge of a wide range of materials and tools necessary for sculpture and construction.

The Hungarian experiment with Dutch expert input

Between 1990 and 1994, a Dutch-Hungarian research project was carried out to investigate the possibilities of introducing a *new, project- and portfolio-based final examination model* (Kárpáti and Schönau, 1997). The two components of this assessment model were as follows:

- Centrally developed *art criticism tasks* in a previously disclosed theme in given epochs of *art history*, containing both multiple-choice and open-ended questions and short art appreciation essay tasks (e.g., "The Role of Ornament in Byzantine, Renaissance, Fauvist and Conceptual Art"). The test is evaluated by the local art teacher according to central scoring guidelines:

  1. Tasks in *studio art* that have to be realized within the school in an examination setting;
  2. Art, design, or media *projects* that develop a theme chosen by the student from a set of 12 central assignments complete with a collection of sketches and background information leading to the visual solution of the theme. Works and documentation are exhibited and judged by the local art teacher and a centrally assigned external evaluator. Projects have to be executed within the confines of school under supervision.

More than a thousand students participated in the experiments that preceded the introduction of this new assessment model. Their work proved that project tasks are not just stimulating but also require a good deal of thinking, planning, and experimenting as well as traditional draughtsmanship. The major argument of those who opposed the idea of the Dutch exam – that it will result in "cheap" solutions and an avoidance of demanding visual problems – was not justified. Contrary to the expectations of teachers in favour of traditional drawing and painting tasks like still life or portrait, students worked harder and produced a variety of high-quality sketches, works of graphic art, paintings, sculptures, objects, and installations. A comparison of a sample of student performance before the exam with examination output proved that *37% of examinees actually produced work well beyond their average drawing level*. Only a small minority (2%) found project-based tasks intimidating and came up with considerably poorer than usual artworks as those in their school portfolios assembled before the start of the project. Challenge resulted in motivation and motivation fuelled intensive experimenting sessions of searching for the right solution. Most students declared in their *logbooks* (that also formed part of the work required for the examination) that they learned a lot during project-based work. Regardless to what extent they were satisfied with their final product, they wished they could have similar, more sophisticated and more demanding tasks for their final examination instead of the traditional, three-hour drawing session. There were of course some students who welcomed the project as a possibility to "get around perspective drawing" (a cherished method of the "old" exam) but even these could successfully find alternative means of visual creation to realize their ideas. Instead of a pen-and-pencil drawing in linear perspective, they used photography, computer animation, collage and montage techniques, and installation to represent distance and open space. Thus, they utilized media and genres typical for our age and employed a visual language deeply rooted in the contemporary art of the last years of the 20th century.

Judging project work

In general, the new assessment challenges found Hungarian art teachers who were used to constant supervision, periodical re-training, and detailed guidelines for an overall prescriptive, central curriculum totally unprepared. Highly qualified, academy-trained artist-teachers in secondary schools were willing to experiment with new fields but unable to develop project-based teaching programs entirely on their own. Judging project work manifests a problem few educators are fully aware of. The traditional belief in expertise and sensitivity to quality resulting from training and experience contradicted our findings about the lack of *reliability of the traditional jury procedure*. We found that several jury members are *ignorant and/or biased* and produce inconsequent scoring results mainly due to the following reasons. Many art teachers have a *strong prejudice based on previous output* of their students and judge actual work according to their preconceptions of the students' presumed level of visual skills and abilities. Those who have a bad record in art will be scored lower even if their work is of much better than usual quality manifest in high estimation by judges who do not know the student. Similarly, students with a good record in technical drawing tasks will fare well even if their project work requiring creativity leaves a lot to be desired.

Several art teachers, who actively practise art, seem to *prefer styles resembling their own* and appreciate planning and compositional methods that reflect their own way of solving visual problems. These teachers arrive at the scoring session with clear assumptions about the "best solution" of the task and find it difficult to accept alternative approaches. The *age* of art teachers also seems to play a decisive role in influencing scoring behaviour. Younger, less experienced educators will be more flexible in judging the correctness of the interpretation of the task in question. (They will be more ready to accept work based on free associations loosely related to the task than their older colleagues.) *Training*, on the other hand, also plays a crucial role in the formation of taste. Teacher training colleges seem to have their own favoured "*school art styles*" and tend to train accordingly. Finally, *experience in teaching through projects and judging process folios* is a crucial prerequisite for reliable judgement. Those inexperienced in attending to all aspects of the collection of works exhibited will base their scoring on individual criteria only. (For example, these teachers will often base their judgements on the masterly final work only and let poor manifestation of planning skills pass as "very good". They easily overestimate a nicely done research report through giving high scores on the less excellent technical execution of the same student as well (Kárpáti et al., 1998)

These results indicate that *traditional jury methods may lack reliability and should not be used for examination.* We planned several teacher training and in-service training courses to see which preparatory methods result in better judgement performance and repeated the project scoring experiment several times. The analysis of the results shows that jurors trained through discussing sample work demonstrating high, mediocre, and poor quality work to establish consensus, will be most likely to judge in agreement with each other. We found that the *topic and genre of the task also influences reliability.*

Design projects that involve more clearly definable technical requirements and less criteria based on aesthetic preference only, can be reliably assessed if at least two, optimally three jurors, are employed who base their judgments on a set of assessment criteria and not on their *global impressions* only. With these tasks, global assessment may work well with two-dimensional tasks as the study of Boughton (in this volume) suggests. However closely related to final results, global impression-based judgments will not assist the improvement of performance or education as such because they do not yield information on the development of individual skills and abilities important for visual creation and perception. Global scores will never reveal which of the criteria was dominant and thus provide no data for the improvement of the teaching process.

The *method of assessment* employed by judges proved to be another key factor in our experiments. "Vertical assessment", judging a work according to all the criteria at the same time, – the traditional "checklist method" used at fine arts competitions – proved to be significantly less reliable than *"horizontal scoring"*. This involved judging all the works according to one criterion at a time. Our experimental judging project proved that results of art education can reliably be assessed through sophisticated tasks representing all genres of the visual arts not just drawing. Our results also revealed, however, that traditional jury practices must be altered for the examination procedure. The employment of trained jurors, preferably *one external and one or two internal* (school-based) *evaluators* who compare all project portfolios according to one given criterion at a time is inevitable for reliable assessment (Kárpáti et al., 1998). The mathematical analysis of results proved that the validity and reliability of the jury process can be significantly increased if there are at least two judges for each work and at least one of them is an external observer, unrelated to the school. Criteria should be described in a more concrete manner, for example, by asking for a judgement report, where decisions have to be given that justify the chosen category. In this procedure, judgements are made "horizontally", applying one scoring criterion at a time for all collections. Thus, the evaluator can compare a certain quality represented by a variety of works. Our jury experiments contributed to the improvement of the jury procedure as an evaluation method that can be successfully employed not only in the classroom, but also at entrance examinations and art and design competitions.

Some of the factors characterizing education in schools (class size, expenditure per pupil) do not have demonstrable effects on student performance while teacher quality (as measured by skills, knowledge, and qualifications) plays a decisive role in students' progress (Darling-Hammond, 2000). Based on an analysis of teacher policies in 25 countries, an OECD report cogently entitled *Teachers Matter* (2010) comes to the conclusion that teacher quality is the most important factor in an education system, and the second most important factor (only preceded by family background) among the variety of influences affecting student achievement. McKinsey & Company investigated the factors behind the accomplishments of the most successful education programmes in Asia, Europe, North America, and the Middle East as evaluated by the OECD PISA survey conducted between May 2006 and March 2007. In their summary of the research results, the McKinsey report comes to the conclusion that certain education systems achieve substantially better outcomes than others because

> they have produced a system that is more effective in doing three things: getting more talented people to become teachers, developing these teachers into better instructors, and in ensuring that these instructors deliver consistently for every child in the system. [...] The quality of an education system cannot exceed the quality of its teachers. (Barber and Mourshed, 2007, p. 36)

This appears to be the area that resources should target; knowledge-intensive training institutions and knowledge-rich teacher development centres should be maintained.

In the 1990s, teacher education in Hungary was modernized in order to suit requirements of the new National Core Curriculum. Between 1986 and today, about 500 teachers with an MA degree in Art and Design Education have graduated at Moholy-Nagy University of

Arts, and created a welcome balance between schools with fine arts and crafts and design focus. Changes in teacher education had a profound effect on the content and form of art and design education in Hungary. In 2009, when the Diagnostic Skills Assessment Project coordinated by the Educational Research Group of the Hungarian Academy of Science and Szeged University was organized with the inclusion of Visual Skills and Abilities as one of the assessment areas, we organized our project team and the in-service training programs connected to it with the participation of nine major Hungarian art teacher training institutions.

The Visual Arts Assessment Database: A tool for evaluating the emergence and development of creative and perceptive visual skills and abilities

The new Hungarian Framework of Visual Skills and Abilities

Our recent assessment effort, started in 2009, targets 6–12-year-olds. Our final goal is to set up a Visual Arts Assessment Database for art teachers, a searchable collection of tasks that are creative, flexible, and still produce measurable outputs to reveal the efficiency of Visual Culture, the Hungarian discipline for art and design education. Documenting continuous development with frequent changes of modes of expression from infancy till the end of adolescence, this model emphasizes the importance of visual language in the interactive and customizable new communication environment of the 21st century.

A group of 12 experts with a background in evaluating visual art performance as art educators and their trainers, artists, art critics, or curators were invited to provide a framework of skills and abilities relevant for the practice and perception of visual culture. The framework was based on the previous studies outlined above and was intended to serve as a basis for further evaluation projects (Bodóczky et al., 2009). First, major areas of expertise in the use of visual language were outlined (Table 5), then, a detailed list of activities were described that would form the basis of the task development process (Table 6).

Table 5:   Skill clusters of the Hungarian Visual Framework.

Observation	Expression and communication	Representation
Interpretation	Visual communication	Design and creation of objects and spaces
Appreciation (of art and visual culture), evaluation, judgment	Visual expression	Design and creation of images

Table 6: Skills assessed in the National Assessment of Visual Skills and Abilities, 2009–2010.

Skills	Activities	Types of tasks (examples)
Observation	a. Observation and recognition of images, spaces, etc. b. Visual memory, recollection of experiences c. Organization of visual information, detection of analogies	Appreciation of works of art Reading visual signs Reading graphs and charts
Creation of 2D and 3D shapes	Drawing, painting, modelling, construction	Map-making Designing and making an object
Manipulation	a. Reconstruction b. Variation (modification of form and meaning) c. Transposition (changing size, location, medium, mood. Etc.)	Completion of ruined building or object Culturally relevant adaptation of signs or things
Abstraction		Designing patterns, maps, signs
Symbolisation	a. Representing non-visual information visually b. Reading and creating graphs and charts c. Depicting a sequence (movement, process, story) d. Representation of an imaginary story, a state of mind, a mood, expression of feelings	
Visual representation and expression	a. Representation of people, things, ideas, actions b. Visualization, imaging	Portrait Comic book Scientific visualization
Representation of space	a. Mental and real manipulation, reconstruction, rotation, etc. b. Use of representational systems	Mental, 2D, and 3D spatial representation tasks Space memory tasks Real life and mental manipulations with objects in space
Design and construction	a. Sensitivity to problems (e. g. form and function, connections, human needs) b. Construction process: planning, tool choice and proper handling, knowing the qualities of and selection of materials, execution of construction tasks c. Fantasy d. Judgment: appropriation of the object constructed to the needs of customers, technology, and materials	Analysis of needs of different social groups in different cultures Constructing everyday and imaginary objects Analysing objects in the immediate environment Deciphering the meaning of culturally loaded objects
Communication	a. Visual rendering of different content b. Preparing graphs and charts c. Modelling and interpretation of models d. Understanding different communication channels (speech, gestures, mimics)	Logo, *ex libris*, and coat of arms Basic typography Posters and presentations Still and moving images for science communication

(continued)

Skills	Activities	Types of tasks (examples)
Creativity	Fluency, flexibility, originality	Open and flexible tasks
Art appreciation and criticism	a. Observation b. Interpretation, meaning-making c. Analysis d. Judgment	Recognition and interpretation of contemporary visual culture Art and cultural history tests

The validation of the Framework and the development of the database

In 2009–2010, a national assessment of visual creation and perception was organized for Grades 2, 4, and 6 (ages 8, 10, and 12) to validate the Framework and pilot the tasks developed to assess its competences. From among the 200 tasks developed, 90 were tested in about 35 schools mainly in the capital, Budapest, and a quarter of it from all over the country. Schools chose to test between two and five tasks, and 8,400 task sheets were collected from 3,400 students aged 6–12 who participated in the survey. No institutions with a special art focus were selected, (but some Waldorf schools), and classroom teachers (non-art specialists), who teach art in the majority of primary schools, took the assessment tasks with their own students. The tasks selected for piloting were in harmony with the objectives and methods of the Hungarian National Curriculum. As they did not resemble "tests" at all, the testing procedure did not differ significantly from normal classroom practice. As the tasks were of different complexity, authentic assessment also involved the embedding of some tasks in a "normal" art lesson as an introductory, warm-up exercise.

Teachers received task descriptions with a detailed explanation of how the tasks had to be administered. After the tasks were piloted, the response forms and accompanying sheets with sketches or other work in progress were carefully collected and handed over for assessment. All evaluators were art teachers with at least five years of teaching practice. Two trained evaluators scored all sheets and in case of disagreement, a third scorer was involved. They received scoring sheets with detailed explanations of every item to evaluate. Examples of average, excellent, and below average works – results of pre-pilots – were also furnished. Evaluators not only judged student performance, but also scrutinized tasks. They oversaw the descriptions and illustrative or explanatory images in order to identify if they could have been responsible for poor performance. Those tasks that were too difficult for pupils (or even for their teachers), were highlighted and corrections of the text suggested. Examples of excellent, good, mediocre, and inferior solutions for all framework items were documented and stored for inclusion in the database along with the corrected task sheets.

Three feedback sessions were organized for piloting teachers to tell their impressions about working with the assessment tasks. One of the most surprising, although very positive results, was their growing enthusiasm. At first, they were not too comfortable with the idea of introducing the element of assessment in the teaching process of a discipline that was supposed to be motivating and inspiring for all. However, the majority of participants was pleased with the tasks and were interested in the results as they provided an "expert look" on their rarely appreciated work in the art room.

Some results of the pilot assessment study

All the tasks were analysed for reliability and validity and were found appropriate for the age level of the students and the skills tested. The level of both indices, however, differed from task to task as the number of students who performed them ranged from 30 up to 200. The uneven distribution of tasks was due to our efforts for authenticity: teachers of the experimental classes could choose tasks to suit their students. In order to build the Visual Arts Assessment Database, we need equally large testing groups and will have to repeat some of the task pilots. However, allowing teachers to preview tasks and then choose those suitable for their teaching needs was a very useful exercise: their preferences outlined the hidden curriculum of art education in Grades 1–6, ages 6–12. This "folksonomy curriculum" is oriented towards creative expression in easy-to-master, two-dimensional forms. Primary school educators prefer open-ended tasks embedded in tales, even if they are longer and require more effort on the teacher's side. They seem to be inclined to integrate art forms (while leading experts in the fields of aesthetic education are not, as postulated earlier). Crafts and design, integral parts of the National Core Curriculum and definitely preferred by pupils, are often avoided because of "dangerous" or "filthy" techniques and the materials or tools required. However, in case they are provided (as was the case in this experiment), they are ready to take risks and submit enthusiastic reports with promises of giving design a larger curriculum space.

This result is especially welcome because *design tasks proved to be more reliable* for evaluating the development of visual skills and abilities than expressive or art criticism tasks. Three-dimensional tasks were found more motivating and their results more pleasing, especially for the 6–10-year-olds, than creating two-dimensional images. Longer, more complex tasks that involved research, planning, and execution – typical for design and construction – revealed a wide range of skills that gave a more sophisticated report on development than expressive or representational tasks did. Therefore, we decided to widen the range of three-dimensional tasks.

Scoring guides that included images of good, mediocre, and inferior solutions (selected by art teachers who developed and tested the tasks in pilots) helped a lot for teachers, and they scored significantly better than those with a verbal explanation of criteria. However, "teaching to test" is a real danger when best (and worst) practice is highlighted. Therefore, the national database will contain a wide range of solutions for all quality levels.

Performance in the arts is no longer independent of school education. In Hungary, PISA studies reveal an extremely significant influence of the school on the performance of the individual (OECD, 2010). This is an issue Hungarian educational policy makers cannot seem to be able to alter although it affects future perspectives of children of low-income families who generally live in neighbourhoods where the local, state-supported school is weak. These children will never be able to recover their educational deficits. In previous studies, (Kárpáti,

1995), we found that the level of visual skills is independent of family backgrounds and school levels. Not any more – the present, large dataset suggests that 6–12-year-olds develop visual expression when and if they are given the chance. Their involvement in art education is significantly related to their performance in more complex art tasks. Follow-up studies will decide if it is the art program, the methodology of the teacher, or the infrastructure of the school (variables that are relatively easy to identify) that is the cause of differences in performance. In any case, this result is a warning sign: if schools will not be more evenly staffed and furnished, the development of creativity will suffer as much as cognition.

The quality of art education is important, but on a primary level, it does not necessarily have to come from an art specialist. *Primary school teachers seem to be excellent art educators.* With only basic training in methodology, they are able to organize art lessons and motivate as well as guide their pupils just as well as specialist art teachers do (who in turn were trained much less in teaching young children). This result is very encouraging as in Hungary, one-tenth of the village schools are small institutions with only two or three teachers to teach all disciplines. Here, more art education may result in more learning. Art can act as the motivating agent for the acquisition of other disciplines as the teacher may use the power of vision to explain and express abstract knowledge.

Results of girls and boys sometimes contradict expectations. In spite of general beliefs, girls are equally as competent in representation and planning as boys, their spatial abilities are significantly different in younger ages only (ages 6–8, Grades 1–3). Later, more complex spatial operations will show similar results for the two sexes. However, boys will excel in one criterion through almost all the tasks: originality. Their plans as well as their expressive drawings or objects reflect divergent thinking more often than those of girls. Therefore, if creative tasks are given, the brainstorming and planning stages have to be carefully monitored with girls to teach them to express their intuitive thoughts, and follow up on their unusual ideas.

The evaluation process was culture fair as it considered specific forms of expression of youth subcultures, idioms of national minorities, and individual uses of visual language. Results suggest a new, multimedia model of child art development that integrates traditional and digital means of expression. Tasks are now being implemented in an online, searchable database with descriptors that enable teachers to retrieve tasks according to grade, age, medium, level of difficulty, and disciplinary area (Visual Communication, Crafts and Design/ Environmental Arts, and Fine Arts/Art Criticism) and use them for training, challenges or evaluation. In this way, assessment is integrated with teaching and training – it becomes an authentic tool for visual skills development.

Acknowledgement

Research reported in this chapter was partially supported by the "Development of Diagnostic Assessment Project, co-ordinated by the Research Group on the Theory of Education of Szeged University. (Phase 1: Project No. TÁMOP-3.1.9-08/1-2009-0001 and Phase 2: Project No. TÁMOP-3.1.9-11/1-2012-0001)

Appendix: Sample tasks of the assessment project of 2009–2010.

Figure 4: Task sheet for Visual Communication: "Everyday signs".

"Visual Culture" assessment task, 2010. ("Development of Diagnostic Assessment Project of Szeged University, Research Group on the Theory of Education. Project No.: TÁMOP-3.1.9-08/1-2009-0001 and TÁMOP-3.1.9-11/1-2012-0001)		
Stamp of the school:	School code:	
	Student code:	
Student name:	Boy / Girl	Grade:

Task number: 0606

Task title: Chairs

Task 1

Chairs come in different forms and functions. Manufacturers use a wide variety of materials to produce them, designers and artists experiment with their forms.

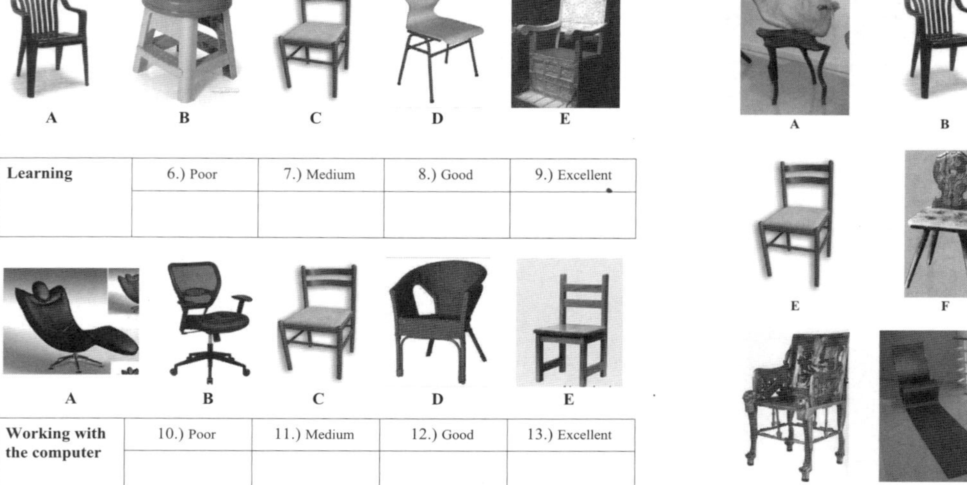

Group these chairs according to function! Choose the one that are best suited to the following functions and write the letter of the picture next to the function that it is best used for.

1.) Relaxation: ....   4.) Work at the office: ....

2.) Patients use it at the doctor's: ......   5.) A work of art: ....

3.) Royal seat: ....

Task 2

The next task is about the usability of chairs.
Group these chairs according to function! Rank the chairs according to their functionality and write the letter of the picture in the appropriate slot in the table.

Learning	6.) Poor	7.) Medium	8.) Good	9.) Excellent

Working with the computer	10.) Poor	11.) Medium	12.) Good	13.) Excellent

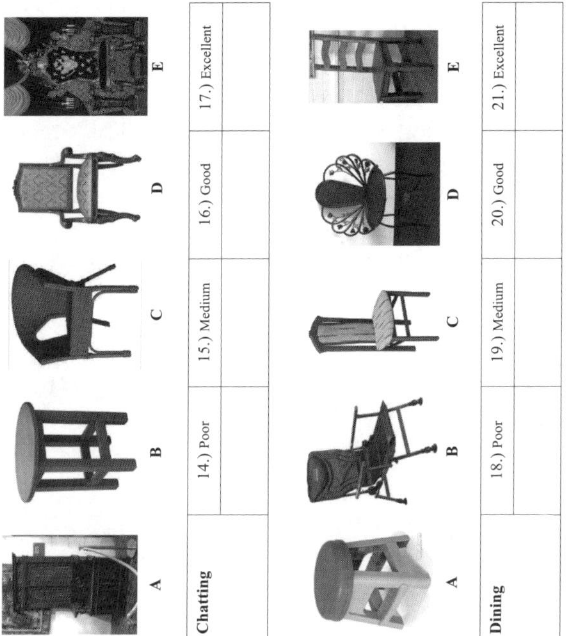

Figure 5: Task sheet for Environment and Design: "Chairs".

References

Bodóczky, I., Pataky, G., Zele, J., Gaul, E., Kárpáti, A. (2009). *Skill clusters of the Hungarian Visual Framework*. Budapest, Hungary: ELTE University.

Barber, M., Mourshed, M. (2007), *How the World's Best Performing School Systems Come Out on Top*. New York: McKinsey & Company.

Carswell, J. H. (1987). Let's Design Objects: The Hungarian Schools Design Competition 1. *Journal of Art & Design Education*, 6 (1), 32–36.

Darling-Hammond, L. (2000). *Reforming Teacher Preparation and Licensing: Debating the Evidence*, *Teachers College Record*, (102) 1, pp. 28–56. http://www.tcrecord.org. Accessed 18 February 2013.

Organisation of Economic Development [OECD] (2010). *Education at a Glance: OECD Indicators*. Paris: OECD, http://www.oecd.org/document/2/0,3746,en_2649_39263238_4863 4114_1_1_1_1,00.html. Accessed 18 February 2013.

Gaul, E. (2006). The structure and development of technological abilities. (Ph.D. dissertation, ELTE University, Budapest, 2006.)

Gyertyánffy, I. (1885). Handicraft Education Congress, Görlitz, Germany. *Néptanítók Lapja*. (XVIII) 83, 689–691.

Halász, G. (2010). The development of the Hungarian educational system, http://www.oki.hu/ oldal.php?tipus=cikk&kod=english-art-bie. Accessed 18 February 2013.

Euroguidance Hungary (2010): Hungarian Educational System. http://www.npk.hu/public/kiadvanyaink/2009/educational_system_of_h.pdf. Accessed 18 February 2013.

Hungarian National Core Curriculum [HNCC] (2007). Budapest: Ministry for Human Resources, http://www.nefmi.gov.hu/english/hungarian-national-core. Accessed 18 February 2013.

Kárpáti, A. (1995). Assessment of Art Education in Hungary: Historical problems in Contemporary Perspective. *Journal of Art and Design Education, 14* (3), 277–288.

Kárpáti, A., Schönau, D. (1997). Examining the Dutch and Hungarian Final Examination System in Art. *Journal of Multicultural and Cross-Cultural Research in Art Education,* 15 (2), 91–102.

Kárpáti, A., Gaul, E. (1998). The Child Study Movement and Its Effects On Hungarian Art Education. In Hernandez, F.; Freedman, K. (Eds.). *Curriculum, Culture and Art Education: Comparative Perspectives.* New York: SUNY Press. 149–164.

Kárpáti, A., Zempléni, A., Verhelst, N. H., Velduijzen, N., Schönau, D. (1998). Expert Agreement in Judging Art Projects – A Myth or Reality? *Studies in Educational Evaluation, 24* (4), 385–404.

Kárpáti, A. (2009). Teacher training and professional development. In Fazekas, K.; Köllő, J.; Varga, J. (Eds.). *Green Book for the renewal of public education in Hungary: Round table for Education and Child Welfare.* Budapest: Ecostat Government Institute for Strategic Research of Economy and Society. 203–226.

Kimbell, R. et al. (1991). *The Assessment of Performance in Design and Technology.* London: School Examinations and Assessment Council.

Pataky, G. (2011). *Értékelés a vizuális nevelésben.* (Assessment of visual skills and abilities of 6–12-year-olds). Budapest: Eötvös Kiadó

Teachers matter. Attracting, Developing and Retaining Effective Teachers. Pointers for policy development. (2010). Paris: Organisation of Economic Development [OECD] http://www.oecd.org/edu/school/48627229.pdf. Accessed 18 February 2013.

Notes

1   The most typical form of schooling in Hungary remained the 8-grade primary school for age groups 6–14, and the 4-grade secondary school for 15–18-year-olds (Euroguidance Hungary, 2010).

2   Shift between the modalities of vision, speech, hearing, touch, or movement, for example: pictorial representation of the written word, oral description of images, creation of a writing or drawing based on an image, etc.

3   Final examinations in Hungary are a version of the German "Abitur", the school-leaving exam that terminates secondary grammar school studies. Compulsory disciplines include Mathematics, World History, Hungarian and World Literature, a science discipline, and a foreign language. The *written part* traditionally consists of centrally developed tests or essays written on topics disclosed only on the day of the exam. Topics for the *oral examination*, developed by the National Examination Authority according to a set of achievement criteria worked out by an expert group of the Ministry of Human Resources, are given to students at the beginning of Grade 12 and teachers help them prepare.

Chapter 5

The competences of visual arts teachers in using performance
evaluation methods: The case of Turkey

Oğuz Dilmac, Atatürk University, Erzurum, Turkey

Abstract

This study aims to assess the competencies of visual arts teachers in using performance evaluation methods, and to examine how these competencies vary by gender, years of service, and the faculty type (education or fine art faculty) that they graduated from. The study is a descriptive one, aiming to depict the present situation. The sample for the study consisted of 78 visual arts teachers working in the primary schools in Turkey.

A three-point Likert type scale was used as data gathering instrument of the study. For the analysis of the data and for calculations, the SPSS 13.0 statistical package was used. Frequencies and percentages were calculated. Of the parametric tests, two samples t-test and one-way ANOVA were used to test for normalcy. In all statistical analyses conducted, a $p < 0.05$ significance level was used. The reliability coefficient of the scale was found to be 0.73.

The findings indicate that visual arts teachers frequently engage in performance evaluation. Visual arts teachers state that they experience difficulties in finding time to prepare and evaluate development portfolios and store them, because classes are too crowded, that they do not have sufficient information on rubrics, and that they need assessment and evaluation experts to help with the use of this tool.

Introduction

There is a need to create new and alternative assessment and evaluation systems that take the learning and knowledge objects created, ways of thinking, and learning styles into consideration. In other words, non-conventional tools or techniques to measure what the student knows and what he or she can do, and evaluations of student development are needed. In education practices, evaluation aims to assess the level of knowledge and ability the student has prior to teaching, to monitor the level of realization of learning targets during teaching, and to produce quantitative data, after the teaching, on the level of achievement of the targets previously set.

Once the process within which the student is going to be evaluated is identified, the next step is to identify evaluation techniques appropriate for the purpose. Different methods can be used in the identification of the process within which the student is going to be evaluated and in the collection of data following the identification of appropriate evaluation techniques. However, in the stage of identifying the appropriate evaluation technique, two important issues require the attention of the teacher. These are how to make the evaluation "meaningful" and "administrable". For an evaluation to be meaningful, it needs to express the operations and criteria clearly, and produce results that provide clear guidance on how to improve teaching. The administration of the evaluation, on the other hand, involves the preparation of resources for teaching purposes (Johnson and Johnson, 2002).

When commonly used assessment methods are examined, it can be observed that we have a system in which the results or the products are measured to evaluate the achievement of the student, and the individual achievement results are expressed relative to group achievement. The most important shortcoming of this system is that there is either insufficient information or none at all and no documents that would help the individual to assess his or her own standing and development. The achievement of the student is expressed as a "GRADE", which usually means some combination of written exam scores and the teacher's subjective evaluation. This traditional method of evaluation, which focuses on measuring the competencies of students in terms of application, knowledge and comprehension, fails to measure higher order competencies.

However, it is important that evaluations also assess student behaviours formed as a result of the knowledge and insights acquired during teaching. This type of an evaluation gives equal weight to the level and quality of cognitive inquiry processes, and to the skills and competencies the student has developed. In our constantly changing and developing world, we need a broadminded educational approach that does not solely focus on rote learning. Paralleling this approach, we also need to create novel learning environments in classes (Johnson and Johnson, 2002). In addition to exams, there needs to be various assessment and evaluation tools and methods to enrich the process of the evaluation of students, and the development of the student that needs to be monitored, so that proper guidance can be provided.

Performance evaluation, which is an alternative evaluation method that measures actual problem solving abilities of the students by focusing upon the performance and upon the process, can serve these needs. Tekin (1991) argues that if education targets include the student following an order of operations, or coming up with a product using any or a specific method in a certain field, then performance evaluation is a must.

In this approach, which does not require the student to come up with a single correct answer, the aim is to evaluate what sort of an impact the new information has on the thinking of the student. Differently from the traditional method, this method of evaluation provides detailed feedback for the students on their development, and encourages personal growth, creative activities, and social responsibility. From 1990 onwards particularly, student-centered evaluations based upon information from multiple sources became important, and various evaluation methods (performance evaluation, portfolio evaluation, etc.) and tools (rubrics, checklists, attitude scales, scoring guides, etc.) started to be used.

Evaluation and Rubrics in Visual Arts Education

In a subject like visual arts, coming up with evaluation criteria is a very difficult task. This is because expression, personal development, creativity, imagination, and originality, the improvement of which is one of the main aims of art education, are difficult to measure. The same work might be evaluated differently by different teachers. Thus, student evaluation in visual arts has to be multi-dimensional. Although there are no single correct answers to arts questions, pre-set targets based upon rubrics would lead both the student and the teacher to make sound assessments.

When evaluating, teachers should take daily performances into account as well as end-of-unit performances. Performance evaluation, defined as a function of the long term learning of the students and an evaluation of their skills, is crucial because constant feedback is provided. With the feedback provided, students will be able to assess their own work.

Tools commonly used for recording observations on student performance include checklists and rating scales. With the development of supplemental evaluation tools, especially since 1990, rubrics, scoring guides, and reflection logs also started to be used for recording observations on performance. Mehrens (1992, p. 3) defines a rubric as follows: "new approaches" that include performance evaluation and actual assessments and separate these from traditional written exams. In addition, we can say that a rubric aims to make a performance based assessment, and to measure how well the student employs the basic knowledge he or she has acquired when performing complicated tasks under authentic conditions. If the performance evaluation is made under authentic conditions, it is called authentic evaluation. The evaluation method that includes performance evaluation and actual assessments and that separates these from traditional written exams is called the "new methods (approaches)" (Mehrens, 1992, p. 5).

A book published by the Ministry of National Education Publications details teachers' competencies, and states that "visual arts teachers identify students that show development above and below certain levels, and help them improve using various tools and methods taking individual differences into account" (Republic of Turkey Ministry of National Education, 2008, p. 130). One of the most appropriate methods for evaluating the class level to assess student development is a rubric. A rubric, which is a scoring tool used in evaluating student performance, helps measure the quality of the student achievement (Strickland and Strickland, 1998).

Dorn (2002) argues that in visual arts education evaluation, rubrics based upon certain criteria need to be used. This kind of an evaluation aims to collect information about the performance level of a certain age group or class, rather than measuring artistic quality. "A rubric is an evaluation method that identifies the standards that a student needs to meet, and can be used to assess which students meet these standards and which do not" (Dorn, 2002, p. 235). Huffman (1998) argues that rubric evaluation in art education can reflect the personal, historical, and cultural understandings of the students about art, as well as their technical and intellectual abilities. This evaluation can be made on the basis of verbal, written, or visual presentation. Stokrocki (2005), on the other hand, argues that preparing rubrics on art education performance may influence design by giving information to the student prior to the work, and thus causing confusion. Stokrocki (2005) also argues that teachers should evaluate themselves first, based upon the rubrics they prepared, so that they can detect mistakes in their own thinking. This way they would also be able to detect differences between what they teach and what students learn.

Various studies on the use of a rubric in painting classes exist. One of these studies is Piscitello's (2002) study on evaluation and the use of rubrics in the arts. The findings of this study suggest that rubrics are successful in helping students assess themselves and develop self assessment abilities. In the process of evaluation, it was observed that over time, students' decisions on their own painting projects grew more independent of their teachers. (Based upon the results of another study on rubrics, Shepard [2005] argues that the use of rubrics in art education should be more widespread.) The results of Borden's (2008) study, titled *Rubrics as an Assessment and Evaluation Tool for Art Education*, indicate that rubrics help develop the self-respect and time management skills of the students, and that evaluations encourage student development both as individuals and in groups. The holistic rubric prepared by the researcher is based upon a literature review and expert opinion (Borden, 2008; Huffman, 1998; McCollister, 2002; Republic of Turkey Ministry of National Education, 2009).

This study aims to examine the competencies of visual arts teachers to use these assessment and evaluation tools, which are part of the primary school curricula, to discover the common difficulties experienced in their application, and to propose solutions for the problems identified. To this end, answers to the following research questions were sought:

- How do the competencies of visual arts teachers vary in using development portfolios, performance evaluation, and rubrics?
- How frequently do visual arts teachers use development portfolios, performance evaluation, and rubrics?
- What are the problems encountered by visual arts teachers in assessment and evaluation, and what solutions can be offered?
- Do the competencies of visual arts teachers to use development portfolios, performance evaluation, and rubrics significantly vary by gender, years of service, and faculty graduated from?

Method

Research design and sample

Because it aims to depict the present situation, the study is a descriptive one. Data collection methods include literature review and a survey.

The sample for the study consisted of all visual arts teachers working in the 2009–2010 academic year in public and private primary schools overseen by the Ministry of National Education. Random sampling method was used to draw the sample. The study group consists of a total of 78 visual arts teachers working in public and private primary schools in Turkey. 42.3% of the participants are female and 57.7% are male.

Distribution of the teachers by whether they took an assessment and evaluation course in college, whether they received any in-service training on assessment and evaluation, and the size of the classes they teach is shown in separate tables.

When we examine Table 1, we see that 15.4% of the teachers teach in classes consisting of 50 to 70 students, 58.5% teach in classes consisting of 30 to 50 students, and 25.7% teach in classes consisting of 10 to 30 students. Most of the teachers, then, teach classes with sizes of 30 to 50 students. Classes with sizes of 50 to 70 are the least frequent.

Table 2 shows that 66.9% of the teachers took an assessment and evaluation course in college, whereas 33.2% did not. Most of those who did not take a university course on assessment and evaluation are probably graduates of visual arts faculties. It is also observed that 47.5% of those who took a course on assessment and evaluation did not have in-service training on the subject. These findings indicate that additional emphasis needs to be placed on in-service training in assessment and evaluation.

Table 1: Distribution of visual arts teachers by the size of class taught.

Size of the class taught by the teacher	N	%
50–70	12	15.4
30–50	46	58.9
10–30	20	25.7
Total	78	100

Table 2: Distribution of visual arts teachers by whether they took an assessment and evaluation course in college or in service.

		Assessment and evaluation course in college					
		Yes		No		Total	
		f	%	f	%	f	%
In-service training	**Yes**	15	19.4	21	26.9	36	46.3
	No	37	47.5	5	6.2	42	53.7
	Total	52	66.9	26	33.1	78	100

Data gathering instruments

As part of the study, a scale for competency in using development portfolio, performance evaluation, and rubric was developed. Prior to the development of the scale the literature on performance evaluation and how it is used in visual arts education was reviewed in detail (Stevens and Levi, 2005; Sezer, 2006; Borden, 2008).

The questionnaire developed aims to measure the competencies of visual arts teachers in using development portfolios, performance evaluation, and rubrics, and the frequency of the use of these assessment tools and methods. The questionnaire was developed taking the views of visual arts teachers on the assessment and evaluation methods used in the second level of primary education into consideration.

In the first part of the questionnaire, there are items on the type of faculty the visual arts teachers graduated from, their years of service, class sizes, whether they took assessment and evaluation courses in college, and whether they received in-service training on assessment and evaluation. In the second part of the questionnaire, there are items designed to measure the competencies of visual arts teachers to use development portfolios, performance evaluation, and rubrics, in the form of statements with three-point Likert type responses: "Disagree, Neither agree nor disagree, and Agree". The data thus gathered were analysed using the SPSS 13.0 statistical package. Following the analyses, 27 items that had t-test results $p > 0.05$ and correlation coefficients $r < .30$ were removed, as well as one item with an item-total correlation value lower than 0.30. Cronbach's Alpha (α) reliability coefficient of the scale was found to be 0.73.

Data analysis

Frequencies, percentages, and averages for the items of the scale for competency in using development portfolios, performance evaluation, and rubrics were examined using descriptive statistics. In addition, one-way ANOVA and when necessary Tukey's test were used to examine whether there are differences in competency by gender, years of service, and the type of faculty graduated from. To examine whether there are significant differences between the genders, an independent samples t-test was used.

Findings and Interpretation

This section examines the frequencies, percentages, averages, and standard deviations for the items in the second part of the scale, reflecting visual arts teachers' views on the methods of evaluation that started to be applied, reported in Table 3.

Table 3 shows that 11.5% to 53.8% of the visual arts teachers agree with the statements designed to measure how competent they perceive themselves to be on the use of development

Table 3: Frequencies, percentages, averages, and standard deviations of the items on visual arts teachers' competency in using development portfolios, performance evaluation, and rubrics.

	Disagree		Neither agree nor disagree		Agree			
	f	%	F	%	F	%	$\overline{X}$	s
1- I can use product portfolio efficiently for evaluation purposes.	27	34.6	9	11.5	42	53.8	3.02	1.13
2- I can evaluate product portfolios easily.	51	65.4	3	3.8	24	30.8	2.33	0.83
3- I can select appropriate criteria in the evaluation of product portfolios.	63	80.7	-	-	15	19.2	2.18	1.16
4- I spend too much time evaluating the product portfolios.	60	76.9	4	5.2	14	17.9	2.21	1.12
5- I need the assistance of an assessment and evaluation expert in the evaluation of product portfolios.	30	38.4	19	24.3	29	37.3	3.13	1.29
6- I have sufficient information on product portfolios.	65	83.3	4	5.2	9	11.5	2.73	1.34
7- I can use product portfolios efficiently in my class.	59	75.6	-	-	19	24.3	2.16	1.27
8- I can use rubrics efficiently in evaluating product portfolios.	69	88.5	-	-	9	11.5	2.18	1.67
9- I can prepare proper rubrics for product portfolios.	63	80.7	3	3.8	12	15.3	2.10	1.21
10- I need assistance from an assessment and evaluation expert in preparing proper rubrics for product portfolios.	45	57.6	17	21.7	16	20.5	4.01	1.09
11- I can assign performance tasks fit for students' genders.	32	41	26	33.3	20	25.6	3.23	1.18
12- I can assign performance tasks fit for students' levels.	11	14.1	16	20.5	51	65.3	4.52	1.46
13- I can assign performance tasks designed to improve the higher order thinking abilities of the students.	37	47.4	31	39.7	10	12.8	3.29	1.22
14- I can prepare suitable environments to evaluate students' performance.	56	71.7	13	16.8	9	11.5	2.13	1.12
15- The performance tasks I assign involve multiple skills.	43	55.1	23	29.6	12	15.3	2.42	1.23

(Continued)

	Disagree		Neither agree nor disagree		Agree			
	f	%	F	%	F	%	X	s
16- I can select performance tasks fit for learning goals mentioned in the program.	35	44.8	14	17.9	29	37.3	3.27	1.21
17- I can select proper criteria for evaluating performance tasks.	42	53.8	9	11.5	27	34.7	2.42	1.32
18- I have difficulty evaluating learning goals mentioned in the program.	39	50.0	14	17.9	25	32.1	3.70	1.16
19- I need the assistance of an assessment and evaluation expert in the evaluation of performances.	41	52.5	4	5.2	30	38.4	4.03	1.43
20- I have sufficient information on performance evaluation.	65	83.3	2	3.6	11	14.1	2.11	1.16
21- I can use performance evaluation efficiently in class/a workshop.	28	35.9	14	17.9	36	46.2	3.23	1.59
22- I can use rubrics efficiently in performance evaluation.	53	67.9	5	6.5	20	25.6	2.42	1.83
23- I have sufficient information on rubrics.	71	91.1	-	-	7	8.9	2.02	1.18
24- I need the assistance of an assessment and evaluation expert for preparing rubrics.	56	71.7	8	10.4	14	17.9	2.88	1.49
Total							X = 2.48	

portfolios. 83.3% of the visual arts teachers state that they do not have sufficient information on product portfolios. 53.8% of visual arts teachers agreed with the item on efficient use of the product portfolio as an evaluation tool. These responses indicate that visual arts teachers perceive themselves to be incompetent in the use of development portfolios, performance evaluation, and rubrics (X = 2.48).

Only 17.9% of the teachers agreed with the item on having time-related difficulties in product selection for preparing product portfolios (X = 2.21). 80.7% of the teachers stated that they cannot select proper criteria for evaluating product portfolios (X = 2.18), 65.4% stated that they cannot evaluate product portfolios easily (X = 2.33), and 88.5% stated that they cannot use rubrics efficiently in evaluating product portfolios (X = 2.18).

8.9% to 65.3% of the visual arts teachers agree with the statements designed to measure how competent they perceive themselves to be on the use of performance evaluation. 83.3% of the visual arts teachers think they do not have sufficient information on performance evaluation (X = 2.11). 46.2% of the visual arts teachers agree with the item on efficient use of performance evaluation in their classes (X = 3.23). 12.8% to 63.5% of the visual arts teachers agreed with the items in the questionnaire on being able to assign proper performance tasks. Of these positive items, teachers who agreed with the item "I can assign performance tasks fit for students' levels" made up 65.3% of the teachers (X = 4.52).

Of the negative items, 38.4% agreed with the item "I need the assistance of an assessment and evaluation expert in the evaluation of performances". Finally, 91.1% of the visual arts teachers think they do not have sufficient information on rubrics (X = 2.02), and 17.9% state they need assistance from an assessment and evaluation expert for preparing rubrics (X = 2.88).

Visual arts teachers' frequency in using development portfolios, performance evaluation, and rubrics

Table 4 reports the frequencies and percentages of the responses given by visual arts teachers to the items in the third part of the questionnaire, designed to measure how frequently the evaluation tools and methods are used.

When we examine how frequently visual arts teachers use the tools and methods of evaluation, we observe that 41.1% of the teachers stated that they never use performance evaluation, and 23.0% stated that they use performance evaluation often. When the use of product portfolios was examined, it was observed that 21.7% of the teachers stated that they use it often, whereas 37.2% state they never use it. 19.3% of the teachers state they often use rubrics, whereas 51.3% state they never use them. These findings show that the assessment

Table 4: Views of visual arts teachers on how frequently they use development portfolios, performance evaluation, and rubrics.

	Never		Rarely		Often		
	f	%	f	%	f	%	Total
Product portfolio	29	37.2	32	41.1	17	21.7	100
Performance evaluation	32	41.1	28	35.9	18	23.0	100
Rubric	40	51.3	23	29.4	15	19.3	100

Table 5: "t" values for visual arts teachers' views on frequency of use of development portfolios, performance evaluation, and rubrics by the independent variable of gender.

Gender	n	x	s.s	s.d.	t	p
Female	33	113.34	12.23	77	0.641	0.92
Male	45	115.78	10.17			

P > 0.05 insignificant

and evaluation tool most frequently used by teachers is performance evaluation (23.0 %), whereas a rubric is the least frequently used (19.3 %). 21.7% of the teachers stated they often use product portfolios, coming second after performance evaluation, and 51.3% state they prefer rubrics the least.

When we examine Table 6, we can see that there are no significant differences between genders with regards to the views of visual arts teachers on frequency of use of development portfolios, performance evaluation, and rubrics (t (77)0. 641; p > 0.05). These findings indicate that male and female visual arts teachers have similar views on the issue.

Table 6: Frequency, mean, and standard deviation of the variable of years of service for visual arts teachers' views on frequency of use of development portfolios, performance evaluation, and rubrics.

Years of service	n	f	x	s.s.
5 and below	24	15.5	142.85	14.36
6–10	38	24.6	118.40	11.56
11–15	46	29.8	115.01	12.43
16–20	28	18.1	111.80	7.13
21 and above	20	12.9	111.46	11.43
Total	154	100	118.70	11.38

Table 7: One-way ANOVA results for visual arts teachers' views on frequency of use of development portfolios, performance evaluation, and rubrics by the variable of years of service.

Source of variation	Sum of squares	Sd	Mean square	f	p
Between groups	5692.35	4	73.22	0.47	.000
Within groups	167622.27	149	138.00		
Total	173314.63	153			

P < 0.05 significant

Table 8: ANOVA results for the type of faculty visual arts teachers graduated from.

Type of faculty graduated from	n	x	s	f	p
Faculty of Education	126	58.75	9.72	7.703	.000
Faculty of Fine Arts	25	53.14	9.21		
Other*	3	43.18	8.53		

*P < 0.05 significant

Discussion and Conclusion

The findings indicate that a great majority of visual arts teachers identify crowded classes and lack of assessment and evaluation experts as the main difficulties they encounter when using these tools and methods of evaluation. Most of the in-service visual arts teachers, never took any classes on assessment and evaluation in college (cf. Table 3). What is more, 47.5% of those that did take such courses never received any in-service training on the subject. Another important issue is the size of the classes the teachers have. Distribution of the sizes of classes taught by visual arts teachers participating in the study is displayed in Table 1. Table 1 shows that 58.9% of the visual arts teachers teach classes of 30 to 50 students. The phenomenon of crowded classes negatively affects the individual assessments of the students, given that visual arts classes are offered one hour a week in the 4th, 5th, 6th, 7th, and 8th grades.

The difficulties encountered by visual arts teachers can be alleviated by having smaller class sizes and more class hours, having assessment and evaluation experts in each school, and offering in-service training seminars on assessment and evaluation tools and methods and their use. Another important issue is to have experts offer these seminars. Mamur's (2004) study finds that arts teachers fail to use different dimensions like testing, scaling (rating), self-criticism, and criticism, which complement each other. The findings of this study also show that as methods of teaching and learning change, assessment methods used to evaluate how much of the aims and the targets that are achieved need to change as well. Otherwise, limited standards would result in limited results. Gelbal and Kelecioğlu (2007), in their study, find that teachers mostly use traditional methods for getting to know their students and evaluating their levels of achievement, and never use methods based upon self-evaluation of the students. Teachers also find themselves to be competent in evaluating student achievement, but state that they have difficulties using assessment tools due to negative factors, such as crowded classes and lack of time. The findings of this study indicate that teachers need training on the use of assessment techniques.

Based upon the interviews made with visual arts teachers and their responses to the questionnaire, we can argue that a great majority of the teachers do not have sufficient information on the subject. For the new primary education program to be successfully applied, and for visual arts teachers to be able to make efficient use of the assessment and evaluation methods of development portfolios, performance evaluation, and rubrics, first, the teachers need to have proper training on these issues.

In-service training seminars on the subject have been organized in certain schools in some of the provinces of Turkey, and the teachers were informed about these methods, but views expressed by the teachers and the findings of the present study indicate that there is a need for more training. The Ministry of National Education needs to organize more in-service training seminars, and inform visual arts teachers about both the new primary education program, and the use of new assessment techniques. The Ministry of National Education could also cooperate with faculties of education in universities on the planning and provision of these seminars. Teachers also state that they experience difficulties due to parents completing painting homework they assign to the students. Parents who complete homework assigned to the students definitely damage the development of their children. What visual arts teachers can do on the subject is identify the parents who engage in this kind of behaviour, and talk to them in person. If that effort fails, then arrangements can be made for school guidance counselors to meet with these parents. Finally, visual arts teachers state that they need the assistance of an assessment and evaluation expert in their schools who can help deal with evaluation problems they encounter. Setting up assessment and evaluation centres in each province and district could alleviate some of these problems. Teachers would thus be able to consult with experts in these centres on the causes of the difficulties they experience and on how to deal with them.

References

Borden, S. S. (2008). Rubrics as an Assessment and Evaluation Tool for Art Education. (Unpublished master's dissertation, California State University, Long Beach.)

Dorn, C. (2002). The Teacher as Stakeholder in Student Art Assessment and Art Program Evaluation, *Art Education, 55* (4), 235–244.

Gelbal, S., Kelecioğlu, H., (2007), Teachers' Proficiency Perceptions of About the Measurement and Evaluation Techniques and the Problems They Confront (Original Turkish title: Öğretmenlerin Ölçme ve Değerlendirme Yöntemleri Hakkındaki Yeterlik Algıları ve Karşılaştıkları Sorunlar), *Hacettepe University Journal of Education*, 33 (2), 135–145.

Huffman, E. (1998). Authentic rubrics. *Art Education: Learning in and Through Art, 51* (1), 64–68. 2010.

Johnson, D. W., Johnson, R. T. (2002). *Meaningful Assessment: A Manageable and Cooperative Process.* Boston: Allyn and Bacon.

Mamur, N. (2004), The Methods of Assessment and Evaluation ın Multi-Disiplinary Art Education: Bolu City Sample (Original Turkish title: Çok Alanlı Sanat Eğitiminde Ölçümleme ve Değerlendirme Yaklaşımları: Bolu İli Örneği), *Elementary Education Online, 3* (2), 1–18, http://ilkogretim-online.org.tr. Accessed 13 January 2013.

McCollister, S. (2002). Developing Criteria Rubrics in The Art Classroom, *Art Education, 55* (4), 46–52.

Mehrens, W. A. (1992). Using Performance Assessment for Accountability Purposes, *Educational Measurement,* 11 (4), 3–9.

Piscitello, M. (2001). Using rubrics for assessment and evaluation in art. (Unpublished master dissertation, Saint Xavier University, Chicago, IL.)

Republic of Turkey Ministry of National Education (2008). *Teacher Qualifications.* Ankara, Turkey: Ministry of National Education Publications.

—— (2009), *National Education Visual Arts and Sports High School Curriculum* (9,10 ve 11. Sınıflar), http://ogm.meb.gov.tr/belgeler/uc_boyutlu_sanat_atolyesi.pdf. Accessed 14 January 2013.

Sezer, S. (2006). A Study on the Use of Rubrics, *Pamukkale University Journal of Education*, 3 (2), 63–71.

Shepard, M. (2005). *The effect of the use of a rubric in teacher assessment.* (Unpublished doctoral dissertation, Boston College)

Stevens, D., Levı, A. (2005). *Introduction to Rubrics.* Sterling, VA: Stylus Publishing.

Stokrocki, M. (2005). Reconsidering everyday assessment in the art classroom: Ceramics and science, *Arts Education Policy Review, 107* (1), 15–21.

Strickland, K., Strickland, J. (1998). *Reflections on Assessment: Its purposes, methods, and effects on learning.* Portsmouth, NH: Heinemann.

Tekin, H. (1991). *Educational Measurement and Evaluation.* Ankara: Yargı Press.

PART II

New assessment practices

Chapter 6

Assessment of performance in the visual arts: What, how and why?

Douglas G. Boughton, Northern Illinois University, DeKalb, Illinois, USA

Abstract

Assessing the creative outcomes of instruction in the arts remains a persistent dilemma for teachers and administrators. This chapter examines three of the most important questions that lie at the centre of most debates about the philosophy and practice of arts assessment. These are "what", "how" and "why". What should be the important focus of assessment in the arts? How might teachers effectively assess the learning outcomes that follow from arts instruction, and why bother? One of the most problematic assessment concerns in the past has been the difficulty of assessing creative products and behaviour since all too frequently assessment methodologies serve to inhibit rather than promote imaginative outcomes. A more productive relationship between the assessment process and creative behaviour is discussed with reference to new ideas about creativity promulgated by the work of contemporary social psychologists. The question of how to conduct assessment in the arts is made more difficult when issues of standards are raised and the perennial challenges of reliability and validity of qualitative judgments are applied to the work of examiners. The strategies outlined below address these issues and conclude with the argument that assessment, properly done, can promote rather than inhibit creative thinking.

Assessing the creative outcomes of student learning has always been a dilemma for educators and will continue to be so for as long as we continue to value imagination as one of the most important underlying virtues of engagement in the arts. I have had the good fortune over the past 45 years to spend time teaching art and art education in Australia, Canada, and the United States, and since 1993 I have worked as an examiner for the International Baccalaureate program with five years of that time as chief examiner for the visual arts. I have seen many models of assessment in the countries I visited, some of the most interesting of which, to my knowledge, have never been formally studied and documented. The International Baccalaureate itself boasts a robust assessment model that is highly regarded in more than a hundred countries. This chapter is a documentation of what I have learned over the years about the what, who, and how of assessment in the visual arts together with recommendations for best practice.

Assessment, of course, is a continuous process in art education. The day-to-day formative judgments made by teachers to assist students' progress towards their learning goals play a central role in any successful art education program. However summative assessment is the force that gives impetus to the direction of the program and defines what is most important to learn. Formative assessment tends to be a private matter between the student and teacher while summative assessments are often a much more public affair. In those countries where art is valued as a core subject the question of how to establish standards is an ongoing debate that finds its way into the public arena. In the Netherlands, for example, the art exam questions are sometimes discussed in the national newspapers.

In this chapter I will discuss summative rather than formative assessment. Good summative assessment models have the potential to improve the quality of student learning in local, state, national, or international contexts, and also gain respect for the discipline. I will use the International Baccalaureate model as a backdrop to the discussion of suggested practices. The International Baccalaureate (IB) program is one that well reflects the challenge of achieving universal excellence variously expressed in multiple personal and cultural contexts. The IB is a system of international education taught in half the countries of the world. As described in documents accessed through the information page of the IB website the centrepiece of the program is its flexibility in responding to local interests but at the same time providing access for students to what is shared and what is different in human experience.

Developing an effective summative assessment model hinges on three questions "what should be assessed?", "who is qualified to assess it?", and "how should it be done?" I address each of these questions separately in the following.

What should be assessed?

For many years educators have argued about specific concepts and skills that should be taught in the visual arts, and which philosophies are most appropriate to direct the selection of such content. I do not wish to enter that debate except to focus on the most problematic assessment issue in the arts, which is how to determine the value of students' creative outcomes.

The assumption that student autonomy is not only important but central to their art making is the assumption that has underpinned art education since the creative free expression movement of the 1940s. Student experience in school art programs is thought to develop the capacity for independent thought and the ability to express ideas in visual form. Individual creative expression has long been valued in education systems in most parts of the world. Recent educational reforms, particularly in the United States, have placed significant emphasis upon testing as a way to improve standards in school subjects across the board. An unfortunate by-product for the arts from these reforms in the United States has been the homogenization of student outcomes expressed as standards that are frequently measured with inappropriate assessment instruments. High-stakes tests, employed by state assessment authorities, in my view, are the epitome of the inappropriate assessment of art learning. These tests require homogenous outcomes reflecting a single set of agreed standards thought to be appropriate for the arts. The casualties in these reforms have been the most valued of all tenets of art education, the freedom of students to pursue independent learning pathways and the autonomy of their expression.

While the accountability problems manifested in the United States have not emerged so noticeably in other parts of the world, the central assessment question remains equally pertinent. How does one assess students' creative behaviour? Creativity is re-emerging as one of the key goals of art learning in the 21st century (Steers, 2009; Freedman, 2010). Determining the level of a learner's technical skills or knowledge of cultural and historical content is a relatively straightforward task that can be satisfied adequately with traditional assessment methods such as tests, projects, or technical tasks. As we have seen in recent years in the United States the intense focus on multiple-choice testing has stripped education to the bare bones of literacy and numeracy and those bones are revealed in schools by multiple-choice tests for the most part. Creative behaviour cannot easily be measured on a state or national scale so it is left to dedicated teachers of art to struggle with the problem alone. In other countries, such as the United Kingdom, creativity has already been repositioned in the spotlight of educational ambition for the visual arts, as is demonstrated by studies initiated at the level of national government (Roberts, 2006; SEED, 2006; Steers, 2009).

New ways of thinking about creativity have suggested a pressing need to reconceptualise the art curriculum and the methods used to both assess and promote creative thinking. One of the most powerful, and possibly the most neglected strategies for the development of creativity, is the apposite use of assessment. No matter how imaginative or robust new creativity based curriculums might be none will be sufficiently robust to survive inappropriate assessment. By inappropriate I mean the kind of quantitative tests national legislators in the United States currently favour.

As I mentioned previously the current educational policy in the United States following from the No Child Left Behind (NCLB) legislation and the conceptions of assessment that followed from this has had devastating impact upon the arts and education generally. NCLB has focused attention upon the so-called basics of reading and maths, diverting attention from social studies, the arts, and almost all areas of curriculum that have anything to do with the analysis of human values and cultural issues. NCLB values objective knowledge and answers that are right or wrong. Many schools now take precious time to train students in test-taking strategies. To do this time and resources are stolen from the arts and injected into reading, maths, and science. Even worse, the arts have been cut from the curriculum altogether in some districts.

Creativity is a victim of this pernicious legislation. National testing practices and punishments associated with poor performance for schools unfortunate enough to be under-resourced or populated by large cohorts of special needs students allow no place for creative thinking. Test results and the achievement of national and state specified standards are the only blips on the educational radar in the United States.

In my home state, Illinois, I have heard multiple stories from my graduate students about educational administrators in their schools who call upon art teachers to demonstrate the success of their art teaching endeavours with test results showing that students have learned something about art. They expect art teachers to use multiple-choice tests to give students practice in filling the bubbles of multiple-choice tests. Good art teachers resist such calls, but with sometimes devastating outcomes to their programs.

Creativity research

Early research in the field of creativity assumed that it was indeed a measurable attribute. Much early research was focused on giftedness and the task of identifying creative individuals. Of particular interest was the development of techniques to identify the personality characteristics and dispositions of creative individuals. The work of Getzels and Jackson (1971) in the early 1970s revealed some fascinating distinctions between the dispositions and performance of high intelligence students compared to high IQ students. In one study two large groups of adolescent subjects were tested and identified as High IQ or High Creative individuals.

The two groups were compared in a variety of ways to determine differences between them. The researchers found that high IQ students valued personal qualities likely to prepare them for adult success. The highly creative group preferred the opposite. Where the high IQ group favoured those qualities they believed the teacher liked, the highly creative group preferred those having no relationship with what they believed would contribute to adult success, and appeared to deliberately select those personal qualities they thought were directly opposite to those that their teachers favoured (Getzels and Jackson, 1971, p.127). Creative students it seems are rebellious, uncooperative and nonconforming.

This study is typical of most of the research that was undertaken in the 1960s and 1970s in the search for answers to the question: what are the characteristics of creative individuals? We now have a good set of understandings that help us identify these individuals by virtue of their behaviour. But this knowledge does not help us much with pedagogy. If we know creative individuals are nonconforming, and rebellious, does it follow that we should try to change the personalities of our students in the hope that they will become creative? Do we direct them to reject authority and seek goals that will not suit them well for adult life? Of course we don't, so what we have to do is look at the problem from a different perspective, and this is to pay attention to the environmental conditions that promote creative behaviour.

For most of human history ordinary people and researchers alike seem to have attributed creative action to personal attributes rather than the context that promotes creative behaviour. Environmental factors contributing to creativity have been largely ignored (Kasof, 1995). To use the distinction specified by Kasof, creative behaviour has been attributed to *dispositional* rather than *situational* causes. "The result has been a highly skewed research literature in which creativity is studied primarily by personality and cognitive psychologists searching for characteristics of 'creative people' and paying comparatively little attention to external influences on creativity" (Kasof, 1995, p. 311).

The creative individuals in an art class are not the students that provide the art teacher with their greatest pedagogical challenges. While it is interesting, and perhaps useful, to know how one might identify a creative individual through personality traits, the major concern for the arts teacher is what to do with those individuals who are *not* inherently creative. These students constitute a far larger number in any given class than creative individuals. Is there anything that the teacher can do to promote creative behaviour in non-creative individuals?

The most powerful support for educators to examine context rather than disposition comes from the field of social psychology and the work of researchers such as Teresa Amabile (1982), Mihaly Csikszentmihalyi (1996), and Dean Keith Simonton (1979). These researchers have addressed the most pervasive misunderstanding about creativity. That is the subjective reception of a creative product. For something to be regarded as creative it must satisfy two basic criteria. First it must be original, rare, or novel in some way. Second, it must be valued by individuals in the context in which it appears. In other words it must be perceived as approved, accepted, appropriate, or "good" (Kasof, 1995, p. 313).

By this definition, creativity is not purely objective and is not a fixed attribute of the creative object that holds true irrespective of its time and place. Whether or not an artistic product is creative in part requires a subjective judgment that must be conferred on the original product (Kaslof, 1995; Amabile, 1982; Csikszentmihalyi, 1988, 1990; Csikszentmihalyi and Robinson, 1986; Gardner, 1993; Weisberg, 1986). As such the determination of creative artistic production becomes an issue of *judgment* rather than *measurement*. It is an *assessment* issue that has a profound effect upon the way art educators need to think about the development of curriculum and the assessment protocols employed for determining student learning.

The fallacy of assuming that creativity is an objective and measurable outcome of learning has significant curriculum implications. Some art curriculums ignore the notion of creativity entirely because of misconceptions about its nature. For example, the current set of state goals in the state of Illinois does not mention the word creativity because it is difficult to measure through testing. So what can we draw from the research that is helpful for the art teacher working with the ordinary population of less creative individuals? First we can dispense with the idea that creativity is contingent upon disposition and is therefore dichotomous, i.e. that one is either creative or not. Instead we need to focus upon the classroom conditions that facilitate creative behaviour. Second we can set up interrelated curriculum and assessment strategies that promote rather than inhibit creative outcomes, and facilitate judgment processes to determine creative outcomes in a social context.

So what are the conditions that can help to improve creative behaviour? Csikszentmihalyi (1996) has offered many positive suggestions for enhancing personal creativity. He interviewed nearly one hundred creative people to gain understanding about the creative process and his recommendations have useful application in the art classroom. They include developing curiosity and interest, cultivating "flow" in everyday life, and ways of thinking creatively. Each of these carries important implications for the creation of conditions that will promote creativity and more importantly defines the nature of assessment that must be used to preserve the integrity of those conditions. I will discuss each of these.

Curiosity and interest

Csikszentmihalyi (1996) says the first step toward a more creative life is the cultivation of curiosity and interest. This seems to be an obvious a suggestion but it is often one that is overlooked. How often have we seen art classes in which students are struggling with media drawing uninteresting or random objects, or simply creating value scales and colour wheels for the sole purpose of learning technical processes? I am not suggesting technical skills should not be taught, or that artists should not be studied. What is of the utmost consequence here, and what is so often overlooked, is the importance of recognizing and engaging the interests students bring to the classroom, and from those leading to new discoveries about technique and artists. Students have a considerable advantage over adults in that their curiosity is easily engaged by many things they encounter in their everyday lives. If invited to bring their interests to the classroom students will willingly oblige. But if art practice is undertaken in the absence of student interest creative production is unlikely to manifest. Interest is an essential prerequisite for creative endeavour.

Journaling and diary notes make experiences more concrete and enduring, and greatly assist students to get in touch with their interests. The point of recording one's experience and surprises is to preserve ideas to make them less fleeting, and after time to look back in order to observe emerging patterns of interest.

Thinking creatively

Csikszentmihalyi's work also suggests creative thinking is characterized by three fundamental activities: (1) in-depth investigation, (2) problem finding, and (3) risk taking in the search for solutions.

In-depth pursuit of ideas related to a particular theme is a well documented hallmark of creative behaviour. Themes develop from interests and provide unique lenses to view the world thus enhancing curiosity and providing opportunity to develop novel outcomes. Investigating a theme requires work, so there is no point investing energy in a pursuit where there is no interest or passion for discovery. For this reason some people need to explore a variety of thematic investigations before settling on something to pursue in depth.

Finding solutions to problems requires divergent thinking and is another key way to engender creative behaviour. This is not so much a function of creative disposition as it is a habit of mind. Such habits of thinking can be learned but this requires an individual to consciously seek alternative solutions to a single problem, to experiment, to play and to take risks. As Elliot Eisner (2005) says producing novelty means one should work at the edge of incompetence. This is risky when you don't quite know what it is you are trying to do but without a supportive and trusting classroom environment risk taking is not likely to occur.

Engendering "Creative Flow"

Csikszentmihalyi is well known for the idea of *flow* which he suggests is the importance of developing habits of engagement with ideas that become self sustaining (Csikszentmihalyi, 1995, p. 349). When one finds an intellectual task that is engaging it is important to be able to pursue it with enthusiasm and sustained interest.

The average school is a very poor place in which to develop creative flow. The structure of a normal school day conspires against the development of any sustained pursuit of creative activity or other kind of intellectual engagement for that matter. In most schools lessons are divided into short time periods of 40 to 80 minutes during which it is scarcely possible for students to collect their materials, let alone their thoughts, in order to generate an idea and begin work. No sooner do they get started the bell sounds and they have to return their materials and move from one classroom to another and repeat the same process over again with a different subject matter. In the course of the day most students start and stop their lessons between five and eight times. Imagine the frustration when one discovers something of interest he or she may wish to pursue only to have to shut down and start something else.

Compared to the intellectual staccato students experience in school, opportunities for out of school visual and intellectual stimulation represent a veritable landscape of treasures. When students can experience the abundance of imagery offered through television, video games, movies, billboards, magazines, the Internet, concerts, exhibitions, community events, and even their phone, it is no wonder they lose interest in school.

There are no easy answers to this problem given the structural limitations of school administration. However, I have seen some hope in the work of gifted teachers who are able to construct the art-learning experience as an integral part of the students' life at school. Once interest is engaged in the classroom these teachers encourage students to return during free periods, recesses, lunchtime and even after the official school day ends. In these classrooms students experience exciting engagement with ideas because their teachers have set up appropriate physical and intellectual conditions, an atmosphere of trust, and the freedom to work in supportive classroom spaces beyond the normal classroom hours.

The role of assessment in fostering creative behaviour

If we know the situational conditions likely to promote creative behaviour then it makes sense to develop assessment strategies that enhance those conditions rather than negate them. We know creative behaviour is more likely to occur If curiosity is fostered, if students are encouraged to pursue interests thematically, if they are prepared to play with ideas and engage in risk taking behaviour in the search for solutions to problems, and if physical conditions support the idea of "creative flow" described by Csikszentmihalyi.

I have long argued in support of the use of portfolios as an assessment tool, (Boughton 1996, 2004, 2006; Boughton and Wang 2002, 2005) because good portfolios do more than provide evidence for assessment. They drive curriculum in such a way that creative engagement is more likely. A good portfolio will demand students to demonstrate their interests and show the ways in which they have integrated classroom learning with their lives. A good portfolio will require in-depth and sustained reflection, and will provide a good opportunity to engage interest through the pursuit of thematic content. For a portfolio to have the best chance of becoming a living record of students' creative thinking less assessment is better than more.

The way to destroy creativity through inappropriate assessment is to structure the art program as a series of directed projects that always receive a grade leaving no possibility for a collection of work to be judged as a record of thinking. If the teacher always chooses the topic, the media, the visual references, the reference sources, the strategy, the style of representation, and the look of the potential outcome, where is the opportunity for student interests to be engaged? Why would a student take risks in the search for solutions when he or she knows they will be graded on every project they do? Instead, assessment practices that require thematic study, that do not assess each project, that require evidence of productive risk taking, and demand evidence of sustained independent investigation are more likely to encourage creative output.

Who is an authentic evaluator?

If we accept the essence of the argument about creativity offered by social psychologists we must then agree that determining the quality of a creative product is a matter of judgment rather than measurement. The task for teachers is to determine if the student work is original, rare, or novel in some way and that it is valued by individuals in the context in which it is created. This means that teachers need to recognize the social context in which student work is produced. And, if we do that it means the teacher is not necessarily the final arbiter of quality. It does not make sense to ignore the significance of collective judgment about artistic production.

The argument that the teacher should not be the sole arbiter of quality in judging student work is not an expression of mistrust in teachers. Rather it is a recognition of the nature of art and the ways in which its quality is determined in social settings. Art in the professional world is judged and valued by many in the art community. Critics, artists, agents, and consumers all play their part in stamping an artist's work as original, valuable, worthy or not. A single critic does not make this decision although some may have more influence than others. In the end it is discourse in the social context that establishes the virtue of the work.

Similarly in the educational context there are many stakeholders who can legitimately contribute to the discourse about the quality of artwork made by students. These include the students themselves, the classroom teacher, the community of art teachers, arts administrators, and professional artists to name some. How is s/he selected and trained? How to overcome cultural differences, expert bias, or the gap between academic and school practice?

There are some good models to guide us with this collective judgment process. Assessment by students of their colleagues' work, and self-assessment within a community context, both help to address the perennial problem of determining the creative quality of artistic products. Moderation processes are employed by school systems in many countries in the world at the senior school level. These have long track records of effectively addressing the need for community determination of the value of art products, and whether or not they contain evidence of creative thinking. More about this later.

In our schools today the demand to demonstrate accountability is extreme and teachers are pressured to produce grades on a regular basis to satisfy the expectations of administrators and parent groups. In the art class this pressure has had the effect of working directly against the development of strategies to enhance creative behaviour in art students.

Assessment against the measure of standards has afflicted maths, reading and the sciences more particularly than the arts. However the search for ways to achieve predictable and agreed standards in the arts deflects attention away from the search for creative outcomes and the exercise of imagination in our students' art-making efforts. Failure to distinguish between standards and standardization in the practice of assessing art destroys the likelihood that students will experience the curricular conditions necessary to stimulate creative thought. It is time to move back towards a more rational relationship between the creative outcomes we desire and the methods we use to assess it.

How to design and conduct summative evaluation?

I have argued above that creativity should be one of the fundamental outcomes of art learning and that an assessment properly conceived and implemented will promote this outcome. The next question is how do we design a summative assessment that will do this in both school and system contexts? The following will focus particularly on the problem of system-wide assessment in contemporary educational settings. By this I mean district, state, or national contexts. The issues to be considered for this purpose include: establishing standards, validity and reliability of assessment judgments in the visual arts, designing authentic assessment tasks, the virtue of portfolio assessment, choosing between analytic and holistic judgment methods, and, moderation models to assist standard setting.

Establishing standards

The singular interest of system-wide assessments is that the achievement of students has common meaning and the standard is understood and accepted by all. The value of an agreed system of standards is that the performance grade awarded to students has common currency. For example, students may transport their documented grades from school to school, or school to university, and there is no debate about the meaning. The creation of standards, however, is a most difficult concept for the arts since the notion of "standard" is often confused with "standardization" and its corollary "homogenization". The simplistic and somewhat naive solution (motivated by fiscal restraint) to the accountability problem for the arts in public school contexts in the United States has been paper and pencil testing (Boughton, 2004). Fortunately this is not so much the case in other parts of the world. Nevertheless, it is still possible that the pressure to define and demonstrate the achievement of standards in school art programs could possibly manifest similarly unpalatable outcomes elsewhere if imaginative solutions to the assessment problem are not identified and implemented.

Validity and reliability of assessment judgments in the visual arts

Efforts to standardize assessment content in the arts often violate content validity. What is content validity and why is it threatened by standardized assessment in the visual arts? "Content Validity is based on the extent to which a measurement reflects the specific intended domain of content" (Carmines and Zeller, 1991, p. 20). An assessment instrument or practice can be said to have content validity if it is capable of revealing learning that is central to the content of the discipline. For example, the demonstration of technical skill and knowledge of formal qualities is easily judged in student work, but possession of this knowledge and skill is peripheral to the core of artistic endeavour. The qualities valued by instructors as the most important defining characteristics of artistic performance are more likely to be attributes such as the degree of imagination exercised, the quality of ideas generated, capacity of students to demonstrate sustained and critical pursuit of themes, and the ability to identify and solve conceptual and technical problems (MacGregor, 1990). These qualities, however, require much more complex judgments from examiners than assessing technical skill and knowledge of the principles of composition.

Herein lies the problem. Accountability pressures to standardize assessment often deflect attention away from the most important content of art learning, replacing it instead with content that is most easily and reliably assessed. Content that is easily assessed, however, does not necessarily represent knowledge that is central to the discipline, even though it may be possible to standardize it and measure it with a high degree of reliability. Testing is not a useful solution to the problem despite the reliability payoff. On the other hand traditional portfolios, as an assessment tool, have long offered the potential to achieve high levels of content validity. The portfolio, once the sole province of studio arts, has now been embraced widely throughout the educational and business communities. Although portfolio assessment had its origins in the visual arts it has, interestingly, been recognized as a useful solution to the shortcomings of paper and pencil testing in other subject areas but is largely ignored by both the state high-stakes assessment programs and by teachers of the visual arts in the United States (Burton, 1998).

Although portfolios offer high content validity in an assessment context, if inappropriate judgment procedures are employed poor inter-judge reliability can result, particularly if individual instructors' judgments are not challenged. Nevertheless, there are some promising solutions to the reliability problem that I will discuss later.

Designing authentic assessment tasks

Much has been written about the concept of authentic assessment in recent years. Howard Gardner (1996) is one who has promoted the concept following from his thinking about the problems of assessment suggested by his theory of multiple intelligences. Authentic assessment (sometimes called performance-based assessment, appropriate assessment, or alternative assessment) simply means that students are asked to perform tasks to demonstrate learning directly related to the nature of the discipline with which they are engaged. For example, if we want to know if a student can make a realistic drawing of a house it is appropriate to set them a drawing task and then make a judgment about the accuracy and skill of the actual drawing. Asking students to answer questions about drawing, media, vanishing points, or value scales would not be an authentic assessment in this case.

However, if we want to know if a student can make an imaginative drawing of the house the judgment of the artwork becomes more complicated but is, on the other hand, more directly related to the nature of the discipline of art in which we expect creative outcomes.

The virtue of portfolio assessment

While much has been written about the portfolio, it is an instrument that is frequently misused or misunderstood. The portfolio, as an assessment tool, can be conceived in many ways, but in its broadest terms is a body of work collected over time. The real value of portfolios is that it is a time honoured performance measure of student achievement, or, in other words, an authentic assessment.

For assessment purposes the collection of work is regarded as assessment data that will be judged by an assessor or panel of assessors relative to agreed criteria. The first step in achieving reliability of judgment is the development of relevant criteria that reflect content central to the discipline, and these need to be agreed by the community of scholars who constitute the field.

Definition of criteria is not enough however. Assessment of artistic performance represented by work in the portfolio is not a matter of measurement in the same way that knowledge of content can be quantified by multiple-choice tests. Assessment of portfolio data requires value judgments to be made about the learning that has taken place and the quality of the work. The nature of the assessment data is therefore critical, so the work within the portfolio needs to be appropriate to the assessment task.

Defining characteristics of good portfolios

The first obvious feature of a good portfolio, mentioned before, is that the work in the portfolio must have been collected over time … typically a term, semester or year. Three other important features that define good portfolios are (1) that the content is embedded in classroom instruction but remains open ended, (2) the portfolio entries are student selected, and (3) that students document their thoughts (reflections) about their work in verbal and or visual notations. These three features, if overlooked, reduce the potency of the portfolio as an assessment tool.

I will discuss each of these characteristics briefly. The first is that the content of the portfolio is work derived in the ongoing program of instruction but *open-ended* in the sense that students are encouraged to develop classroom experiences into independent explorations of ideas. Stecher and Herman (1997) use the term *embedded* to describe the way in which students are expected to independently develop ideas and apply techniques that have their origins in the classroom (or studio).

The central intention here is that portfolio entries should be derived from regular instructional events and are not to be the result of "on-demand" tasks. The student should be free to interpret the ideas encountered both inside and outside the studio and to develop independence in their exploration of art ideas. This characteristic, if present, enables students to take risks and move beyond classroom exercises.

Taking responsibility for learning, and developing the capacity to work independently, are important indicators of good art learning. A good example of this kind of portfolio can be seen in the IB program (Boughton, 2004). Not only does the portfolio serve as an assessment tool it also plays a vital role in the meaningful elaboration of curriculum intentions. In short, the portfolio becomes integrated with the art curriculum in very important ways, and is not simply a repository for all class assignments set throughout the year.

Burton (1998) found in a large-scale survey that 52% of all visual arts teachers in US public schools assess their students at the completion of each studio project or written assignment. A portfolio that contains only a collection of assigned work and lacks open-ended content is one where the instructor defines both the content and the outcome of each project. Such practice ultimately defines the complete form and content of the portfolio. At the end of the term, semester, or year students in the classes of these teachers will typically present portfolios that look very much the same as each other with products that meet the common project criteria demanded by the teacher. These kinds of portfolios do not reflect the student's capacity to work independently, nor do they reveal the degree to which students are willing to take risks in order to extrapolate from, and interpret the ideas presented in class. By definition, the only thing these portfolios can do is showcase the teacher's capacity to invent tasks for student response, and to direct their outcomes.

Good portfolios in contrast may contain some common features of students work, but for the most part will be comprised of work that will be unique to each individual, will represent the particular artistic interests of each student, may be very different in content and dependant upon the teacher's background, and may even represent a wide array of media as well. Students will certainly have worked outside the classroom and be encouraged to bring their spontaneous work to the studio/classroom to include in their portfolio.

The second feature of good portfolios identified in the literature is that they contain *student-selected entries* (Stecher and Herman 1997; Castiglione, 1996). While the idea of educational portfolios is prominent in the professional art world the educational application of portfolios is different (Castiglione, 1996). The artist portfolio is usually a display of a person's public professional persona and does not usually contain works indicative of process, doubts, or failed explorations. The purpose of education portfolios is to promote students' knowledge of their own progress, and to support their ability to demonstrate independence in researching and evolving projects of their own. Thus, works in progress, sketches, and re-worked pieces are as important as portfolio entries because they provide insight into student growth, and the pattern of decisions students have made in relation to their evolving work.

Without student choice there is no indication of the student's capacity to make informed decisions about their own ideas and progress. Often it is possible to discover as much about a student by what they choose to include as it is from the quality of the work itself. Clearly, the degree to which this is possible is determined to some extent by the age and sophistication of the students involved. Less is expected of younger students, while more fully resolved work can be anticipated from senior students. Nevertheless, some choice is possible at all levels of schooling. The IB assessment criteria provide useful guidelines (International Baccalaureate Organization, 2000), Purposeful Exploration (Studio), and Independence of Research (Research Workbook) reflect the capacity of portfolios to effectively reveal these qualities in ways that other assessment instruments cannot.

A third, and most important, feature of good portfolios is the significance of *student critical self-reflection*, which may appear in journals or portfolios in written or taped form (Wolfe, 1988). Interviews are commonly used methods in conjunction with portfolios to determine the degree to which students understand their own growth and development. The IB and Arts PROPEL (PROduction, PErception, refLection), programs in the United States both use this methodology (Blaikie, 1994). Ross et al. (1993) found, during reflective discussions with students, that teachers tend not to listen carefully to students; appear to drive their own agendas through teacher talk; and that students understand more about their own feeling states and sensibilities than their teachers comprehend. Ross claimed that dialogue, properly conducted, can reveal valuable insights into the process of arts making, particularly students' understanding of the quality of the work, the manner of its production, the reasons for choices, influences on the work, difficulties encountered, new ideas to explore, and so on.

Choosing between analytic and holistic judgment methods

The old adage that the whole is equal to more than the sum of the parts still bedevils judges. One of the perennial dilemmas of judgment strategies in the visual arts is determining the role and value of *holistic judgments* versus *analytic judgments*. Analytic assessment strategies require the specification of discrete criteria which serve to focus attention on those aspects of the work that are thought to be most important. For example, the IB program, prior to 2000, used the following analytic criteria: Imaginative and Creative Thinking and Expression (30%), Persistence in Research (15%), Technical Skill (15%), Understanding the Characteristics and Function of the Chosen Media (15%), Understanding of the Fundamentals of Design (15%), and Evaluation of Own Growth and Development (10%).

The assumption underpinning analytic judgments is that the sum of all the elements defined by these criteria together equals the whole. In some cases application of the analytic method employs criteria that are weighted to reflect their relative significance. For example, the percentages following the IB criteria above indicate that "Imaginative and Creative Thinking and Expression" is twice as important as each of the other criteria except for Evaluation of Own Growth and Development, which is worth only 10%.

The holistic assessment approach, on the other hand, assumes that a single set of criteria cannot be expected to accommodate adequately all genres of visual artwork likely to be presented by students in multiple contexts. It may well be the case that the relative emphasis or type of criteria, employed for appropriate judgement of studio work in different contexts may need to vary somewhat depending on the kind of attention demanded by the work. Indeed, even within a single cultural tradition, the criteria used for judgement may demand different emphases according to its genre. For example, contemporary work using new technologies and recycled imagery may raise different issues for judgement than work undertaken within traditional styles using older media.

Those who advocate for the holistic approach hold the belief that it is important to avoid the imposition of specific biases, such as cultural or modernist, by the use of criteria that are weighted to reflect a particular view of art. A single set of weighted criteria may be appropriate to some cases, but not to others. For this reason the criteria provided for holistic assessment of studio work are intended only to direct the attention of examiners to values which are important to consider initially in relation to students' work.

Typically the holistic assessment method proceeds as follows. The examiner will first view the work in relation to each of the program criteria. Then the examiner will view the work again to form an overall impression of its qualities considering the particular genre of the work, its cultural emphasis, and any other important characteristics not taken into account by the stated criteria. Finally, a holistic judgment is made taking into account all considerations relevant to the work.

Diederik Schönau (1996) reported at a Getty sponsored Visual Arts Evaluation Conference in Bosschenhoofd the work done by CITO to examine the Dutch Central Practical Examination (CPE) in terms of the potential for achievement of common standards against national prescriptive criteria. Schönau's report of research showed that holistic judgments tended to produce higher judge agreement than judgments using criterion analysis. My own interviews with five chief art moderators in Australia indicated a preference for holistic judgment over strict adherence to criterion based referencing. Judges admit forming an overall impression, then checking the criterion judgments against that overall impression to confirm the final score.

While considerable work is being done in other fields little research is available in visual arts education about the relative value of holistic versus analytic assessments on complex tasks. Other disciplines provide some parallels, for example Walker (1983) found that problems of objectivity in assessing language speaking skills could not be improved with the use of detailed mark schemes. She claimed that the division of language into separately assessed components was inappropriate in oral tests, and did not necessarily provide greater reliability than holistic judgments. In fact, her study confirmed earlier findings by others that dividing oral performance into separate parameters to increase a marker's ability to assess objectively found little difference between the reliability of holistic as compared to analytical mark schemes. Also, the strategy admitted by markers using analytical schemes was to make some kind of general assessment, then apply it to each scale. "Alternatively, experienced markers frequently decide on the total score ('That's a 25 out of 30') and then distribute it among the separate scales" (Walker, 1983, p. 44). Walker also found that the degree of agreement between judges' holistic impressions was remarkably high.

When I took office with the IB as Chief Examiner for Art/Design in 1994 I raised the question about the appropriateness of an analytic assessment model for art students who are examined across multiple cultural contexts. It seemed to me that the weighted criteria described above represented a universal definition of art that was anchored in a modernist Eurocentric view of art which was not sufficiently flexible to accommodate the full range of work likely to be produced by students in all parts of the world in which the IBO (International Baccalaureate Organization) program was taught.

Since the reliability of examiners' judgment is an important precondition for validity in large-scale assessments I proposed a research project to investigate the reliability of the analytic model as opposed to a holistic impression of the quality of studio work. The IB assessment system at the time was structured to ensure examiners could not easily check their final score against their holistic impression in order to preserve the integrity of a criterion-based analytic assessment system. Pre-determined weightings for each criterion were scaled to a maximum score of five and then the final weighted judgments were computed out of a total seven making it very difficult for examiners to anticipate the final score. This was a highly specified criterion-based judgment system that pre-determined the relative significance of criteria and disallowed holistic judgment by examiners. The rationale that underpinned this method was that judge agreement would be increased, and this is a very serious concern for any assessment system administrator. The downside was that the method was not as flexible and responsive to emerging new forms of art and design as it should be to achieve the greatest validity of assessment of learning.

The research proposal to examine the reliability of information gained from weighted criterion based judgments vis-à-vis holistic judgments was undertaken in 1998 as a joint project with Dr George Pook, Director of Assessment for the IB Diploma Program. The research employed a balanced distribution model in which 12 student exhibitions were selected from students in varied cultural settings. These exhibitions, reproduced in slide sets, were split into groups of six and sent to 12 reliable examiners also selected from different world regions. Examiner subjects were identified as those IBO external examiners with a history of reliable judgments over at least three years. Six of these examiners assessed the first half of the slide sets by the holistic method and the second half of the slide sets by the analytic method. The other six examiners did the reverse, assessing the first half of the slide sets by the analytic method and the second half by the holistic method. Thus, every collection of students' work was judged by both methods.

The data were analysed using an inter-rater reliability coefficient to determine the degree of agreement using both assessment methods. It was found that there was no significant statistical difference between the reliability of the analytical method as compared to the holistic methods. This study was an IB in-house research project and was not formally published. However the findings were sufficient to enable the examinations office to confidently move to a holistic model for studio assessment which was implemented for first examination in 2002.

The benefits to validity of the holistic model are significant in our postmodern age. While "postmodernism" is still not a cohesive, or well-defined notion, it is sufficiently evident in the discourse of academic groups within the broader cultural context, to indicate the emergence of a new intellectual mood which has shown itself in the past decade or so. Some philosophers, such as Foucault have claimed that we are experiencing a reconfiguration of western thought and action on a scale equivalent to the Renaissance. This revolution has been characterized by the rejection of many ideas and practices that began with the Enlightenment of the eighteenth century (Shumway, 1989).

Some elements of postmodern thought are already impacting art education. One of the most obvious is the value placed upon the "eclectic" and "bricolage" – the habit of using whatever comes to hand (MacGregor, 1992). The "new architecture" which emerged during the 1970s uses architectural elements from the past, combining them in eclectic configurations that often verge on the bizarre. Jencks (1992) popularized the term "postmodern" in his discussion of these kinds of architectural images.

The practice of plundering the past for inspiration is now as evident in fashion and popular music as it is in other facets of our culture. In the art world ideas from the past now sit comfortably with those of the present. Similarly ideas from different cultures can be accommodated together in the context of pluralistic societies. Many of the old cultural distinctions within and between cultures are breaking down. In societies where many different cultural groups are living together the cultural activists express their values through artworks in curious combinations of imagery and materials. Distinctions that once had meaning are no longer clear or significant. What is the difference between the "original" electronic computer image and the "copy"? Is the distinction important? What is "authentic" in Aboriginal art ... ochre on bodies? ... Acrylic on canvas?

Other distinctions between high art and popular art are no longer as significant as they once were. In questioning old dichotomies the postmodern age has produced a world of tension between the old and the new, popular culture and high art, conservation and renewal, and western traditions and other cultural practices, in which one is not supposed to be valued over the other.

Several issues arise for educators who have to judge student art learning works, particularly at the senior school level. What is the relationship between postmodernism and modernism in curriculum structure? The issue of originality is challenged by eclecticism, and technical mastery may be even less significant in relation to the idea carried in both visual and verbal forms.

Should the balance in emphasis of socially critical theoretical analysis and studio practice be reconsidered? Aesthetics within a postmodern paradigm may be less significant than social consciousness as a focus for learning. Should the balance of language and image be reconsidered in the total program? Text and image are frequently combined in postmodern expression. At times the image is incomprehensible without the text.

The traditionalist argument suggests established concepts and processes ought to be learned before new expressions can be properly understood. Postmodernism is the newly emerging form, but is only the newest of many other forms of artistic expression which possess their own unique integrity. This debate is a perennial one.

Given the above questions arising from the influence of postmodernism there is a very strong case in support of the flexibility of holistic judgments as a means to accommodate the dynamic nature of artistic expression in schools. The value of criteria in judgments is not under question, but strict adherence to them can lead to restrictive conceptions of the field.

Moderation models to assist standard setting

Moderation is a judgment process undertaken by teachers within the educational community of peers to ensure that the equivalent work done by students in different classrooms and different schools is rated equally. The grades issued by both external examiners and teachers are not the final grade. Moderation is a system of multiple judgments made by different examiners about the students' work. The intention of moderation is to reduce variations of interpretation among different examiners, and serves to promote a climate of debate and discussion about the quality of student work. This debate is essential in assessment context where students are required to push the limits of their own understanding, to take risks, exercise imagination, and interpret the visual world critically. The best students frequently produce work that will perplex examiners and this is the way it should be if art is properly taught in a postmodern context. A second and sometimes third look at student work is often necessary to determine its qualities and to serve students fairly.

This process in many countries in the world is particularly important to the IB program given the wide geographic distribution of students who participate in the program. Different IB examiners are employed to visit schools in almost half the countries in the world.

Subsequent to the examiner visits to schools photographic and photocopy samples of candidates' work is sent to a central location where a team of experienced and trained moderators, under the direction of a chief examiner, compare the visiting examiners' and teachers' judgments against agreed benchmarks of performance. Benchmarks of the best work are drawn from the international student community and posted year by year on the IB virtual gallery. These works are available for access by teachers, students and examiners. Benchmarks illustrating the range of achievement at specific levels from highest to lowest are sampled from student work and made available to examiners.

The benefit of this process, in addition to ensuring more reliable judgments of the quality of student work, is that examiners and teachers receive feedback about their judgments thus developing a community of agreement about standards. The IB is not the only program to employ moderation procedures. Moderation is used on national scale in the United Kingdom (Steers, 1988), the Netherlands Schönau (1996), Australia (Boughton, 1994), and by the AP program in the United States (Askin, 1985).

Benchmarking

Central to the moderation process is the practice of benchmarking. In simple terms benchmarks are samples of student work selected by moderators to exemplify specific levels of achievement. The work samples clearly indicate the limits of performance within each level. If, for example, five levels of performance are specified by performance descriptors, five collections of studio work are selected to define the limits of each level. Written performance descriptors alone tend to be limited in their ability to represent the qualities of visual art. Therefore the benchmarks take the form of actual examples of student work.

Benchmarking is an idea that has been much practised in the United States businesses (Codling, 1998), and is now finding favour in higher education (Alsete, 1996; Barak and Kniker, 2002; Tucker, 1996). However in the United Kingdom and Europe benchmarking has been practised for many years in art assessments as well as other fields. There are many approaches to the selection of benchmark work (Boughton, 1997). It is possible to select benchmarks each year from the cohort of candidates who are to be assessed. It is also possible to choose work from past years to represent benchmark standards. A combination of both past and present work may also be chosen. Irrespective of these choices, the idea is to choose multiple samples of work that represent the lower bound, the centre and the upper levels specified in the system. The visual arts are dynamic and unpredictable thus the intention is *not* to choose examples that must be matched by student candidates' work. Rather it is to choose samples of work that represent qualities rather than specific models of performance. In other words an excellent painting of a scene depicting poverty in Zimbabwe is not intended to provide an image for students to copy in order to receive high grades. The painting is intended to exemplify an imaginative representation of a political statement, superior understanding of media and, expressive use of form that is supportive of the content of the work. Students who attempt to make copies of benchmarks are penalized in their assessment.

The IB program provides benchmarks of student work to examiners, selected from previous students' work. Teachers and students are provided with examples of high-level work chosen from previous years' examinations on the IB website (IBO.org/gallery).

The IB moderation process is based on an external examiner model. That is a model in which teachers do not provide grades for their students' work and an external, impartial expert visits the school to interview students and award the marks. Following the examiners' work a team of moderators will review samples of the examiners' marks and make adjustments were necessary to bring them in line with the agreed benchmarks.

There are many other models of moderation. These include peer agreement models in which a committee of instructors review each others' students work. Schönau (1996) reported the system used in the Netherlands in which various committees of peers travelled to schools to review students work at the end of each year. It was found that there was little difference in reliability of judgment between groups of five colleagues and groups of two in which experienced and inexperienced teachers were paired to review each other's schools.

Some school district systems employ direct supervisory review models in which instructors grade work and experienced supervisors moderate. In the United Kingdom a cascade moderation model (Steers, 1996) is employed in which moderators are trained centrally and then in turn train regionally-based moderators to work in remote regions. In New South Wales, Australia senior school students ship their work to a central location in Sydney to be moderated by large teams of centrally located moderators.

Conclusion

In this chapter I have argued that one of the most important and most difficult outcomes of art programs to assess is creative thinking. I have suggested that assessment properly conceived and implemented can foster creative outcomes. To achieve valid assessment outcomes authentic assessment tasks should be employed and one of the most appropriate ways to do this is to employ portfolios both as a source of data for assessment, but also as a central support for the instructional process.

Portfolios need to be appropriately employed to achieve the best results. Good portfolios systematically collect work over time, extend students beyond the classroom, engage student interests, and require a reflective component. Summative, system-wide assessment of student studio work is probably more appropriately conducted by experienced evaluators who employ holistic judgments, clear assessment criteria illustrated by performance descriptors and visual benchmarks. Finally the process of moderation is an essential contributing process for establishing agreed standards, reliability of judgment, and the promotion of healthy discourse in the community of stakeholders in education programs.

References

Alsete, J. (1996). *Benchmarking in higher education: Adapting best practices to improve quality.* Washington, DC: The George Washington University.

Amabile, T. M. (1982). Social psychology of creativity: A consensual assessment technique, *Journal of Personality and Social Psychology, 43* (5), 997–1013.

Askin, W. (1985). *Evaluating the Advanced Placement Portfolio in Studio Art.* Princeton, NJ: Advanced Placement and the College Board.

Barak, R., Kniker, C. (2002). Benchmarking by State Higher Education Boards, In *Using benchmarking to inform practice in higher education: New Directions for Higher Education, no 118,* ed B. Bender and J. Schuh. San Francisco: Jossey-Bass. 93–102.

Blaikie, F. (1994). Values inherent in qualitative assessment of secondary studio art in North America: Advanced Placement, Arts PROPEL, and International Baccalaureate, *Studies in Art Education, 35* (4), 237–248.

Boughton, D. (1994). *Evaluation and Assessment of Visual Arts Education.* Geelong: Deakin University Press.

———(1996). Evaluating and Assessing Art Education: Issues and Prospects. In Boughton, Doug; Eisner, Elliot. W.; Ligtvoet, Johan (Eds.). *Evaluation and Assessment of Visual Arts Education: International Perspectives.* New York: Teachers College Press. 293–310.

———(1997). Reconsidering Issues of Assessment and Achievement Standards in Art Education, *Studies in Art Education, 38* (4), 199–213.

——— (2004). Assessing Art Learning in Changing Contexts: High-Stakes Accountability, International Standards and Changing Conceptions of Artistic Development. In Eisner, Elliot; Day, Michael (Eds.). *Handbook of Research and Policy in Arts Education.* New Jersey: Lawrence Erlbaum Associates. 585–604.

——— (2006). *Assessment of Student Learning in the Visual Arts.* Keynote paper presented at the *Daxia Forum,* 19 September. Shanghai, China: East China Normal University Publication.

Boughton, D., Wang, S. (2002). The implement of electronic portfolio in student assessment in art education, *Journal of Aesthetic Education, 129,* 69–75.

——— (2005). Electronic portfolio and visual arts assessment: Conceptual and technical issues in art education. In Wang, S. (Ed.). *Think outside of the box: Visual literacy in the new century.* Taipei: National Taiwan Arts Education Center. 48–57.

Burton, D. (1998). A Survey of Assessment and Evaluation among U.S. K-12 Teachers of Art. Meeting of the NAEA Task Force on Demographic Research. *National Art Education Association Convention,* Chicago, IL, 2 April.

Carmines, E. G., Zeller, R. A. (1991). *Reliability and validity assessment.* Newbury Park: Sage Publications.

Castiglione, L. (1996). Portfolio Assessment in Art and Education. *Education Policy Review, 97* (2), 2–9.

Chapman, L. (2005). No child left behind in art?, *Art Education, 58* (1), 6–16.

Codling, S. (1998). *Benchmarking.* Brookfield, VT: Gower.

Csikszentmihalyi, M., Robinson, R. (1986). Culture, time, and the development of talent. In Stemberg, R. J.; Davidson, J. E. (Eds.). *Conceptions of giftedness*. New York: Cambridge University Press. 264–284.

Csikszentmihalyi, M. (1988). Society, culture, and person: A systems view of creativity. In Stemberg, R. J. (Ed.). *The nature of creativity: Contemporary psychological perspectives*. Cambridge, UK: Cambridge University Press. 325–339.

——— (1990). The domain of creativity. In Runco M. A.; Albert, R. S. (Eds.). *Theories of creativity*. Newbury Park, CA: Sage. 190–212.

——— (1996). *Creativity: Flow and the Psychology of Discovery and Invention*. New York: Harper Collins Publications.

Eisner, E. W. (2004). Response to Arthur Efland's and Richard Siegesmund's reviews of "The Arts and the Creation of Mind". *Journal of Aesthetic Education, 38* (4), 96–98.

——— (2005). *Reimagining schools: The selected works of Elliot W. Eisner*. New York: Routledge.

Freedman, K. (2010). Rethinking Creativity: A definition to support contemporary practice. *Art Education, 63* (2), 8–14.

Gardner, H. (1993). *Creating minds*. New York: Basic Books.

——— (1996). *The assessment of student learning in the arts*. In Boughton, Doug.; Eisner, Elliot. W.; Ligtvoet, Johan (Eds.). *Evaluation and Assessment of Visual Arts Education: International Perspectives*. New York: Teachers College Press. 131–155.

Getzels, J., Jackson, P. (1971). The Highly Intelligent and the Highly Creative Adolescent: A Summary of Some Research Findings. In Muuss, Rolf E. (Ed.). *Adolescent Behavior and Society: A Book of Readings*. New York: Random House Inc.

International Baccalaureate Organization (2000). *Diploma Program Visual Arts Guide: For First Examinations 2002*. Geneva, Switzerland: The International Baccalaureate Organization.

Jencks, C. (1992). *Post-modern Triumphs in London*. N.Y. John Wiley and Sons.

Kasof, J. (1995). Explaining Creativity: The Attributional Perspective. *Creativity Research Journal, 8* (4), 311-366.

MacGregor, R. N. (1990). Reflections on art assessment practices. *Journal of art and design education, 9* (3), 315–327.

——— (1992). Post-Modernism, Art Educators, and Art education. *ERIC Digest ED348238*. Bloomington, IN: ERIC Clearinghouse.

Roberts, P. (2006). *Nurturing Creativity in Young People: A report to Government to inform future policy*. Department of Culture Media and Sport, UK (July), http://www.ltscotland.org.uk/creativity/aboutcreativity/nurturingcreativity. Accessed 13 February 2013.

Ross, M., Radnor, H., Mitchell, S., Bierton, C. (1993). *Assessing Achievement in the Arts*. Buckingham, UK: Open University Press.

Schönau, D (1996). Nationwide assessment of studio work in the visual arts: Actual practice and research in the Netherlands. In Boughton, Doug; Eisner, Elliot. W; Ligtvoet, Johan (Eds.). *Evaluation and Assessment of Visual Arts Education: International Perspectives*. New York: Teachers College Press.156–175.

SEED [Scottish Executive Education Department Promoting Creativity in Education] (2006). *Overview of Key National Policy Developments Across the UK*. An Information paper by SEED, http://www.hmie.gov.uk/documents/publication/hmiepcie.html. Accessed 15 May 2011.

Shumway, D. (1989). *Michel Foucault*, Twayne Masters Series. Boston: Twayne.

Simonton, D. K. (1979). Multiple discovery and invention: Zeitgeist, genius, or chance?, *Journal of Personality and Social Psychology, 37* (9), 1603–1616.

Stecher, B., Herman, J. (1997). Using portfolios for large scale assessment. In Phye, Gary, D. (Ed.). *Handbook of Classroom Assessment*. London: Academic Press Limited. 491–516.

Steers, J. (1988). Art and design in the national curriculum. *Journal of Art and Design Education, 7* (3), 303–323.

——— (1996). Response to papers by Gardner and Schönau. In Boughton, Doug; Eisner, Elliot. W.; Ligtvoet, Johan (Eds.). *Evaluation and Assessment of Visual Arts Education: International Perspectives*. New York: Teachers College Press. 176–193.

——— (2009). Creativity: Delusions, Realities, Opportunities and Challenges, *International Journal of Art & Design Education, 28* (2), 126–138.

Tucker, S. (1996). *Benchmarking: A Guide for Educators*. Thousand Oaks, California: Corwin Press Inc.

Walker, C. R. (1983). The whole is more than the sum of the parts: Evaluation criteria in oral tests, *British Journal of Language Teaching, 21* (1), 41–44.

Weisberg, R. W. (1986). *Creativity: Genius and other myths*. New York: Freeman.

Wolfe, D. (1988). Opening up assessment. *Educational Leadership, 45* (1), 24–29.

Chapter 7

Developmental self-assessment in art education

Diederik Schönau, Cito Institute for Educational Measurement, Arnhem, the Netherlands

Abstract

For education to be effective, assessment is essential. Without assessment, no conclusions can be drawn on the effectiveness and quality of an educational activity or program. Traditionally, assessment is driven by predefined educational goals, standards to be met, and a teacher who is in charge of the learning and assessment process.

In this chapter another approach is suggested: art education based on developmental self-assessment. In this type of assessment, the student plays the central role. He[1] is the person in charge of what he wants to show through his work of art. This not only relates to the content, but also to the means used to convey this content through the work. Content and artistic means are the main tools to give form to the meaning of a work of art. The way this is done defines the expressive quality and effectiveness of the meaning the student has in mind.

This approach is demonstrated by an example from Dutch final examinations. Although not designed as a form of developmental self-assessment, the approach taken there exemplifies what is possible when developmental self-assessment is used as a means to organize art educational activities

Need for assessment

The issue of assessment in arts education is not an easy one. When it comes to the assessment of studio work, the traditional assessment instruments like paper-and-pencil tests are not applicable. More importantly, the products of studio work are highly individual, both in character and in level of accomplishment. Where in many disciplines students who take a test are expected to come up with highly comparable or – in many cases preferably – identical results, in the arts assignments generate highly diverse work. The resulting products are unique, personal and often also unpredictable – and this is in many cases what is hoped for.

Although art products do not fit the format of traditional assessment instruments, this is no reason to conclude that work made by students should not be assessed. When art is included in compulsory education, a certain amount of specification of educational goals is inevitable. Both students and parents – and society at large – have the right to know what is taught, and why, and whether a school has been able to meet these goals. The concept of curriculum itself, as an array of activities that give direction to and develop the cognitive abilities of a person (Eisner, 2002, p. 148), can only come alive when it is possible to decide as to how far a school has been able to reach the goals of the curriculum. So almost by definition the introduction of educational goals implies the need to use assessment to know whether these goals have been met in the expected way.

The arts address a broad array of cognitive abilities, varying from perceptual skills, to motoric, intellectual, social, emotional, and artistic skills. Like in all other subjects, student assessment in art should be taken seriously as it helps to get insight into a student's learning, thinking, and understanding (Boughton, 2004a, p. 589), but also in the growth of their skills (Davis, 2008, p. 34). By giving no feedback at all, students would be left with no clue as to how effective their work has been, nor how they could improve their skills. Students like to be informed about the effect of their artistic activities. These activities are a means of communication, and when this attempt to communicate is not understood or answered, it will loose its value. When no one reflects on their work, students have little reason to continue and improve, and will lose interest in making art in the end. In fact, most teachers and adults do respond to the artworks made by students, but it is uncertain whether this feedback is relevant and helpful for the student or not. Doing so, they might use criteria about which the student is not informed, or which may be only relevant in the eyes of the person who is giving comments, but which are irrelevant to the student. The teacher's comments might unintentionally result in a loss of interest on the part of the student in what he is trying to communicate.

Studio work in the arts made as part of general education therefore deserves careful assessment for two reasons. As part of the curriculum, teachers need to know whether their educational goals have been met. For the students, their art is a way of communication, and therefore their efforts are relevant for them. They need to know whether their work is worthwhile and effective.

Assessment goals and standards

Generally, educational assessment is oriented towards intended outcomes. These outcomes are formulated in educational goals and specified into assessment goals. To make these goals more instrumental, they are sometimes translated into educational standards. These standards define a minimum level of competencies to be met by students in a specific area of education. Standards can relate to a minimum body of knowledge (e.g. knowledge on the history of one's country), predefined skill levels (e.g. mathematical skills), or examples of behaviour that should be shown in a specified professional situation (e.g. the activities of a doctor while examining a patient). As such, standards reflect what is considered relevant by society.

There are four types of standards: learning standards, professional standards, social standards, and personal standards. First, students need to acquire knowledge and skills that support their learning now and in the future. When leaving school, students must be able to continue their studies at a higher level. Next, students are prepared for a job, in which job-related competencies are central. Education also helps students to be ready to take part in society as citizens, who are knowledgeable on political, legal, and social issues. Finally, education supports students to develop their individuality, personal interests, and talents.

Many subjects and activities in education relate to the acquisition of basic skills that are considered necessary for learning other subjects and skills and in becoming an active and successful learner. The three "R"s are the best known and most universal, as they are instrumental for learning in other subjects. Also strategies to acquire knowledge, to process information, to do research and to reflect on the results are general skills that are independent of subjects. They are central to becoming a successful learner, not only in school but in life as well.

When it comes to the content learned, many subjects – especially at higher levels of education – concentrate on competencies that are needed in professional life. These competencies can be seen as professional goals, which are codified in a diploma. The occupational group decides on who can enter its domain as a professional and take the responsibilities that go with the profession. All vocational education and most university studies as well, are preparing for professions. To become a construction worker, a teacher, a medical doctor, or a researcher, one has to adhere to strict rules laid down in the curriculum. These rules reflect the fundamental areas of knowledge, skills, and attitudes that go with the profession. Standards are necessary to make sure a professional has the minimum level of competency needed to do his job properly. Also artists, being trained at art academies, are educated to become professionals, and their diploma is seen as a ticket to enter the field of professionals in the arts. It is even because of this diploma that an artist can say that what he makes, is a work of art, because it is a made by an artist-by-profession, – although the public might sometimes fail to appreciate the work as such.

The third group of standards are those related to social goals. Education and schools are culturally-based institutions that make sure that all persons living in a country will be able to participate in society as citizens. They are guided in their social development, learning how to interact socially and adhere to the norms and values that are essential to make a society work. As a consequence, certain areas in education are compulsory to all students, as it is considered to be impossible to take part in society without a basic level of competency in these areas. Educational areas, like knowledge of the history of one's own country, its political system, its cultural identity and traditions come to mind. As to the art subjects, social standards can include issues in society or aspects of culture and art that are considered relevant for students to explore and learn about. The history of the arts – the canonical ones and the alternative ones – can be seen as such: they can be described in terms of desired knowledge and thus transformed into standards. Learning to appreciate art as it is presented in its social context in a museum, a gallery, in a theatre, or in a community project, can be part of basic education. Most people do not by themselves learn to value all art forms and the great diversity in it. Engaging in artistic activities as a social phenomenon must in many cases be learned as well. Going to a classical concert and remaining seated in silence for some hours is not a behaviour most people will show spontaneously. Finally, social interaction – including ways to cooperate with others – can be part of education, as this interaction is also guided by social standards through norms and values. The norms are laid down in laws and rules, while the values are the more fluent medium that makes social interaction possible and sustainable. These rules are not always evident per se, and they need an ongoing effort from the part of educators to have them internalized in the social make-up of the students.

This fluency of values is strongly related to the fourth area: personal standards. A person can decide on the importance of exploring his own feelings, opinions, and attitudes towards reality. He can also decide to develop his own talents and work on issues that pertain to his personality and interests. It is for this reason that in most countries students can choose subjects in which they wish to take exams. Actually, the existence of so many types of educational courses also reflects to a certain level the importance given to the development of specific talents and the interest to give students the freedom to make their own choices. When this fourth area is appreciated in the education system, the system should give the students the space and freedom to explore their personal ambitions and standards. The arts are the area in education where this can be done in a fundamental and "natural" way.

When related to the issue of assessment and testing, each type of standards has its own merits. They do not exclude one another, but they all reflect aspects of learning and education that are worth being developed. Depending on the type of standard or the task given, the use of an assessment tool must do justice to the intended learning outcome. So in the arts a variety of assessment tools can be used. For instance, professional skills, like technical and historical skills, can be learned and tested in a clear and transparent way. Technical skills can be trained, by repetition and by working towards specified levels of competency. The levels of accomplishment can be assessed by using rubrics that show what is expected or possible. Historical knowledge and skills and theoretical insights can be assessed by paper-and-pencil tests. When it comes to personal standards, these can be chosen as goals in themselves, for instance to develop one's own artistic talent, irrespective of social and professional standards. In many cases personal goals will be connected with social issues or professional expectations. Thus a student can investigate social and professional standards by making them part of explorations of his own personal standards. Professional and social goals are impersonal by definition, and because of this, students must make them personally understandable, acceptable, relevant, and interesting. It will also help them explore what it means to take part in professional activities and to define to what culture and subcultures they feel attracted to and why.

Students need time in the educational setting to come to terms with learning goals and standards presented to them. More often than not, these standards are unrelated to the students' own views of learning and understanding. But when, for instance, they learn to see that investigation, cooperation, engagement, reflection, and perseverance are general learning goals that are part of art education, they can understand that art is more than entertainment, and that it can be challenging in its own right.[2]

Art education can present a forum where all types of learning goals and standards can be addressed, next to offering students a place to explore their own individuality, talent, and concerns. These latter issues are often seen as the core of art education. True: the arts are a very effective means to investigate personal issues and help to develop the student's individual talents and personality. But the arts, as a social phenomenon, do not limit themselves to being a platform for the exploration of personal strengths and weaknesses only. They also help to understand the world as it is codified and formed by others.

Growth

Education is organized in such a way that students gradually become more competent by acquiring and developing knowledge, insights, skills, and attitudes. There is no limit to this development, and practice shows that many people look for challenges to learn till the last day of their life. This innate drive is a strong power to learn new things and improve or refine what has been acquired.

The learning process can be seen as accumulative by nature. But in this accumulation process the content of what is accumulated, is also continually reorganized. The same goes for insights, skills, and attitudes. When new understanding takes place, sometimes accompanied by a new insight that opens new ways to look at reality, this process is almost irreversible. It becomes very difficult and even irrelevant to go back to the situation before this understanding originated. So also, one's skills and attitudes change over time, not only by being replaced by other skills and attitudes, but also by an irreversible reorganization.

This development can be defined in terms of growth. While in nature growth takes place almost spontaneously, in the human mind, part of the learning can be understood as an intentional form of self-guided growth in learning and understanding. But, like in nature, this learning is guided by internal dynamics in the (growing) human mind and the drive of human beings to understand what they are doing. With regard to art education, under the influence of Piagetian developmental psychology, researchers have sought for "natural" phases in learning in general and in art education in particular (Lowenfeld and Brittain, 1947; Arnheim, 1974, pp. 162–217; Gardner, 1980; to name a few). It turns out, that this approach is too limited, and that it might be more helpful to start from the idea that there is a diversity of skills that can be trained independently from one another. There is not always a compulsory order in which things will or even should be learned. The acquisition of the same skill can start for each individual at different moments (Kindler, 1997). When translated to the acquisition of artistic skills, children develop individual repertoires of artistic skills not only because of the developmental phase they are in, but also because of their current interests and the skill level needed.

Not all learning is guided by preset goals, however. In practice, many events occur in one's life that were not sought for, but that can offer learning opportunities and challenges. In hindsight, the experience and the way one has handled the situation can be evaluated.

This evaluation, which is not based on preset goals, but on the outcomes as they appear, can be compared to "responsive evaluation". This form of evaluation, introduced by Robert Stake in 1973 (Stake, 1975a), was originally used for the evaluation of educational programs. Responsive evaluation has three central characteristics: it is more directed towards program activities than to program objectives and it responds to audience requirements for information and different value-perspectives that are referred to in reporting the success and failure of the program (Stake, 1975b, p. 14). By transferring this approach from program evaluation to individual student assessment, student evaluation can be made more meaningful for the student, especially in the arts, where much learning takes place without clearly defined learning objectives. Not without reason Elliot Eisner connects this concept of responsive assessment to the evaluation of so-called expressive outcomes: outcomes that students realize in the course of a curriculum activity, but which were not intentionally sought for (Eisner, 2002, p. 161). These outcomes can be seen as a side effect of what a student was supposed to achieve, but one can also look at this type of outcome as something that is fundamental in artistic assignments. In many art forms, the artist is not just making what is already present and finished in the mind. On the contrary, by working in the medium, the work itself is guided by the creative process and the final result is partly undefined until the moment the artist decides the work is finished. So growth is not a clear-cut series of activities that develop in a predictable way and at the same time in all children.

Assessment

The common characteristic of traditional student assessment is, that the teacher decides on the assignment and the result, while the student is supposed to concentrate on completing the assignment as "good" as possible. Students are in most cases informed about the characteristic of the task and about the intended outcome and the criteria used to assess the result – or at least this should be the case. They are also informed about the results and, when needed, how to improve on a subsequent assignment or test. The teacher is in charge, while the student has to follow.

Like their colleagues in other school subjects, art teachers are prone to define the assignments students have to work on in their lessons. These assignments relate to educational goals as laid down in the curriculum or the book used. When there are specific techniques and effects to be learned, this prescriptive approach to what students must do in an art class, can be very helpful and relevant. But in many cases the students can contribute little to make an assignment more meaningful from their personal point of view. The solution for this problem could be to ask students to develop their own assignments. But for the students to be successful, they have to be trained in deciding what to do in order to make their work effective and efficient.

The decision on what will be effective or efficient when making a work of art is a complicated one. It depends on the unique combination of the problem as seen by the student, the learning in which the student is currently involved, and the expectations and criteria of the people who will look at the result. In teacher-guided assignments, the problem is usually defined in relationship to learning goals common to all students. They address the students as if they were on an equal level of accomplishment. In student-guided learning, these aspects become diffuse and can even get lost.

One solution might be to have the students develop a clear insight into what they have to have learned in the end. But then teachers should inform students from the very beginning about the final goal of the educational programme and about the level to be attained at the end of formal instructions. This is not common practice in art education, nor in education in general. It is easier to make these final goals operational in assignments that address what students should know or be able to do at that moment. This is characteristic for teaching and testing. The final goal is thus reached in predefined steps.

Developmental self-assessment

Here another approach is suggested, based on the concepts of personal standards and growth: developmental self-assessment.[3] In this type of assessment, the student is given more freedom and responsibility with regard to the interpretation of the assignment itself and to the criteria on which he wishes the final result to be judged. Both this freedom and responsibility are relative. The freedom is limited by the general goals set by the teacher. The student has the freedom to choose within those limits what to make and how to make it. Technically speaking, in the arts this situation is quite normal, as most assignments give the student a lot of freedom to generate his own ideas on content and on the artistic techniques and elements to be used. Not without reason, many classroom assignments result in a great variety of artworks.

But to make an assignment developmental in character, a student must define a *meaning* of the work to be made (Schönau, 2011). This meaning is first of all dependent on content: the student's personal knowledge, opinion, interpretation, or feeling with regard to the content of the assignment. Thus the work to be made becomes a research by the student about what the work should reflect from the point of view of content. One could also say that the work to be made has to reflect the meaning given by the student to the content as suggested in the assignment. In this way, the personal standards of the student are taken as a starting point. From these personal standards, the student can relate his opinions, interpretations, or feelings with regard to the issues at stake.

The second step is to decide on the visual qualities of the work to be made. These qualities should visualize and reflect the intended content. The visual quality is defined by the choice of representational elements, the materials and technique, the elements and principles, and by the skill of the student to apply these tools. A work of art is made to communicate, and a good work should be a "visual seduction" to the observer (Boughton, 2004b, p. 266). It invites an observer to have a good look and to get an understanding of what the artwork wants to communicate. It is the seductive and artistic quality that makes a work effective as a work of art and not a mere illustration of an idea.

In the third step a student is challenged to improve his skills in visualizing meaning by rendering content through a visual work of art. This challenge can be defined by the student. It can be based on the evaluation of the work the student has finished shortly before. This evaluation can be done by the teacher, but also by the student or his classmates. The teacher can, of course, challenge the student and coach him in making the work more convincing. The student may also decide to make learning standards into a starting point for research into his personal standards. Or he can define his own goals within the general limits set by the teacher (for instance a prescribed theme, or the use of a specific material or technique). His goals may also be unrelated to what other students in the classroom are doing. What counts, is that the student must clarify the meaning or character of the work to be made and the ways this meaning is expressed by the artistic tools used by the student. This prevents students from merely producing illustrations to an idea, but engages them in transforming meaning into a work of art. The artwork is then the artistic equivalent of the idea expressed.

Finally, a student is asked to write down the criteria on which he wants his work to be assessed. This assessment will be done by the student himself in the first place. Then classmates and the teacher can give their comments. This is a criterion-referenced way of assessing, as the student himself defines the criteria. Of course these criteria will also be related to what his classmates are doing, but the assessment is not norm-referenced, as is the case when the group results define the relative position and level of each student within the group.

This may seem very abstract, but in practice things are not that complicated. Even very young children can be asked what they want to show in their artwork and how they are going to make that visible. When completed, they can also judge the effectiveness of the visual result.

This approach is closely connected to the social constructivist learning theories, more specifically to the concept of the "zone of proximal development" as conceptualized by Lev Vygotsky. According to this learning theory, students learn most, by striving for the "next" level of skill or accomplishment, using the skills as mastered in the preceding phase. "*It is the distance between the actual developmental level as determined by independent problem solving and the level of potential development as determined through problem solving under adult guidance or in collaboration with more capable peers*" (Vygotsky, 1978, p. 86, original emphasis). The roles of the teacher and peers are essential. Thanks to them the student is challenged and guided to master the next level in relationship to what he is capable of at that stage of his cognitive (intellectual and artistic) development. So the tasks set by the teachers or the students should be challenging, but realistic and not too complicated. To make this approach an educational activity, a student's learning must take place under the guidance of a teacher. Outside school this dynamic is used by children spontaneously as they challenge themselves to "try to do better". It is a dynamic best known in sports. In the arts, the idea of "better" is closely related to the specific skills and techniques that are subservient to the actual goal of art: to communicate meaning through artistic tools. "Better" communication is not dependent on the originality of the idea or the concept, but on the way this idea is presented with representational and symbolic elements into a work of art, through the effective use of elements and principles, skills, and techniques. The work made should show what the student is after and express the intended meanings through the artistic way the representational aspects, the elements and principles, and the material and techniques have been used. The work made should express the intentions, not illustrate them, to make it artistically interesting and convincing.

To make this process work, students must take time to think about what they are going to do. Before starting to work, the student could be asked to write down or tell what he intends to make and how he thinks he will use the artistic means to visualize the ideas in mind. By writing down or formulating his intentions the student is stimulated to think about the meaning of the artwork and about the best way to arrive at a convincing result. The next step is to write down the choices with regard to the representational elements and symbols, material and techniques, and the elements and principles to be used. As any idea can be given form in a limitless amount of ways, choices are inevitable. These choices indicate the contents to be shown, and the effects and expressive meaning sought for by the student. They also limit the amount of criteria on which the work can be judged. The student can do this by choosing from a long list of criteria, or by formulating the criteria himself. Through this limitation, the student – and the teacher alike – can concentrate on the relationship between the intended meaning of the work and the way this is given form in this specific way.

Starting from his intention, a student can then specify the criteria he wishes his work to be judged on, both by himself and by others, including his teacher. One could compare the way these criteria are used with an analysis that is normally made after the work has been completed. In the latter situation, students describe what they have done in relationship to what they intended. They can also comment on the quality of the technical and artistic aspects of the work. But doing so in hindsight, this process risks being guided by ill-defined or opportunistic criteria, formulated on the spot. These criteria may be closely related to the general expectations of the teacher about what the student should be able to do in that phase of his educational career. What normally is being described by the teacher in advance are general aspects that are considered characteristic and desirable for a work of art made by students at that age level. Using a developmental approach, the student himself can change these general aspects into personal goals by selecting what he thinks relevant. He can attach beforehand weights to each goal and describe how these goals relate to one another in relationship to the intended result. During the work, changes and adaptations will take place. These adaptations can result from new ideas with regard to content and representation, but also from problems or inventions in handling the artistic means. The final work is the result of a series of decisions at the start, and of intentional changes made by the student while creating the work of art.

By formulating in advance what he is after, the student becomes more responsible for what he creates and how he creates it. The teacher can coach the student to help him develop ideas and make these ideas visible. Besides plain instruction and exercises, teachers not only develop the technical knowledge and skills related to the materials used, but also the skills of the student to judge the (intended) effects of their own work.

The teacher's responsibility is defined and limited by the context of the educational situation. Art education, as a school subject, has a curriculum that exemplifies what students should learn during the years. This curriculum is defined by national guidelines, adapted by the goals set at school level, and given form by the ideas of the art teacher. At the same time, the way the curriculum is translated into assignments is dependent on the age of the student. Each assignment can be seen as a step towards the completion of the curriculum and will relate to what the student has done before the current assignment. The result itself will, ideally speaking, influence the characteristics of the next assignment. It is the teacher in the first place, who, as an expert on artistic development, should advise the student about the next step. But it is up to the student to interpret this next step in terms that are relevant for him and that reflect his personal choices in the improvement of his artistic skills. During the course, a teacher can help the student to improve his technical skills. Here assessment will be teacher-guided, for instance, by using rubrics that show how well a student is doing compared to what is technically possible. Students can adjust their technical skill level to the level they need or would like to reach (Wiggins, 1998, p. 153 ff.).

To make this process work from an educational point of view, students must be aware of what characteristics of the work to be made are regarded as essential, relevant, and worthwhile. Otherwise they might get lost, without knowing what to look for and what to improve. The art teacher, as an expert in artistic visualization processes, can teach students about the aspects of artworks and their contribution to effective communication. So setting personal goals in an educational context requires a well-informed teacher who is able to guide the student in his developmental process.

Authentic and evaluative assessment

The model as presented here in many ways reflects other types of performance assessment like educative and authentic assessment (Wiggins, 1998; Zimmerman, 1997). In those types also more importance is given to assignments that are meaningful and realistic.

In educative assessment, the assignment is seen as a teaching tool, not a measurement tool in the first place (Wiggins, 1998, p. 12). But in the end it is the teacher who is in charge of what is taught, learned, assessed, and reported (Wiggins, 1998, p. 242). It is also more normative in character as benchmarks are given that reflect normative levels students have to reach. In developmental self-assessment these normative levels are in most cases absent as there is no external norm a student should meet. The student predefines his own goals and norms. This does not mean the teacher has no role to play, on the contrary. The teacher is the professional who knows how to stimulate the student, give guidance to his search, and to enter a discourse in which the student is triggered by questions, not by solutions or instructions. Of course a teacher can challenge students by limiting the potential choices in content, material, or elements and principles, but this limitation should stimulate productivity and prevent loss of time. Although it might be enriching for students to get acquainted with a great variety of techniques, styles, and approaches, it limits time for students to improve their skills in a technique, style, or approach they feel comfortable with.

Only at final examination level, absolute norms will play a role, but maybe only in the form of minimal fluency in ideas and of predefined grades of technical skills. To assess the latter, "rubrics" can be used, but for the arts this type of assessment tool has limited possibilities. The "final examination level" can function as a general goal for students to reach a certain amount of proficiency. The way to arrive at that goal, however, can be very different for each student.

In authentic assessment the tasks given should engage students in real world problems and situations (Zimmermann, 1997, p. 150; Burke, 2005, p. xxi). The work made by professionals or artists is often taken as a point of reference. The tasks must be meaningful and challenging for students, but in the end, it is the teacher who sets the norms and decides what students should demonstrate. Although the students play a role in the assessment, it is the teacher who defines or shows examples of what the student is supposed to show (Burke, 2005, p. 87).

Developmental self-assessment has one other element that is essential to make it work. The criteria as formulated and used should reflect ambitions to improve on the quality of the work made. This "quality" can relate to many aspects: the general effect a work will have on an observer (matching between intended meaning and the meaning as observed by an outsider), the recognizability of the objects and symbols represented in the artwork, and the effectiveness of the techniques, and the elements and principles used. Many students will spontaneously try to improve on the work they are doing. The next work is always different from the last one. What might happen is, that the quality is not improving and that the student will repeat the tricks learned so far. In an educational setting, a student should be stimulated to be critical about his work and to think about expanding his repertoire, both in content and in means. By asking the student to make explicit what he intends to do before actually starting the work, a teacher can play the role of the coach, while the student becomes more and more responsible for his own learning process.

How to make developmental self-assessment work

When the student is made more responsible for his own assignments, he should be able to think about his goals and how to get there. This process includes three steps: formulating the intention and goals, choosing the ways and means to get there, and deciding whether the goals have been met. These three steps are critical.

The first step is to define the goals of the work to be made. In art education, goals and means are not always easy to separate, as the way the means are used is often considered a (sub)goal of the assignment. Where in other subjects the result can be assessed in terms of correctness, the way this result was reached can be of secondary importance. This, however, is not always the case. In science and mathematics, for instance, not only the result is assessed, but also the way the student has arrived at the result. In this way the student is assessed, in most cases, on the correct application of the rules of logic. The correct use of these rules is part of the assignment. They give the student some flexibility, as the same solution can be reached through different approaches. But this freedom is restricted and can be judged in terms of correct or false, elegant or sloppy.

In art, the relationship between process and product is more complex and insecure. Therefore, to specify, from the start, criteria for both the process and the product might limit the flexibility needed by the student to arrive at the intended goal. Before arriving at the final solutions, a student can decide to make a series of sketches, make investigations on the physical and expressive characteristics of the material used, or train himself in creating results that meet his expectation. By being in charge of the process, a student can research what he is doing.

Practically, a student must learn to think about what he is going to do before starting. This can done by asking the student to write down (or tell) what he wants to make and what characteristics the final work should express. The next step is to choose the materials, technique, representational and visual elements, and to think how these can be combined in such a way, that the final work best reflects his intentions. Writing down what one wishes to accomplish and how this can be done in the best way possible, is one thing. To make an artwork "work" in the intended way, is something else. While working, a student – and this goes for artists as well – changes ideas, adjusts the means used, or makes new choices. In the end, the result can be quite different from where the student started. He can have excellent reasons to do so. Therefore, a student should be allowed to revise his choices made at the start, and even revise his intentions. But he should be invited to lay down the arguments that led to the changes and the adaptations in his working process. Being in charge of his own artistic process gives a student the right to revise and adjust this process when necessary. It is up to the student to reflect on these changes and make clear how these changes have affected the result. In this way, it is possible to understand how the process has guided the student and why the final result looks the way it does.

An example from the Netherlands

Since 1972, it is possible in the Netherlands to take an art as a final examination subject. In almost forty years this possibility has evolved into a system in which students of most school types in secondary education are offered the opportunity to take an art discipline as a final examination subject. As part of this evolution, a special examination format has been developed: the Central Practical Exam (CPE) (Schönau, 1996; Ministry of Education, 2007).

This type of exam is limited to the visual arts subjects. It has been introduced at the pre-university level of secondary education (age level 17–18 years) and in the highest level of lower vocational education only (age level 15–16 years).

Both exams make use of an approach that can be compared to what has been introduced here as developmental self-assessment. However, due to its character as final examination, the freedom of the students is much more limited. By definition, the exam is not meant to be a developmental test.

In both levels (pre-university and lower vocational) students are given assignments from which they can choose. The next step is, that students have to write down what they intend to make. The way a student is addressed in the assignment very much reflects what has been suggested above (also see Appendix). Within these set limits, students have freedom to make their own choices, with regard to content and meaning expressed, as well as to the means used to give form to this content. By writing down what they think essential in their work, students indicate the relationship between content and form on which their work should be assessed.

The CPE at pre-university level (VWO) was introduced in 1979, being the first central practical exam in secondary education. The acceptability and objectivity of this exam has been discussed vehemently on several occasions, but in the end it still is part of the final examination system.

When they start to work on an exam, students at pre-university level have to answer the following questions:

1. *What assignment have you chosen?* (They can normally pick one out of a choice of six offered.)
2. *How do you take the content into account, or how do you want to interpret the assignment? Describe the starting point with regard to the content and/or the goal you intend to reach.* If needed, they can also describe the visual effect or the function of the work. *You also have to give an interpretation of this content or goal.*
3. *In order to reach this goal, the following aspects seem to be relevant:*
   (a) Representation:
   (b) Elements and principles of design
   (c) Materials and techniques

At the final session of the exam[4] the student is asked to give a short summary of the way he has worked on the assignment. Any changes can be clarified.

At lower vocational education level (VMBO) students are guided by a more structured format to prevent them from loosing time or getting lost in the task. The original format of this exam was developed to assess individual student results in basic education in the early 1990s for students aged 14, and has been officially introduced in lower vocational examinations in 2004. Since 2004 a variety of practical exams has been developed for central exams in most vocational subjects.

The form used in CPE at VMBO-level follows the structure of a predefined working process, which is composed of six parts: orientation, artistic research,[5] decision on what to do, production of the work, a comparison of the final work made with a work made by another candidate in the same class, and a presentation.[6] The assignments are all organized around a central theme (e.g. "Collected", "Water", "Like a beast") that are introduced to the students two weeks before the actual start of the exam period in March. This introduction is done through a small booklet with a description of the theme, many small photos of artworks, and some exemplary artists, with additional information on how these artists work. Also a series of some 100 keywords are given that all relate – or can be related – to the theme. After two weeks the students receive the actual assignment and a form of 16 pages. This form has a series of questions students must answer during the exam period. In doing so, they document their own thinking during the six phases of their working process.

In the orientation phase, students are asked to write down their very first ideas when reading the assignment. In the 2012 exam (Theme: "Green space", see Appendix) the general assignment is, to design and make a work of art about a green space that has a special meaning or function for the student. This work should be made in the medium related to the subject, in which the student has specialized (two-dimensional art, three-dimensional art, textile art, or audiovisual art). First the student must write down what he would like to visualize in his work (what type of space, what activity, what atmosphere) as starting points for the work to be made.

In the next phase – artistic research – the student is given more specific instruction to make small sketches. In these sketches he must pay attention to representation, elements and principles, and material(s) and technique(s) to be used in the final work. He can also make sketches by using computers or three-dimensional materials.

Then student is then asked to decide what 'green space' he is going to visualize. He also makes choices about the use of visual aspects like form, colour, texture, and the like. He indicates what materials and techniques he is going to use and why. He is also invited to think of a title for his work.

In the fourth phase, in which the student is actually making his final piece, he can adjust his choices, depending on how his work develops. If so, he must write down these changes in the official form. He can also give the definitive title to their work.

After having completed their final piece, the student must analyse his own collection of work and compare it with that of a fellow student. He must choose a work that is very different from his own, and explain his arguments for this choice. He has to compare the two works on the differences in content, representation, and elements and principles. He must also give his opinion on the meaning of the work made by another student in relationship with the meaning of his own work.

Finally, the student has to present their work in a favourable way, showing what he has done, but also indicating how he have reached his goals and whether the result meets his own expectations.

Conclusion

When the development of a student's learning process is central in art teaching and assessment, the assessment process should also be given a central position as well. Instead of starting the learning process from the assignment, the product, or the process, it starts from the student's intentions and goals, and encompasses the process, the product, and the match or mismatch between selected goals and intended results. The student will be the first to give an opinion about the quality of the work done, using the goals and criteria set at the start. From here the assessment will become a joint enterprise of the student, the teacher, and, when possible and relevant, other students or experts.

Goal-setting at the beginning and reflection at the end, both related to start level and end level, should be part of this process. The self-assessment is based on criteria formulated by the student, with the help of the teacher. These criteria must be specific enough to prove that improvement has taken place. This can be done by using rubrics that describe the qualitative aspects of the process and/or product. Rubrics are put in an increasing order, from start level, through an intermediary level, to the end level. An extra level can be added to register accomplishments that go beyond the level aimed for.

Judgment can also be done through a version of a Likert scale. Here the level to be reached (or criterion) is put in the middle as the "expected level", and the assessment is done by indicating as to how far the result agrees to the criterion. In this last case the judging takes place in terms of the deviation of a result from the expected outcome. This can either be "(much) better than expected" or "(much) worse than expected". As stated before, the "expected level" can be represented by an example showing the relevant qualities or by a well-formulated description.

When assessing the work made, a student should be able to point to the aspects at stake, either in words or by pointing to characteristics of the artistic characteristics involved. The assessment needs to follow a strict procedure to make sure that the result is compared to all goals set from the very beginning, taking into consideration the use of artistic means to arrive at that goal. Both the teacher and the student judge the work in this way.

The final judgment is formulated in terms of aspects (visual, technical, artistic) or characteristics of the work that were successful when compared to the goals set at the start, and in aspects that can be improved in a forthcoming assignment. Both student and teacher must strive for agreement on the final conclusions. The next assignment is then defined on the basis of these conclusions.

It will be clear, that through this way of instruction students are encouraged to be more articulate on what they are after and to become more critical about the results of their work. They are challenged to combine exploration of content with artistic expression. The format used here is the one used at final examination level in the Netherlands. When seen in a larger context, it is easy to understand that this method can be very helpful to organize assignments given to students. In earlier phases of the education process, a student can be given more freedom to make his own choices on content and meaning. It will make their work more authentic, as it is more related to their own concerns, the individual circumstances, and cultural context of the student, and their level of understanding.

To make this approach really developmental, students should learn to formulate their own standards for each assignment they are working on. These standards do not relate to the content of the meaning of the work per se, as these cannot be "good" or "better". What counts is the relationship between what is intended and what is finally made. Does the work effectively express what a student had in mind? Or, to put it differently, are all visual aspects of the work made adding up to the intended effect? To give form to ideas and feelings students – like artists – must rely on their skills to give form to what they want to express, convey, or communicate. Each work is a step in a long learning process, in which these skills – artistic, technical, intellectual, and social – are improved. The teacher can help the student to overcome blockades and to solve technic al, artistic, and visual problems. He can also stimulate students to make bigger steps, or to try again. It will be clear, that this way of working and teaching will generate a great diversity in works in the same class. This diversity reflects what is characteristic of the arts: the individual meaning-making of life.

The paradigm of developmental self-assessment, as presented here, can be a starting point when we wish to assess constructivist learning process in other subjects, or in learning in general. Developmental self-assessment is part of an active learning process in which both students and teachers take responsibility. It is oriented towards a recurring feedback between reflection on results at the end of an assignment and the ambitions and goals set at the start of the next one. Each new assignment is something like a new contract between the student and his teacher, but it must always be a challenge for the student. It is up to the teacher to insert in-between assignments that help students develop their technical skills and their understanding of visual elements and principles. These tasks can be assessed by a teacher using sets of criteria reflecting clear-cut levels of competency or skill.

The divergent, volatile, and social aspect of the art learning process is no longer a problem for assessment, but the starting point for a meaningful learning process. It is the teacher's responsibility to ensure that the student has realistic expectations and does not get lost in the working process. It is the student's responsibility to think about what he wants to do and how to do it, and to reflect on both the resulting product and the process that went with is. Developmental self-assessment is, in the end, a process that might help students to develop their learning potentials, including the artistic ones, in a more effective way.

References

Arnheim, R. (1974). *Art and Visual Perception: A Psychology of the Creative Eye: The New Version*, Berkeley, CA: University of California Press.

Boughton, D. (2004a). Assessing art learning in changing contexts: High-stakes accountability, international standards, and changing conceptions of artistic development. In Eisner,

E.; Day, M. (Eds.). *Handbook of Research and Policy in Arts Education*. Mahwah, NJ: Lawrence Erlbaum, 585–605.

—— (2004b). 'The Problem of Seduction: Assessing Visual Culture', *Studies in Art Education* 45 (3), 265–269.

Davis, J. Hoffmann (2008). *Why Our Schools Need the Arts*. New York, London: Teacher College, Columbia University.

Eisner, E. W. (2002). *The Arts and the Creation of Mind*. New Haven, CT, London: Yale University Press.

Gardner, H. (1980). *Artful Scribbles: The Significance of Children's Drawings*. New York: Basic Books.

Hetland, L., Winner, E., Veenema, S., Sheridan, K. (2007). *Studio Thinking. The Real Benefits of Visual Arts Education*. New York, London: Teacher College Press.

Kindler, A. (1997). Map of Artistic Development. In Kindler, A.; Darras, B. *Child Development in Art*. Reston: NAEA. 17–44.

Lowenfeld, V., Brittain, V. L. (1947). *Creative and Mental Growth*. New York: MacMillan Company.

Ministry of Education (2007) *Examination program Visual Art VWO.*, http://www.examenblad.nl/9336000/1/j9vvhinitagymgn_m7mvh57glrndzx7/vhkxaygcroys/f=/bestand.pdf. Accessed 28 November 2011.

Schönau, D. W. (1996). Nationwide Assessment of Studio Work in the Visual Arts: Actual Practice and Research in the Netherlands. In Boughton, D.; Eisner, E.; Ligtvoet, J. (Eds.). *Evaluating and Assessing the Visual Arts in Education*. New York, London: Teachers College, Columbia University. 156–175.

—— (2011). Towards developmental self-assessment in the visual arts: supporting new ways of artistic learning in school. *International Journal for Education through Art*, 8 (1), 49–58.

Stake, R. (1975a). *Program evaluation and particularly responsive evaluation*. Paper presented at the *New Trends in Evaluation* conference, Goteborg, Sweden, October 1973. Published as an Occasional Paper of the Center for Instructional Research and Curriculum Evaluation, University of Illinois at Urbana-Champaign in November 1975. https://www.globalhivmeinfo.org/CapacityBuilding/Occasional%20Papers/05%20Program%20Evaluation,%20Particularly%20Responsive%20Evaluation.pdf. Accessed 8 January 2013.

—— (1975b). *Evaluating the Arts in Education: A Responsive Approach*. Columbus, OH: Ch.E. Merrill Publ. Comp.

Vygotsky, L. S. (1978). *Mind in Society: Development of Higher Psychological Processes*. Cambridge, MA: Harvard University Press.

Wiggins, G. (1998). *Educative Assessment: Designing Assessments to Inform and Improve Student Assessment*. San Francisco, CA: Jossey-Bass Publishers.

Zimmerman, E. (1997). Authentic Assessment Research in Art Education. In La Pierre, Sharon D.; Zimmerman, Enid (Eds.). *Research Methods and Methodologies for Art Education*. Reston, VI: NAEA. 149–169.

Appendix

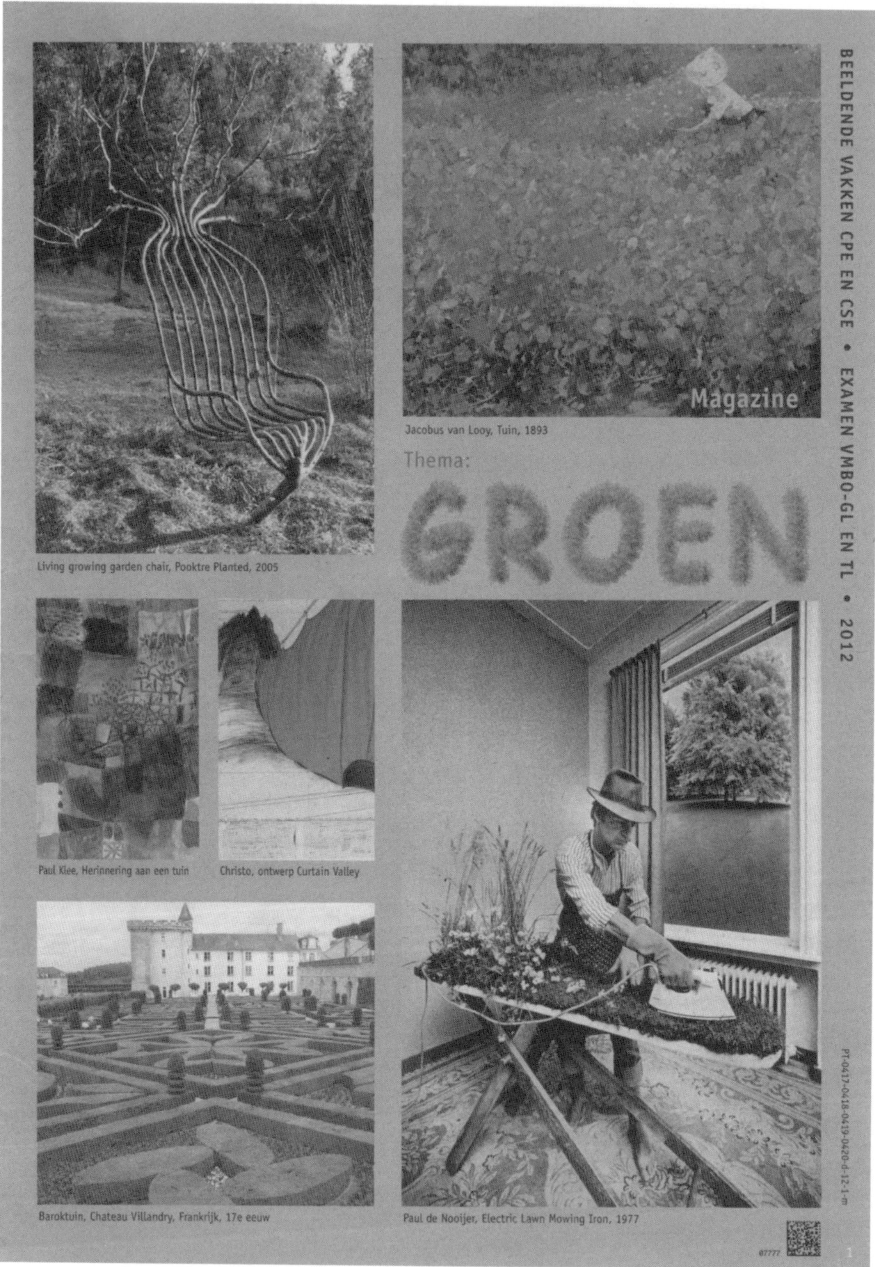

Figure 1: Page 1 from the magazine of the 2012 vmbo-exam.

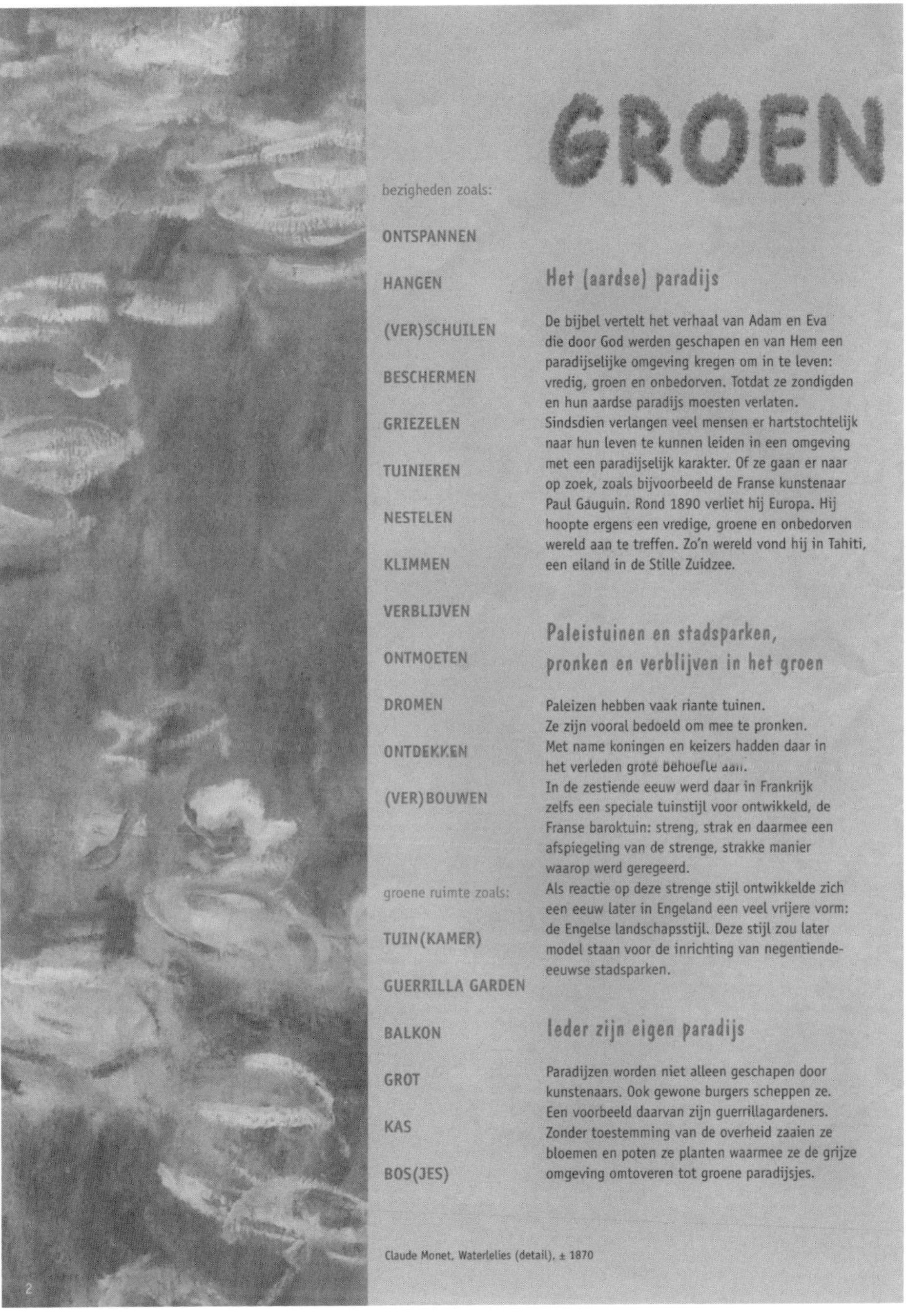

Figure 2: Page 2 from the magazine of the 2012 vmbo-exam.

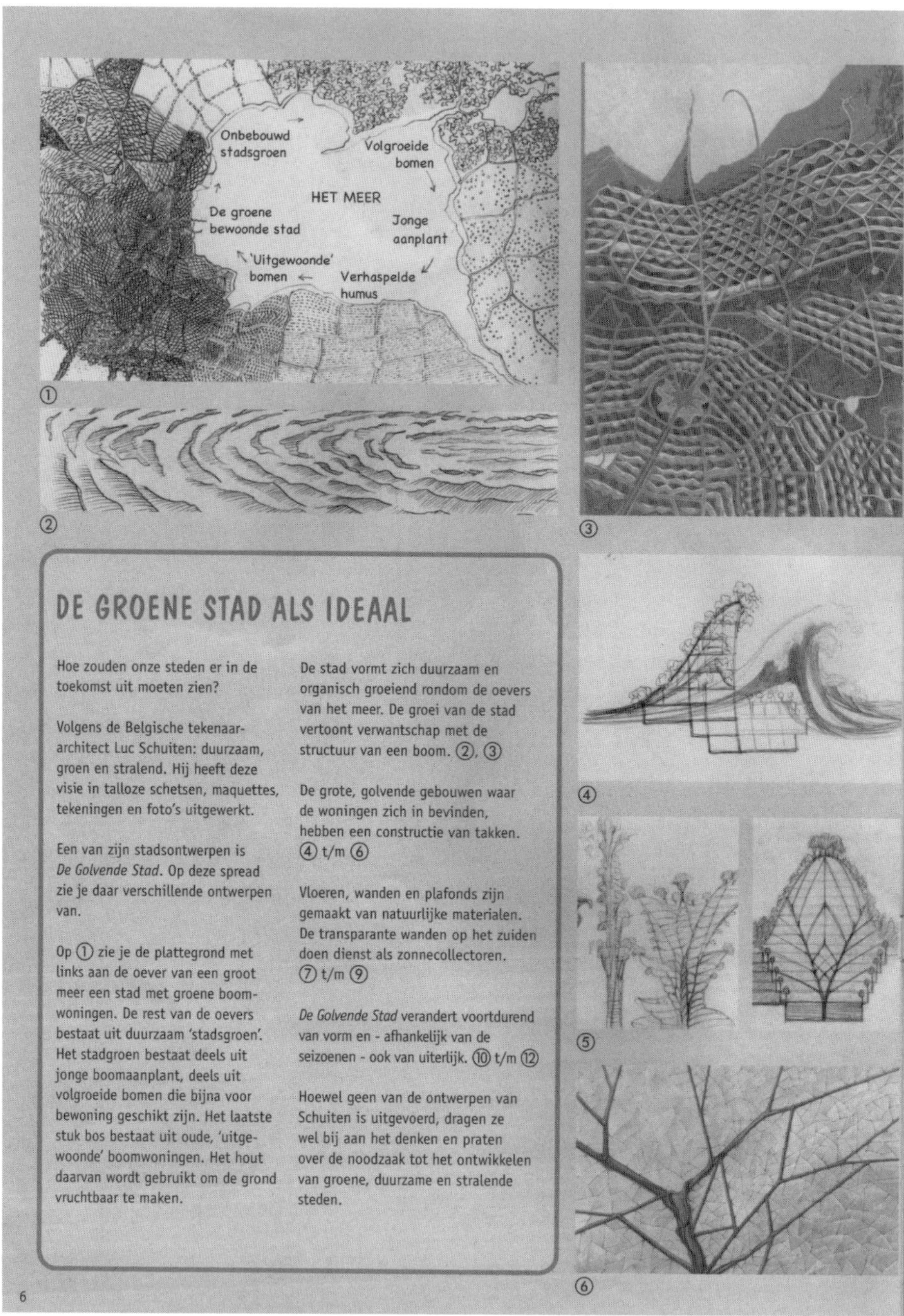

Figure 3: Page 6 from the magazine of the 2012 vmbo-exam.

Final examination assignment for the Central Practical Exam for the visual arts in lower vocational education 2012 (the Netherlands).

Theme: 'Green space'[7]

Name of the candidate: ……………….   Examination number: ……….............

Assignment booklet

This exam consists of the parts A, B, C, D, E, and F.

You have to execute all parts.

Make use of the information given in the magazine.[8]

'Green space'

Design and make a piece of work in which you visualize a green space in which you would like to live.
On page 4 off this booklet you find columns with suggestions you can choose as a starting point. Select one suggestion out of each column.
You can also formulate your own starting points in these columns.

Attention!
- The piece of work has to be made in a technique that is used in your art discipline.[9]
- In this exam you have to work in a process-like way.
- Collect all your sketches, studies, and technical trials.
- Indicate in what order they were made.
- If needed include notes and remarks to clarify the choices you have made.
- At the parts A, B, C, D, and F of this exam the maximum amount of scores to be given to this part are indicated at the top of the page.
- The maximum amount of scoring points for this exam is 50.

Below you can see the maximum score for each part.

Part A: Orientation	4
Part B: Artistic research	9
Part C: Decision on the design	2
Part D: Execution of your piece of work	25
Part E: Analysis of your own work and of one of your fellow students	7
Part F: Presentation	3

Timeline

The assessment of your time line is included in part F: Presentation.
Make use of the scheme below to check your investment in time.

Part		Actual time spent
A: Orientation	(about 50 minutes)	.... minutes
B: Artistic research	(100 minutes)	.... minutes
C: Decision on the design	(10 minutes)	.... minutes
D: Execution of your piece of work	(500 minutes)	.... minutes
E: Analysis and evaluation	(45 minutes)	.... minutes
F: Presentation	(15 minutes)	.... minutes
Total	720 minutes	.... minutes

A: Orientation   *about 50 minutes*

At this part you are assessed to what degree you have oriented yourself in a broad and varied way on the possibilities of this theme.

In this part you have to investigate possible approaches to this theme.
Mark the possibilities in the columns below you wish to investigate
and/or write down other possibilities at the bottom of the columns.

activities like	green spaces like	atmospheres like
relaxing	garden (room)	paradisiacal
hanging	guerrilla garden	peaceful
hiding	balcony	lively
protecting	grotto	unspilled
shuddering	greenhouse	creepy

activities like	green spaces like	atmospheres like
nesting	woods	thrilling
climbing	verge	mysterious
staying	(roof) terrace	moving
meeting	hollow in the dunes	lightharted
dreaming	oasis	grand
(re)building	jungle	
	moor	
	garden center	
	farmyard	
	cemetery	

Design a mood board which shows that you have investigated the possibilities above or written down by yourself in a broad and varied way.

B. Artistic research
about 100 minutes

At this part you are assessed to what degree you have made a deep and coherent artistic research.

Now you have to elaborate on the possibilities written down or marked under A.
Make sketches, studies, and technical trials and keep them.
They do not have to be perfect. What counts is, that you can show you have done research and what this research has brought you.
Do this research using the following research questions.
Research what you wish to represent,[10] how you think you do this, and with what means.

What: content
What kind of green space would you like to visualize?
For what activity would this space be fit?
What features of the atmosphere should such a space have?

What: characteristics of the representation
What characteristics of the representation are you going to investigate?

How: visual elements
What visual elements (like form, light, space, colour, texture, order) are you going to investigate?

With what: material and technique
What materials ands techniques are you going to investigate?

C: Decision on the design *about 10 minutes*

> *At this part you are assessed to what degree you have processed the results of your research at point B into your final design.*

At part B you have researched what green space you would like to represent, what activities might be fit to do there and what atmosphere this space should have. Now you have to take decisions and finalize your design.

What: content

Describe the green space you are going to visualize, the activities for which this space is fit, and the atmosphere the space should have.

Green space: ....

Activity: ....

Atmosphere: ....

What: characteristics of the representation

Name the two most important characteristics of the **representation** you will use to visualize the content and give short explanations for each element.

1. ....

2. ....

How: visual elements

Name the two most important visual elements you will use to visualize the content and give short explanations for each element.

1. ....

2. ....

With what: material and technique

Name the (most important) material you are going to work with and also the most important technique.
Give a short description for both the material and the technique.

....

> Give a preliminary title that fits your work.

D. Execution of your piece of work   *about 500 minutes*

> *At this part you are assessed to what degree your have visualized the green space you would like to be in.*

Make your piece of work.
During the work you may have made changes in your original design. If so, describe these changes below. Clarify why you have made these changes.
Give your work its final title.

If you have not made any changes, write down the final title at the bottom of this page and go on to the next page.

Main changes with regard to the content:

Space: ....

Activity: ....

Atmosphere: ....

Clarification: ....

Main changes with regard to the characteristics of the representation:

....

Clarification: ....

Main changes with regard to the visual elements:

Clarification: ....

Main changes with regard to material and/or technique:

....

Clarification: ....

> Give your work its final title:
> ....

E: Analysis and evaluation *about 45 minutes*

> *At this part you are assessed on the way you have analysed and evaluated your own work and the work of another student.*

Analyse and evaluate your own work and work process using the questions on page (...)
Next choose a work of a fellow student that is highly dissimilar to your own work.
Write down this analysis and evaluation on page (...)
Also analyse that work and write down this analysis on page (...)

Evaluation is done by giving a judgement about the way in which the work made agrees with the choices with regard to content, activity and atmosphere. Your judgment can exist of "good", "sufficient" or "insufficient". Indicate what judgements (good/sufficient/insufficient) are relevant and clarify your judgement.

Analytic scheme for the student's own work and working process

> Title: ....
> The work made by me is:
> 0 a drawing[11]
> 0 a painting
> 0 a collage
> 0 something different, namely a ....

What: content
In my work I have visualized the following green space:...
because I would like to be able to do...(name activity) there.
Because of this the atmosphere has to be...

What: the two most important characteristics of the representation with regard to the content
Indicate as to how far (good/sufficient/insufficient) the two most important characteristics of the representation links up to the content.
Clarify both characteristics.

1. ....

2. ....

How: the two most important visual elements with regard to the content
Indicate as to how far (good/sufficient/insufficient) the two most important visual elements links up to the content.

Clarify both elements.

1. ....

2. ....

With what: material and technique with regard to the content
Indicate as to how far (good/sufficient/insufficient) the chosen **material** links up to the content.
Clarify your answer.

....

Indicate as to how far (good/sufficient/insufficient) the chosen **technique** links up to the content.
Clarify your answer.

....

<table>
<tr><td>What makes you enthusiastic about your own work, and about what aspects are you less enthusiastic?

Very enthusiastic ....

Less enthusiastic ....</td></tr>
</table>

The name of the student whose work I will analyse and evaluate is...

The title of the work is ....

The reason I want to analyse and evaluate this specific work is ....

Analytic scheme for the other student's work and working process

<table>
<tr><td>Title: ....
The work made by him/her is:
0 a drawing[12]
0 a painting
0 a collage,
0 something different, namely a ....</td></tr>
</table>

What: content

In this work he/she has visualized the following green space: ....
because he/she would like to be able to do... (name activity) there.
Because of this the atmosphere has to be ....

What: the two most important characteristics of the representation with regard to the content

Indicate as to how far (good/sufficient/insufficient) the two most important characteristics of the representation links up to the content chosen by the student.
Clarify both characteristics.

1. ....

2. ....

How: the two most important visual elements with regard to the content

Indicate as to how far (good/sufficient/insufficient) the two most important visual elements links up to the content chosen by the student.
Clarify both elements.

1. ....

2. ....

With what: material and technique with regard to the content

Indicate as to how far (good/sufficient/insufficient) the chosen **material** links up to the content chosen by the student.
Clarify your answer.

....

Indicate as to how far (good/sufficient/insufficient) the chosen **technique** links up to the content chosen by the student.
Clarify your answer.

....

What makes you enthusiastic about his/her work, and about what aspects are you less enthusiastic?
Very enthusiastic ....
Less enthusiastic ....

F: Presentation   *about 15 minutes*

> *At this part you are assessed if your work is shown to full advantage in your presentation, what starting points you have used, and to what extent your presentation gives insight into your timeline and working process.*

Make a presentation in which

- Your work is shown in full advantage.
- You show what starting points you have used.
- Your timeline and working process are clearly visible.

Notes

1 The male version should also be read in its female version.

2 The distinction into four types of standards can also be helpful to (re)organize the so-called studio habits as discerned by Hetland et al. (2007). Some of the habits are not specific for art education, but can be seen as learning standards.

3 The concept of "developmental assessment" is also used in early childhood care, where it refers to the ongoing observation of the young child with regard to their development on critical aspects and circumstances. Assessment is related to diversion form the mean development. The concept as presented in this chapter is much broader and less normative.

4 The CPE VWO normally takes place in 28 sessions of 50 minutes (or combinations) during 4 months, with a minimum of 7 weeks.

5 The concept of "artistic research" is a poor translation of "beeldend proces". This process is a research on the ways how to give form to what one is after, using all the artistic means available.

6 Orientation: 50 minutes; visual research: 100 minutes; decision on what to do: 10 minutes; production of the work: 500 minutes; a comparison of the final work made with a work made by another candidate in the same class: 45 minutes; and a presentation: 15 minutes. In total: 12 hours during two months

7 The original Dutch word is "In het groen". This expression has a layer of meanings: "In (to) nature", "A space in nature", but also "Dressed in green". The examples and tasks in the magazine are best covered by the concept of "Green space".

8 This magazine (identical for all four art subjects) is a full colour booklet of eight pages with some 20 examples of artworks (varying from a French baroque garden, Caspar David Friedrich, and Renoir, examples of Chinese and medieval art, to Monet, Christo, Robert Morris, and Giuseppe Penone). A two-page description of the contemporary Dutch artist Anouk Vogel who has made an artwork of a tree into the façade of a newly built school, and another two pages are devoted to examples of fantasies of cities by the Belgian artist Luc Schuiten. The theme itself is described by a short text in which a variety of approaches to nature in religion (paradise), history (palaces) and art (landscape painting, land art) is

introduced, and some forty words that refer to objects, activities or moods related to nature. The magazine is given to the students at the same time as the assignment booklet.

9   The same theme is given to all students in the visual arts, but adapted to the specific discipline: two-dimensional art, three-dimensional art, textile art, audio-visual art. In this appendix only the example of two-dimensional art is presented. The instruction here is adapted for each discipline.

10   The Dutch word is "verbeelden": giving form into an image. In this translation this word is translated as "represent".

11   This choice varies with the discipline taken by the student.

12   This choice varies with the discipline taken by the student.

Chapter 8

The assessment of visual knowledge and communication in art education

Kerry Freedman, Northern Illinois University, DeKalb, Illinois, USA

Abstract

In recent years, visual information systems have increased in use to such an extent that specialized abilities are necessary for navigating visual culture communications. Good visual communication has become as important as good textual communication and at least some standards for visual learning and methods of assessment should be applied across disciplines, just as we assess students' use of spelling and grammar. In this chapter, the purposes and methods of assessing visual knowledge and communication will be discussed. First, I will discuss art curriculum as a necessary foundation for learning about visual culture and communication. Second, the importance of creative, artistic production as a reflection of students' visual learning will be explored. Third, a section on methods and techniques of assessing student art will follow. Finally, the importance of group cognition as a vehicle for visual learning that is assessed through group critique will be discussed.

Assessment and visual information systems

As well as the acquisition of knowledge from the past, two aims of 21st century education are the preparation for innovative forms of work and the creation of new knowledge. In order to fulfill these contemporary purposes of education, educators and policymakers need to consider the types of information systems that people use to bring their definitions of an educated person in line with the ways students learn now.

In recent years, visual information systems have increased in use to such an extent that specialized abilities are necessary for navigating visual culture communications. These abilities depend on what has been called "visual literacy". The idea of a need for visual literacy highlights the fact that people interpret meaning from countless images and objects each day and that this process of interpretation demands concepts and skills that differ from those used in interacting with texts. For example, when we encounter visual images, we use eye movements to collect various types of information around the picture, rather than following a textual sequence; we tend to interpret the codes of a picture in layers, from simple to complex, rather than deciphering textual codes in a linear fashion; when decoding images, we tend to form an associative context for holistic analysis, rather than figuring out what words mean as the story unfolds. Images can have a powerful, and subtle, impact on people in ways that text cannot and we have a much larger memory capacity for images. Of course, when we read a novel, we form images in our minds, but most of these are dependent on some form of visual experience, including previously seen visual images.

So, visual literacy now means a working knowledge of the highly influential and unique ways that images and objects mediate the construction of meaning. As Michael Polanyi (1958) pointed out in his seminal book about tacit knowledge, we know more than we can say in words. Images pervade post-industrial cultures and, with increasingly sophisticated media capabilities, visual culture has actually overtaken the written word in its effectiveness to transmit some forms knowledge. Visual culture is used to convince as well as inform. As a result, visual literacy demands both creative and critical engagement to construct and understand knowledge derived from visual sources. These skills are necessary for effective participation in advanced democratic societies and to succeed in today's creative economy.

To understand the wide range of ideas, concepts, and skills tied to visual culture requires a visual education that too many students lack. For the purposes of this chapter, visual literacy has to do with communication through visual and material culture, which includes both images and objects; this should be considered basic to art education (although art education is much more than just visual literacy) and all disciplines.

Good visual communication has become as important as good textual communication and at least some standards for visual learning and methods to assess the acquisition and use of visual knowledge should be applied across disciplines, just as we assess students' use of spelling and grammar. Educators have begun to see the application of an increasing visual consciousness in the use of portfolio assessment across disciplines. The ability to create and use visual information to communicate is important if students are to stay current in any profession and critical for those who seek to become leaders in the Information Age. And yet, the development of visual literacy standards across disciplines has yet to be established as a goal of 21st century education.

Methods for assessing visual learning are not mysterious; they are used every day in the visual arts, information technology, and media communications. For example, all students should be expected to use basic presentation media. Most important, the quality of students' visual communication through expressive forms in all school subjects should be assessed along with their quality of writing.

Visual culture curriculum in art education

Visual literacy should be supported throughout education; however, as with reading and writing, it requires a level of specialized learning through planned educational experiences. A good visual arts curriculum is the foundation of such learning.

Contemporary art education is dependent on a conception of curriculum that is both meaningful in content and structured in design. Such a curriculum must have stated aims that represent the purposes of the curriculum at the cultural and/or societal level and goals that function as a translation of those aims for a discipline. From these, appropriate learning objectives and instructional procedures can be established for particular students.

Such a curriculum must enable students to fuse emotion and cognition in the visual expression of ideas. It must relate art and design education to students' present interests and experience while preparing them for a postmodern future. It must respond to the expansion of the visual arts in forms and influence. It must infuse diverse, historical, and contemporary visual arts to enable students to gain broad and deep knowledge about making and viewing contexts. And, it must address artists' and educators' growing social concerns and students' demand for change. These are the characteristics of a visual culture curriculum.

Teaching visual culture is not based on a single model of curriculum or instruction; it plays out differently in different educational contexts. As such, it builds on teachers' specialized knowledge of student populations and interests as it supports local culture and programs. However, some characteristics are common across visual culture perspectives of art education.

Visual culture is best understood when students are able to learn relationships between art concepts and skills through their infusion in curriculum. Modelled on a spiral since the mid-20th century, a good art curriculum will be designed to add information, increase complexity, and allow for rehearsal. That is, the spiral metaphor for curriculum refers to the adding of information while looping back to persistently revisit concepts (rehearsal) at continually higher levels of complexity.

However, a contemporary visual culture model of curriculum is eclectic as well. That is, it is open enough to provide opportunities for alternative, self-directed curriculum experiences, which can motivate students to take different pathways to learning. Better than the spiral, a metaphor for contemporary curriculum is that of a web or network that enables curriculum to be conceptualized and structured in non-linear ways unique to individual students' interests and needs.

Artistic production is critical to the development of visual literacy, in part, because the processes and products of artmaking enable students to find those individual pathways to expression through connections among form, feeling, and knowing (Freedman, 2004). Creative production empowers students through their unique learning and identity construction as it provides insight into the artistic motivations, intentions, and capabilities of social groups.

Creative production as evidence of visual learning

As a way of knowing and a form of literacy, artistic production demonstrates human learning. Student creative production in the visual arts is an illustration of the didactic influence of the broad range of visual culture students encounter both inside and outside of school. For example, many assignments that result in student art depend on problem-finding and/or problem-solving processes that lead to situated learning about design. Such learning enables students to construct authentic knowledge based on the experience of designing (McCormick, 2004).

Art is basic to human existence and psychophysical responses to it are shared across individuals and communities. However, Individual or communal value of any particular work of art is socially and culturally constructed. Value emerges out of a range of conditions, from the politics of artistic production to historical and contemporary meanings for a single viewing audience. We cannot assess such complexity of value using a single, simple method.

Students learn about the complexities of assessing art when instructors model for them the ways that serious artistic judgments are made (Freedman, 2003). These are not made based solely on personal preference, but rather on community debate and consensus. Likewise, experienced teachers' assessments of student art are not merely personal; they are an expression of expert opinion based on education and experience, including a large imagic store of student art examples in each instructor's memory that acts as a group of benchmarks against which any new example is judged. Assessment of art is not a matter of being "subjective" or "objective," it is a matter of responding to evidence. In fact, artistic production by students can be understood as an exhibition of their acquisition of visual knowledge. The assessment of that knowledge is accomplished based on having seen the ways that other students and adults have revealed similar knowledge in art education and the history of art. The assessment of student art involves processes of determining the amount and quality of what students demonstrate they have learned in and through visual culture.

From this perspective, we must make judgments about student visual learning through the assessment of their artistic and design-based production. For example, students demonstrate what they have learned by recycling images. Despite the fact that teachers often try to prevent children from copying, students' drawings rely heavily on a variety of graphic sources ranging from mass media images to other student art (e.g. see Duncum, 1988, for a review; Wilson, Hurwitz and Wilson, 1987; Wilson and Wilson, 1977). As is the case with learning to write, students learn from copying images, and through education, extend their learning beyond the copy.

In an educational setting, rather than a focus on conceptions of artistic quality per se, assessment of art should focus on discovering the knowledge that students have constructed and revealed. The learning that accrues from a good art education that can be revealed through student art and design includes, for example, richness of expression, clarity of communication, formal and technical skills, basic visual literacy, inter-arts knowledge, and knowledge of other school subjects.

Assessment of student art: Techniques and processes

Social and cultural conditions have both positive and negative influences on learning, such as the negative effects of high-stakes testing on students. Assessment procedures linked to any type of literacy should "include observations, clinical interviews, reflective journals, projects, demonstrations, collections of students' work, and students' self-evaluations"

(Shepard, 2000, p. 8). As I discuss more thoroughly in my book, *Teaching visual culture* (Freedman, 2003), these complex assessment procedures have long been common to the arts and have gained interest in other school subjects.

Procedures to assess visual knowledge

Art educators develop large stores of mental images, based on art and other forms of visual culture, which they rely on as benchmarks to assess student work both formatively and summatively (Freedman, 2003). Rubrics, checklists, and other forms of textual and numerical assessment can be used in conjunction with comparisons to this imagic store, or with physical benchmarks on small or large scales, to aid reliability in assessment. For example, rubrics can result in a numerical score representing quality; however, descriptions of level must be associated with a *visual equivalent*.

The assessment of student work should involve oral and written documentation based on peer- and self-assessment and other forms of student response (Boughton, 1996). When teaching contemporary concepts and skills, such as suggestiveness, which demand multiple, varied, and extended responses, one teacher alone may not be the best determinant of the overall success of the work (Freedman, 2003). This is particularly the case when the teacher is inexperienced or has a relatively narrow imagic store. In such cases, student response through small group or large group discussions or written feedback may be effective in helping teachers judge whether a work is successful. Also, the form of student art may indicate alternative forms of assessment. For example, installations, performances, and community projects may be most effectively assessed through the inclusion of audience/community response.

Assessments should relate to the concepts and skills that students are intended to learn, but must also allow for those students who go beyond "the box" of instructional objects. Students are often particularly interested in the suggestive, symbolic attributes of visual culture, which go beyond the formal qualities of the objects (Freedman, 1995). Secondary students can become deeply involved in making and viewing, but usually not because of formal qualities per se, rather through the ways in which possible meanings have been artistically presented and their personal and group extension of those meanings.

Making "alternatives" standard

Such "alternative" methods of assessment should be considered standard procedures for assessment while protecting their unique strengths in helping educators grasp the complexity of visual knowledge revealed in student art and design. For example, portfolio assessment should not be a matter of assessing each individual work of art as much as holistic assessment processes that can take into account the breadth and depth of student learning. Portfolios can involve one-to-one interactions between student and teacher in which an exploration of the relationship between the visual and textual work can be done to extend ideas and increase the complexity and sophistication of future work. Such assessment strategies can inform students about the process of critical thinking that is involved in making and assessing works of art.

At an early age, students can begin to learn about the connections between art and social life, which is an important step towards understanding why a particular work of art, and art in general, is valued. At the elementary school level, children begin to learn distinctions, categories, and generalizations of many types and are able to discriminate among a variety of styles, subjects, forms, meanings, and purposes of visual culture. At this level, students can begin to understand why different individuals and cultural groups have made different visual representations of the same subject matter (such as people, animals, events, etc.) and grasp the value of this variety of representation. At the same time, comparing artifacts from different cultures must be done carefully, because what may be similar in appearance may be fundamentally different in purpose and meaning. By pointing out such relationships, teachers can help students see that an understanding of art requires a search beyond the surface so that students develop skills in investigation and sensitivity to visual culture forms and conditions.

Determinations of quality by a community

Students can develop an awareness of quality in the visual arts early in life. By adolescence, many have a preference for realism in art and may judge the quality of art in terms of closeness to life. Students can learn the production skills necessary for them to feel comfortable about producing their own imaginative work, as well as gaining an appreciation for the qualities of art made by others, by working in a safe environment for producing, writing, and talking about a range of visual culture.

Students do not need a high degree of representational skill in order to demonstrate that they have successfully learned art concepts. For example, although basic drawing techniques are important for all, students can demonstrate their learning about formal qualities and visual communication using photography, video, and computer technology without advanced drawing skills. Teachers can help to convince students that art has many forms which may be determined as good in quality and that a diversity of forms is judged as one of the strengths of art and design in a democracy.

Critical making and viewing

Because students are becoming increasingly aware of local and global social conditions, and are immersed in the culture of their peers, they should be encouraged to develop a critical awareness, including making critical statements through their own art. Students can use sociological and anthropological methods, such as interviewing and bringing artists and designers from the community into the classroom to gain knowledge of visual culture contexts that can lay the groundwork for their own statements through artistic production. Through the use of critical methods, such as analysis and commentary on social issues, students develop an understanding of the ways that social groups and issues are visually represented and judged.

Critical investigations through artistic practice should give attention to issues relevant to students, as well as to adults, and should be done with students as soon as they begin to attend to their social surroundings. In excellent elementary- and middle-level school programs, I have seen even early adolescents do forms of cultural critique through their art, making visual commentaries, for example, on their fears of terrorism and war, make-up testing on animals, student bullying, skateboarding laws, and environmental concerns.

Verbal and written critiques aid assessment of student art that enhances understanding of the culture and sub-cultures in which it was created. Critical analysis of adult art and design reveal reflections of and influences on sociocultural and sub-cultural contexts; this is no less the case with regards to student forms of expression. Such critique can be done individually or in a group, initiated by students or teacher, and done during or after production. On-going, formative critique is part of any good art lesson and the types of critical analysis used in art education are useful methods for developing reflective, general educational practice (Eisner, 1982, 1985; Schon, 1987).

When students participate in a verbal or written critique, they make connections between visual and textual learning by articulating related concepts and skills, stating reasons for their decisions, and explaining what they believe to be successful or unsuccessful about the work. Through in-class critique, educators provide students with ways to reflect on art that will enrich their learning. Well-handled, student interaction during a critique disperses control and responsibility in the classroom and promotes student interpretation as part of the construction of knowledge.

The critique process provides another modality for learning, just as music adds to the visual art of dance and dialogue of theatre. Critique can be done to enhance learning and illustrate the point that knowledge in and through art is interactive and interdisciplinary. Critique is often most effective in small groups and can be facilitated through the use of several different formats discussed in the next section.

Assessment and the social conditions of art education

In art education, as in other school subjects, it is extremely important to relate change in curriculum to change in the professional field. Such change in international arts communities now includes growing attention to the social conditions of art. The crossing of cultural and historical borders, the construction of multiple and group identities, and the importance of contexts of production and appreciation are all part of these social conditions. As a result, issues of artist collaboration, the world art market, art as social statement, and audience response are becoming increasingly important in curriculum.

These conditions reflect the group cognition that occurs in the learning communities of art classrooms. Group discussions, study groups, and group critiques help to foster the fusion of emotion and cognition in the production of art. The promotion and assessment of learning can be accomplished through social interaction among students around many forms of visual culture.

Group cognition and cooperative learning

One way to promote group cognition not generally used in art classrooms is through collaborative learning and assessment techniques. David Johnson and Roger Johnson's (1996) seven principles of assessment and reporting are essential components of the form of collaborative education referred to as cooperative learning: (1) design an assessment plan that takes account of teaching and learning processes, outcomes, and educational settings; (2) use cooperative student groups in assessing; (3) do not use "pseudo" groups which involve an unfair distribution of privilege or responsibilities, hostility, and other dysfunctional social behaviours; (4) use groups that function cooperatively which "are characterized by positive interdependence, individual accountability, face-to-face interaction, the appropriate use of interpersonal and small-group skills, and group processing" (Johnson and Johnson, 1996, pp. 25–26); (5) integrate assessment practices into instruction; (6) involve students in reporting assessment results; (7) use cooperative groups to help students individualize instructional and assessment goals and procedures.

Fundamental to the plan described by Johnson and Johnson (1996) is that cooperative learning should help students focus on assessing content outcomes. Truly cooperative groups should provide educational advantages for all students. Cooperative learning groups should work together to achieve shared goals, one of which is to promote the learning of all of the individuals in the group. As a result, Johnson and Johnson recommend criterion-referenced assessments and the continual checking of both individual and group progress.

The place of assessment in students' responsibility for learning

Blumfeld et al. (1996) support the Johnsons' argument that group learning should result in group, as well as individual, assessment. They stress the importance of teacher understanding of the processes that promote group learning and that group assessment should be part of the learning process. They state, "effective group work requires that students share ideas, take risks, disagree with and listen to others, and generate and reconcile points of view" (Blumfeld et al., 1996, p. 38). As a result, the types of tasks given to students, conditions of giving and seeking help, individual accountability, and group composition are important considerations in teacher planning. Collaboration is an essential element for success because it involves students in constructing shared meanings that will aid their understanding of disciplines and discipline communities.

Unfortunately, few art educators currently use group forms of assessment, primarily because they assume that creativity and the production of art is the domain of the individual. However, group assessment is being used in an increasing number of teacher education programs to help teacher educators become aware of its strengths as a process through which students can learn about the many social influences on art and design practices.

One of the important aspects of cooperative learning in school is that it shifts responsibility for student learning to the students themselves. Students' ability to criticize their art and the work of others is a vital consideration with regard to group assessment. Students should be able to participate in group critiques of individual student work, respond to group learning as a group, and respond as a group to professional artistic production and performance.

Fundamental to students taking increased responsibility for their own learning, and to several types of group forms of assessment, are student peer- and self-assessment. If students are to monitor group activities in-process and be, at least in part, responsible for the success of the group, they must be taught how to analyse constructively and improve their own work and the work of others. Research has suggested that students who take part in self-assessment activities learn more about the arts than those who do not (Carole, 1995).

Critique as cooperative assessment

The studio in an educational setting is not one of single artists working alone. Rather, it is the foundation of a learning community and a socially interactive environment that involves individuals and groups in viewing, analysing, debating, and making art. As a result, any discussion of the assessment of student visual culture must include some consideration of the interaction between and among students (Freedman, 2003).

As discussed above, group critique is an established activity of the visual arts community and the idea of group cognition suggests new possibilities for critique procedures through which groups of students can assess works of visual culture. Through such procedures, students can discuss, debate, and judge the quality of visual and interdisciplinary concepts and skills. As students develop social knowledge about visual culture in the process of making and viewing art and design, they can begin to understand the relationship between their art knowledge and its social value.

Several aspects of group critique are similar to those of individual assessment. For example, student self- and peer-assessment and the relationship of student production to lesson objectives are important to both. However, some aspects of group assessment are different, and involve changes in lesson design to accommodate, and even enhance, student collaboration and peer-assessment. Such changes require a shift in thinking about the responsibilities of students for their own learning and the learning of their peers. This means that students must be made increasingly aware of the social conditions that enable, nurture, and limit judgments about quality in the arts.

Among the difficulties instructors find with student group critique, at least at the adolescent stage, is that students become very concerned with being correct and the ways in which they are seen in the eyes of their peers. For this reason – and so that students can become more engaged in learning – student-directed critiques and small group critiques are often most practical. Small group methods include small group conferencing and peer–pair critique.

Group methods of assessment are particularly important in the assessment of group works of art. Group works of art, including for example, those of fine artists who work in pairs, television producers, advertisers, muralmakers, graffiti artists, and film-makers are highly complex and are assessed on multiple levels by many people. Group assessment of public visual arts occurs even when fine art, television, and film critics work alone in their authoring of criticism because even these individual efforts are part of a discourse community.

Three components of assessment are of particular importance when attending to the development of group forms of student assessment: *methods of procedure, methods of analysis,* and *analysis criteria* (Freedman, 2003). Methods of procedure are the ways in which evidence of performance and achievement is gathered, such as checklists, observations, or portfolios. Methods of analysis refer to the means by which decisions are made about the evidence and can be quantitative or qualitative. For example, a checklist usually leads to a quantitative analysis involving counting (for example, the number of techniques used by a student), whereas observation notes (which can be analysed numerically, such as through a count of social interactions between students) provide opportunities for qualitative analysis involving an interpretation of student dialogue. The analysis criteria should determine the appropriate methods of procedure and analysis. In other words, as is the case with individual assessment, what and how group assessment should be done are dependent on the goals of instruction.

Collaborative forms of portfolio assessment

Doug Boughton's chapter in this text will provide a more complete discussion of portfolio assessment. However, for the purposes of this chapter, I will present group uses of portfolio processes in brief.

Wolf (1988–89) describes a portfolio as "a chronologically sequenced collection of work that records the long-term evolution of artistic thinking" (p. 27). Portfolios have historically been used for student assessment in the arts. Generations of art students have benefitted from type of individualized assessments that portfolios can help to provide.

Similar types of portfolios used for individual assessment can be used to facilitate group assessment, which can reflect the best of the work of the students as a whole (Robinson, 1995). The procedures for developing and analysing group portfolios are similar to those for individual portfolios. For instance, several types of evidence should be included, such as examples of work and information about the work. In the visual arts, this involves examples of works of art, records of production processes, and student reflections about the art, including sketchbook/journal entries. Group portfolios can be developed in the same way for the production of group art and, at the same time, provide evidence of individual accountability and contribution. Group portfolios can also be used to assess group responses to professional art or the work of other groups of students.

Many group activities that support student learning, but may not directly result in the production or performance of art, can be assessed through the use of portfolios. For example, teaching-back, which involves students teaching peers what they have learned, can be documented using evidence of lesson planning.

Observation and recording

Observing and recording group learning is an important part of teacher-based group assessment. These components of group assessment facilitate the analysis of social interaction, which, as we have seen, should be considered part of the learning objectives in group work. Students' performance, cooperation with others, work habits, and so on can be recorded using checklists, rubrics, and anecdotal descriptions.

Videotaping is a particularly powerful assessment tool in the arts. It is a concrete record of words, actions, and sounds, can be viewed repeatedly to allow for reflection and analysis, and it enables students to watch and critique themselves (e.g. Carlin, 1996; Zimmerman, 1992). For formative assessment, teachers might video record the production process of a group making a work of visual art or students may choose what and when to record. For example, they may wish to record a particularly difficult performance so that they can analyse it. For summative assessment, public performances and exhibitions can be taped and can include student commentary.

The difficulty with this method of procedure is to develop careful methods of analysis. Several questions should be addressed for an effective strategy: How will the observation/recording be done? What social interactions will be used to illustrate student learning? What visual characteristics of the creative process, exhibition, or performance will be assessed? Will the analysis depend on qualitative or quantitative methods?

Summary of group assessment issues

The important points from the review and analysis of literature surrounding the topic of group assessment in the arts are highlighted in the following (Freedman, 2003):

- Individual assessment is important, but learning may be limited in focus and characterized by competition, exclusion, and social isolation.

- Group assessment in art education reflects the recent attention to the importance of collaboration and community in the arts.
- Group assessment is consistent with empirical research that suggests the educational importance of socially shared cognition and cooperative learning.
- Group assessment can reflect group learning and help students take responsibility for their own learning.
- Individual accountability should be maintained as a part of group assessment.
- Self- and peer-assessment are fundamental to successful group assessment.
- The analysis of students' ability to work as a group and conduct self- and peer-assessment is essential for effective group assessment.
- Group assessment can be done with formal, informal, or base groups.
- Any group assessment plan must include predefined methods of procedure, methods of analysis, and analysis criteria.
- Ways of gathering evidence include portfolios, observations, videotaping, and peer- and self-critique.

In sum, three central issues are of particular importance in group forms of assessment. First, determining the appropriateness of the lesson for group learning and students' capacity to work in groups should be an essential part of planning any group assessment. Second, group assessment should include measures of individual accountability within the group. Third, measures of individual accountability should include evidence of reflection on self- and peer-performance.

Conclusion

Creative studio production is vital to helping students understand the visual arts and visual communication in general. It is the creation of unique images and objects, the freedom of making a statement, enrichment gained through the investigation of visual media, and the power of symbols to communicate that enable students to go reach outside of themselves, going beyond consumption and appropriation to become contributing members of larger communities and cultures. Although studying art through various visual and textual processes is helpful, making art is the surest way for students to come to understand the most fundamental reasons to value art.

Assessing what students come to know about art through their studio work can be difficult without the aid of a range of visual experiences and knowledge of methods for determining value within visual culture communities. Experience should include a focus on the most up-to-date student and professional art being produced at any given time. Methods of determining value must include the continual challenge of rewarding students who go beyond the hopes stated in instructional objectives.

References

Blumfeld, P. C., Marx, R. W., Soloway, E., Krajcik, J. (1996). Learning with peers: From small group cooperation to collaborative communities. *Educational Researcher, 25* (8), 37–40.

Boughton, D. (1996). Assessment of student learning in the visual arts. *Translations from Theory to Practice, 6* (3).

Carlin, J. (1996). Videotape as an assessment tool. *Teaching Music, 3* (4), 38–39, 54.

Carole, P. J. (1995). Alternative assessment in music education. (Unpublished Master's thesis, Nova Southeastern University, 1995.) ERIC doc., no. ED398141.

Duncum, P. (1988). To copy or not to copy: A review. *Studies in Art Education, 29* (4), 203–210.

Eisner, E. W. (1982). *Cognition and curriculum: A basis for deciding what to teach.* New York: Longman.

———— (1985).*The educational imagination: On the design and evaluation of school programs.* New York: Macmillan.

Freedman, K. (1995). Educational change within structures of history, culture, and discourse. In Neperud,R. W. (Ed.).*Context, content, and community in art education.* New York: Teacher College Press. 87–107.

———— (2003). *Teaching visual culture: Curriculum, aesthetics, and the social life of art.* New York: Teachers College Press.

———— (2004). The importance of student artistic production to teaching visual culture, *Art Education, 56* (2), 38–43.

Johnson, D. W., Johnson, R. T. (1996). The role of cooperative learning in assessing and communicating student learning. In Guskey, T. T. (Ed.). *Communicating student learning.* Alexandria. VA: ASCD Yearbook. 25–46.

McCormick, R. (2004). Issues of learning and knowledge in technology education. *International Journal of Technology and Design Education, 14* (1), 21–44.

Polanyi, M. (1958). *Personal Knowledge: Towards a Post-Critical Philosophy.* Chicago: University of Chicago Press.

Robinson, M. (1995). Alternative assessment techniques for teachers, *Music Educators Journal, 81* (5), 28–34.

Schon, D. A. (1987). *Educating the reflective practitioner.* San Fransisco: Jossey-Bass.

Shepard, L. (2000). The role of assessment in a learning culture. *Educational Researcher, 29* (7), 4–14.

Wilson, B., Hurwitz, A., Wilson, M. (1987). *Teaching drawing from art.* Worchester, MA: Davis.

Wilson, B., Wilson, M. (1977). An iconoclastic view of the imagery sources of the drawing of young people, *Art Education, 30* (1), 5–11.

Wolf, D. P. (1988–89). Opening up assessment, *Educational Leadership, 45* (4), 24–29.

Zimmerman, E. (1992). Assessing students' progress and achievements in art, *Art Education, 45* (6), 14–24.

Chapter 9

A national assessment of learning outcomes in art in the Finnish comprehensive school 2010

Sirkka Laitinen, the Viikki Teacher Training School, University of Helsinki, Finland

Abstract

In Finland the National Board of Education assessed learning outcomes in music, art, and craft in the final ninth grade of basic education in 2010. This chapter will report the the outcomes of visual arts in this assessment. It will also handle some problems of the assessment. The assignments were used to assess the standard of pupils' skills and knowledge and their understanding and command of art processes. It also involved surveys for principals and teachers covering teaching arrangements and opportunities for and barriers to learning.

Pencil-and-paper assignments were considered necessary also in the assessment of art subjects, as the material had to be in a form allowing statistical processing. In art education the essential things are the experience-oriented nature of learning and the processes of picture making: production assignment suited for art was developed. Satisfactory results were achieved only in the content area of media and visual communication. In the key content area of art instruction, visual expression and thinking, the performance level of more than one-third of the pupils was low. Teachers and pupils appreciate the same thing in art instruction: pupils' own creative artistic activity. This assessment shows that it is important to reinforce pupils' performance as a whole and their cultural performance and knowledge of art in particular.

***

I am going to present assessment of learning outcomes in art carried out in Finland. The National Board of Education assessed learning outcomes in music, art, and craft in the final ninth grade of basic education in March 2010 (Laitinen, Hilmola, and Juntunen, 2011). A more detailed account of the discussion on the assessment of art subjects can be found in an article that I have written together with Marja-Leena Juntunen (Juntunen and Laitinen, 2011).

It is often wondered if assessment of learning outcomes is at all necessary in art subjects. The matter is seen as problematic, to say the least. In these subjects assessment has been seen to prevent creativity or focus on the pupil's personality or abilities regarded as innate, which it would be unfair to assess. In people's minds the concept of talent is such an inseparable part of art that assessment in art subjects is easily understood as measurement of talent. Assessment of art and making of art has also been considered subjective, relying on individual preferences to the extent that it should be eliminated form these subjects. As far as I can see, assessment of learning outcomes is meaningful also in art, providing that assessment methods are developed to suit art subjects. It must be as transparent, reliable, and representative as in any other field.

In art subjects learning also signifies realization of cultural equality. In addition, it means versatility of culture transmitted by the school and of the school's support to pupils' growth as well as every child's and young person's right to self-expression and cultural participation. From this point of view, also assessment in art subjects can be regarded as an essential tool for the development of education.

In the assessment under study, data was collected through stratified sampling from 152 comprehensive schools representing a comprehensive cross-section of different parts of Finland. The sample included 12 Swedish-language schools, which is in keeping with their relative proportion. Pupils from the ninth grade were selected to take part in the assessment using systematic sampling. A total of 4,792 pupils participated in the assessment, consisting of 2,411 girls and 2,381 boys.

At different stages of the assessment, pupils performed a wide variety of assignments assessing achievement of the objectives set for art in the 2004 National Core Curriculum for Basic Education (National Core Curriculum for Basic Education 2004). The assignments were used to assess the standard of pupils' key skills and knowledge in these subjects and their understanding and command of music, art and craft processes. The assessment also involved surveys for principals and teachers covering teaching arrangements and opportunities for and barriers to learning. Pupils were asked to provide background details and perceptions on studying and learning these subjects.

At the first stage of the assessment, pupils completed common pencil-and-paper assignments covering all three subjects at all schools. For the second stage, the schools were divided into three segments. At each school, pupils performed advanced pencil-and-paper assignments in music, art, or craft. Furthermore, some of these pupils also completed production assignments in the same subject, which aimed to assess their skills in making music, art, or craft.

The assessment of several thousand pupils had to be committed to the objectives of learning in art subjects and feasible in various schools. Pencil-and-paper assignments were considered necessary also in the assessment of art subjects, as the material had to be in a form allowing statistical processing. However, the use of statistical methods set restrictions on the versatility of the assessment. The tools of assessment were partly of the type used for years for assessing learning outcomes in mathematics, mother tongue, natural sciences, and foreign languages. They have been devised to measure levels of competence. Adapting a formula used in national follow-up assessments of learning outcomes in other subjects to art subjects presented some problems, however.

In one follow-up assessment it is possible to examine pupils' performances only in some areas. Some teachers wrote in the connected survey that pencil-and-paper assignments focused too much on assessing pupils' knowledge of art. It is true that pencil-and-paper assignments easily concentrate on questions regarding knowledge. This problem has been discussed by Persky (2004, p. 615) in his presentation of assessment in art subjects carried out by NAEP in the United States. Yet it is also true that knowledge of art and visual culture is clearly emphasized in the National Core Curriculum, along with pupils' own picture making. In art the form of pencil-and-paper assignments presented some challenges for reliable assessment based on the National Core Curriculum. Poor understanding of written instructions may have weakened some pupils' performance, but ninth graders should have had no difficulty in understanding instructions in clear standard language. However, when completing pencil-and-paper assignments pupils did not have the same feeling of making something as is characteristic of picture making in art lessons.

In the 2004 National Core Curriculum for Basic Education key content areas for art education are visual expression and thinking, knowledge of art and cultural performance, environmental aesthetics, architecture and design, as well as media and visual communication. In the assessment under study each art assignment concerned one or more of these four content areas. These assignments can, however, only be used to assess some of the objectives set in the National Core Curriculum.

The assignments varied as to their level of difficulty. Some of them can be said to have assessed learning of the key issues emphasized as early as grades 1–4. Among these worth mentioning are mixing intermediate colours, depicting movement in comic strip frames, identifying an artist of the Golden Age of Finnish art, and describing art pictures as well as assignments concerning pairs of complementary colours, the concept of primary colour, and identifying picture sizes and the source of inspiration for Akseli Gallen-Kallela's and Mauri Kunnas's works.

In intermediate assignments pupils were urged to interpret, understand or explain works of art. In assignments concerning their own concepts of art pupils could use the art exercise books for providing many kinds of answers stemming from their own ideas. In these assignments the objects of assessment were the grounds given by pupils, their command of concepts of art, and versatility in the handling of the subject.

Some assignments were so demanding that their successful completion presumed good performance in the final ninth grade of basic education. Among these worth mentioning are the ones that concerned concepts of art, cinema, or product development and those regarding the history of art and architecture.

In art education essential things are the experience-oriented nature of learning and the processes of picture making. For the assessment of these matters a production assignment suited for art was developed. In these assignments pupils were informed beforehand of the objects of assessment. When assessing production assignments teachers had also been informed of the objects of assessment and the exactly defined assessment criteria. In the art assignment objects of assessment were the use of comic art expression, use of visual expression, originality of ideas and communication of the message. In addition, in both art and craft working skills and skills of self-assessment were assessed. In the assessment criteria, performance levels for each object of assessment had been defined using school grades.

In the production assignment in art it was essential that it allowed a comprehensive, even if short, assessment of the process of making pictures. Skill in making separate pictures would not have been sufficient as an object of assessment. It was important that each pupil's performance was assessed in terms of his or her own intentions and in a situation that allowed interaction between pupils and between pupils and teachers. The US assessment in art subjects (Persky, 2004, p. 615; Soep, 2004, pp. 570–583) also emphasized the socio-cultural nature of the assessment and the fact that in an assessment situation it is worthwhile to simulate usages of art lessons.

The production assignment in art had been devised in a way that allowed assessment of pupils' skills in visual production, working, and self-assessment. Pupils were asked to draw a comic strip on the basis of four pictures: a comic strip frame, a photo, a painting, and a graphic sheet. The assignment thus combined media and art imagery as inspiration for work; making pictures on the basis of other pictures is today commonplace in art and communication. The purpose of the pictures was also to make it easier for pupils to start working.

In the instructions for the assignment pupils were urged to start by sketching. Available at the session were ordinary tools used at schools, among which the pupils could choose the ones that they preferred. The content of the assignment was free, as the purpose was also to assess pupils' creative abilities. The relatively great freedom in the assignment also brought out the pupils' skills in independent work and command of the process of picture making, and at best also inspired them to complete the assignment.

When performing the assignment pupils were allowed to talk to each other and look at the pictures that others were making. The criteria for assessment were given in the instructions. At the end of the session pupils had to fill in a form in which they were asked to assess their performance. During the assignment pupils' working skills were assessed by teachers. In the assessment of picture making skills attention was paid to the use of comic art expression, originality of ideas, communication of the message, use of visual means of expression, and working skills. The same criteria were used by pupils when assessing their own work and the comic strips which they had produced. The pupils' self-assessment skills were afterwards assessed by teachers.

Judging by the assessment under study, the general level of performance in art of pupils in the final ninth grade of basic education in Finland seems to be adequate or fair in comparison to the objectives set in the National Core Curriculum. Satisfactory results were achieved only in the content area of media and visual communication. In the key content area of art instruction, visual expression, and thinking, the performance level of more than one-third of the pupils was low. More than half of the pupils showed at best adequate performance in the content area of knowledge of art and cultural performance. The results were at best adequate also in production assignments assessing visual expression, comic art expression, communication of the visual message and creative skills.

Learning outcomes and data collected from teachers and pupils showed that instruction had been focused in fairly differing ways in some of the key content areas of art. More than 16% of the teachers stated that they had not taught digital image processing at all. More than half of the pupils for their part stated that they had learned no digital image processing in art lessons. The pupils of some schools had never visited art museums or exhibitions during art lessons. Reasons for this were the location of the school far from cultural services, scarcity of instruction time, and lack of funds.

As a general rule, irrespective of the location or the language of instruction of the school, the results showed only small differences between schools. There were considerable deviations in the level of performance only in the two to three highest- and lowest-ranking schools. The schools that had provided art-oriented instruction were among the ten highest-ranking ones both in pencil-and-paper and production assignments.

Most of the pupils probably have failed to achieve the key basic skills and knowledge of art in the lower grades, and in the upper grades there has been no time for correcting these shortcomings. In the upper grades, virtually all pupils (96%) had participated in art instruction in the seventh grade, whereas in the eighth grade only slightly less than half, and in the ninth grade one third of the pupils had received art instruction. In all three grades of the upper school pupils who had studied art did definitely better than those who had studied art only in the seventh grade.

One-fourth of the art teachers at lower secondary level (grades 7–9 of basic education) were not formally qualified to teach this subject. As most of the art lessons in basic education are given by class teachers of lower grades, one fourth of the pupils fail to receive education provided by a subject teacher in this subject throughout basic education.

In art boys achieved considerably weaker outcomes than girls. The deficiencies in boys' performances were evident in all content areas of art. The girls also had a more positive attitude towards art as a subject than boys.

As a general rule, pupils consider art an interesting but not very useful subject. They find that art lessons encourage creativity and pupils' own activity. Teachers and pupils appreciate the same thing in art instruction: pupils' own creative artistic activity.

Assessment can be defined as comparison between set objectives and achieved results (Jakku-Sihvonen and Heinonen, 2001) When assessing learning outcomes pupils' results are compared to the objectives set in the Core Curriculum. This provides ideas for planning of instruction. At first sight it is possible to draw one clear conclusion from the follow-up-assessment of art subjects: it is important to reinforce pupils' performance as a whole and their cultural performance and knowledge of art in particular.

References

Jakku-Sihvonen, R., Heinonen, S. (2001) Johdatus Koulutuksen Uudistuvaan Arviointikulttuuriin [Introduction to the New Evaluation Culture of Education]. Helsinki: National Board of Education, Evaluation 2/2001.

Juntunen, M-L., Laitinen, S. (2011). Musiikin ja kuvataiteen arvioinnin kysymyksiä/Issues in the Assessment of Music and Art. In Laitinen, S. Hilmola, A. (Eds.). *Taide-ja taitoaineiden perusopetuksen oppimistulosten arviointi – toteuttamisen and tuloksien tarkastelua/Assessment of Learning Outcomes in the Basic Education in Art and Craft Subjects – Discussion on the Implementation and Results.* Helsinki, Finland: Opetushallitus, http://www.oph.fi/download/131643_Taito-_ja_taideaineiden_oppimistulokset_-_asiantuntijoiden_arviointia.pdf. Accessed 24 January 2013.

Laitinen, S., Hilmola, A., Juntunen, M-L. (2011). Perusopetuksen musiikin, kuvataiteen ja käsityön oppimistulosten arviointi 9. vuosiluokalla/Assessment of Learning Outcomes in Music, Art and Craft in the final 9th Grade of Basic Education. *Koulutuksen seurantaraportti 2011:1/Follow-up Report on Education.* Helsinki, Finland Opetushallitus http://www.oph.fi/julkaisut/2011/perusopetuksen_musiikin_kuvataiteen_ja_kasityon_oppimistulosten_arviointi_9_vuosiluokalla. Accessed 24 January 2013.

National Core Curriculum for Basic Education (2004). http://www.oph.fi/english/publications/2009/national_core_curricula_for_basic_education. Accessed 24 January 2013.

Persky, H. (2004). The NAEP Art Assessment: Pushing the Boundaries of Large-Scale Performance Assessment. In Eisner, E.W.; Day, M.D. (Eds.). *Handbook of Research and Policy in Art Education.* National Art Education Assocation. Mahwah, New Jersey: Lawrence Elbaum Associates Publishers. 607–635.

Soep, E. (2004). Assessment and Visual Arts Education. In Eisner, E.W.; Day, M.D. (Eds.). *Handbook of Research and Policy in Art Education.* National Art Education Assocation. Mahwah, New Jersey: Lawrence Elbaum Associates Publishers 579583.

Chapter 10

How to create competency-based assignments in the visual arts?

Ernst Wagner, University of Erlangen-Nuremberg, Germany

Abstract

Assignments touch the core of teaching more than any other issue. This concerns all teachers, but perhaps in a special way, art educators. The following text shows, using one concrete example, how an assignment can be developed in regards to the new concepts of competence-oriented teaching and learning.

In central Europe, it seems to be accepted in general that the new curricula in art education, will and should be based on the concept of comepetences, and there is a broad consensus on how a competence-model should look. (As an example see Figure 5.) But lively and even controversial discussions start as soon as one talks about the assignments, which claim to develop these competences, or which claim to test the competences of the students. So assigments seem to touch the core of teaching in a very direct and intensive way. That is why it is important to develop them with special care, especially in regards to the wording and to the expected outcome in the terms of competence.

The use of a concrete example helps to explain different aspects that one should pay attention to. Two years ago a group of authors discussed this example, publishing a special edition of a German journal (Schuster and Wagner, 2010) titled "New Ways to Conceptualize Classroom Assignments". One of the proposed assignments that they discussed intensely, was:

Competency-based Assignment - Version 1

1. Take a picture of your MP3-player with headphones – or any other object – in different ways.
2. Choose three different photos and present them in a sequence.
3. Search the Internet or print media (e.g. advertisements) for pictures of the same object and compare one of your photos with a picture taken by a professional photographer.

Comments about this proposal

This is an assignment which follows a quite common structure in German art education. And the person who proposed it was convinced that it is "modern" because it involves digital media, which is definitily not common in Germany. But what is the basic idea of this assignment? What core competency do students possess, or better show, if they are able to complete this assignment? When can we say that the students have done a good job?

1. In the first part of the assignment (Take a picture of your MP3-player with headphones – or any other object – in different ways.) students can show that they are able to create different varieties. This is a competency that is generally called creativity. Thus, perhaps one could call the core competency being tested here – creativity – or more precisely: the skill to come up with a variety of solutions.
2. In the second part, students show their willingness to make a choice and show their ability to judge their own product. As a further step in this process they show their skills to present their product well. One can see that the main competencies demanded in this part of the assignment are the ability to judge and to present.
3. In the last part students can show their analytical ability when they compare two pictures. This stresses the skills of awareness, perception, and analysis.

A diagram can explain the relationship between the different competencies that are asked for in this assignment.

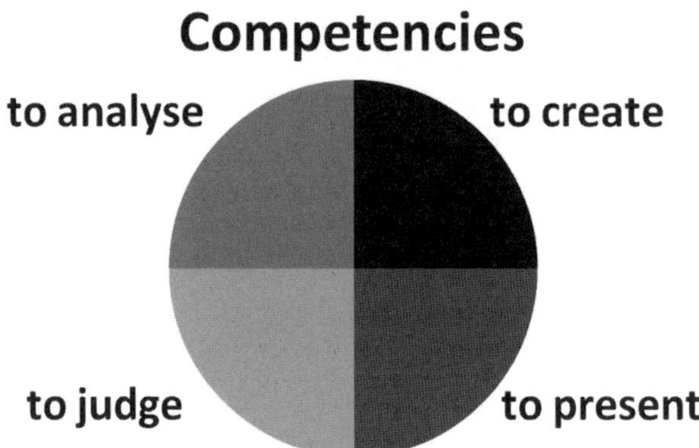

Figure 1: Dimensions of visual competency.

Furthermore, when we look at the relationship between the two most important dimensions of competency in art education, which are reception and production (receptive and productive elements of a lesson), we see a ratio that may be typical for Germany. The third part of the assignment stresses the receptional processes (analysing and interpreting pictures), whereas the first two parts are supposed to encourage a production of pictures (creating, arranging, and composing). The term "picture" is used as a synonym including all visual products from art lessons.

One can describe the relationship between reception and production in terms of literacy, as the ability to read (perceive) and write (produce). The whole assignment combines both dimensions: reception and production. The combination of these dimensions is a typical characteristic of assignments in Germany, at least for written assignments in tests and examinations (Figure 2). I want to emphasize here the necessary differentiation between

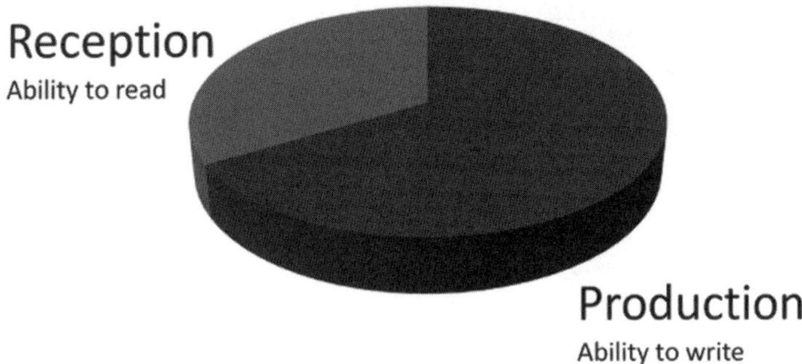

Figure 2: Relationship between different competencies.

written and oral assignments: I would phrase a written assignment differently from an oral one. In Germany, assignments are usually given orally, unless you are dealing with final exams. With oral assignments, the teacher is able to correct and explain them during the regular classroom discourse. The precise language I am dealing with here is only necessary for written assignments and examinations. But there is an imbalance between productive and receptive approaches and activities. Looking at art lessons in German schools, productive processess are clearly dominant, thus fostering and demanding creative products.

The assignment I am presenting here does not give the students any clues for criteria that may help them to complete the assignment successfully. Possible criteria might be, for example,

- Use of focal length
- Depth of field
- Cropping the picture
- Camera perspective
- Lighting
- Arrangement and presentation of the object

These criteria are also very useful clues for the teacher because they help grade and assess the assignment. (Grades and assessments are considered in this context as a diagnostic tool, i.e. to give feedback. The students can use this feedback to find out in which areas they are already firm and in which areas they need support.) Usually it is not necessary to phrase the criteria in such a precise way because students, as well as teachers, will understand the assignment without them. However, this is only true for those who are familiar with these kinds of assignments as well as the criteria that are taught in the lessons before.

If one looks at the assignment in regards to the definition of competency (including knowledge, skills, and attitude), the dimension of knowledge is missing in the assignment.

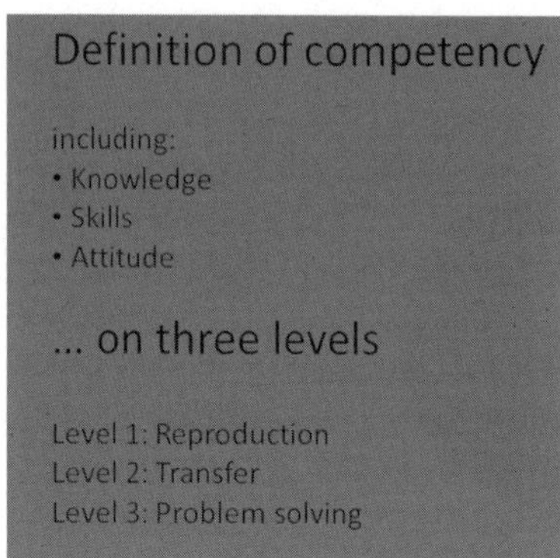

Figure 3: The concept of competency.

Depending on the age of the students to whom the assignment is given one can also distinguish between different levels of expected performance. In Germany, we are used to differentiating between three levels (s. Figure 3).

Discussion of the proposal

The assignment we are dealing with led to discussions between the authors, where the following aspects were criticized:

- Using MP3 players that belong to the students: consumption is very important for teenagers, at least in Germany. Status symbols, such as MP3 players, lead to social distinction. If a student does not own the "right" MP3 player, this can lead to social exclusion.
- Using MP3 players also seems problematic regarding artistic aspects. An MP3 player is a product which is very flat and plain. Its streamlined design may be interesting – if you are dealing with design history. But it is not a good reason for an artistic activity especially for average students in a normal school. There are other objects that might be more challenging and motivating.
- It is not clear, what criteria students could use to choose their photos for the second part of the assignment? Should they choose a picture according to their own personal preferences? Or should they choose one which could be used for an advertisement? A photo which has been transformed? A picture which could be used for a wanted poster? Should the photo be used as a graphic gag for the cover of an art magazine? One has to consider the context, in which the picture should be used, as part of the assignment.
- Furthermore, the comparison between the professional and the student's solution seems to be problematic. Calling one of the photos "a photo taken by a professional

photographer" already includes a judgement, which may probably be correct, but which is rather demotivating for students. They will read: "Your solution is not professional."

- Finally, the main point of criticism was that the decisions the student has to make are not reflected during the whole process of completing the assignment. How the assignment is structered now, students will never reflect on a meta-level about what they are actually doing, they will only use their learned skills in creating, analysing, presenting, and judging.

Further development of the assignment

As a follow-up, the authors discussed possibilities of alternative phrasing, which was meant polemically at first. Although it was not meant to be serious then, certain qualities became visible later on. The assignment was rewritten as follows:

1. Take a picture of anything, in any way.
2. Choose anything from your results and present it anywhere and anyhow.
3. Look for another picture somewhere and compare one of your photos with it.

This phrasing was originally meant to expose an open assignment as an assignment that you can complete however you like. But this assignment, which gives the student a lot of freedom, is probably the version that is most competency-based, in regards to Level 3, problem solving (Level 2 refers to transfer, Level 1 to reproduction). Students are asked to be as organized and self-reliant as possible. Over and above that, this assignment makes students define the goals they want to reach on their own. It makes students think about and understand the actual assignment and it makes them find strategies to reach their goal.

The ability to act in such an autonomous way is closely linked to a corresponding attitude of the student. From the point of view of the psychology of learning, high motivation in the student is a prerequisite to find a good solution for the assignment: is the student motivated at all to create something new? Will they be motivated long enough, until a (good) solution is found? Are they willing and able to structure the assignment reasonably? Are they able to find their own approach to the topic? Are they willing to interpret the topic creatively and especially independently? These are important characteristics of *methodical and personal skills* which have to be taken into account.

Another version might be interesting here, although it was quickly rejected as being too narrow because it does not leave any scope and, thus, no possibility for *methodical and personal* competences and capacities. (Even though Internet research at google.at already gives a wide range of possible solutions – see Figure 4.)

1. Take a picture of a clothes pin. Use different photographic means to reach different statements and effects.

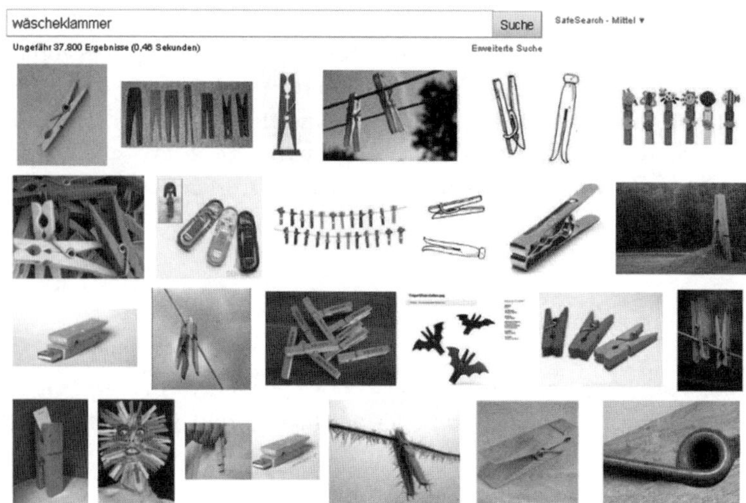

Figure 4: Screenshot google.at search for "Wascheklammer" (25 March 2011).

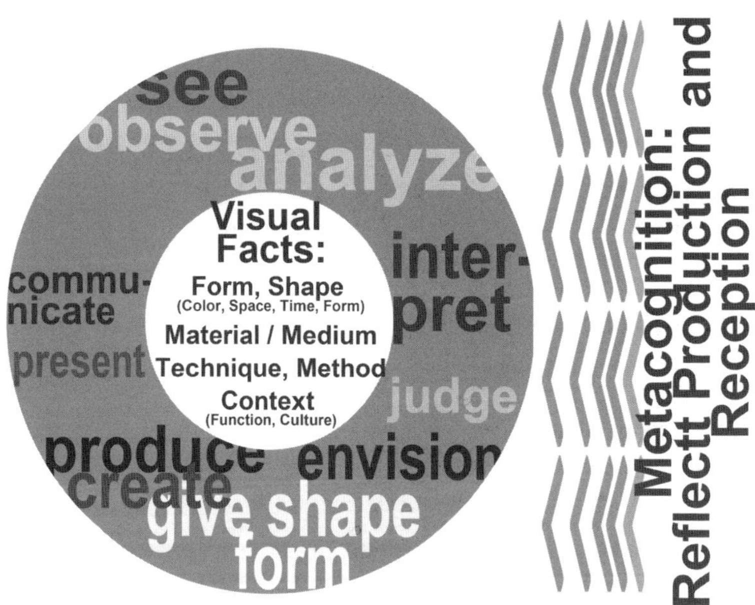

Figure 5: Competency model of "visual literacy".

2. Choose three of your photos for a fancy photo story. Use image editing software and print your pictures. Comment on your course of action.
3. Choose one picture of a clothes pin from the Internet and compare one of your pictures with it in a written text. (Make a comment as well about how much the pictures are comparable.)

In the end, we chose a fourth version, which was finally published:

1. Look at the object you have chosen carefully and draw or take notes about aspects that come to your mind.
2. Take pictures of the object, which show different meanings. Be careful to use photographic techniques which fulfil your purpose.
3. Choose three different photos from your results to reach an aim which has been defined by you. Present your pictures and your ideas in a short presentation of about five minutes.

The discussion was based on a competency model of "Visual Literacy". It might be helpful for a better understanding of the discourses, to show this model in a visualization at the end.

Reference

Schuster, U., Wagner, E. (2010). New Ways to Conceptualize Classroom Assignments, *Kunst+Unterricht*, 341, 5–32.

PART III

Research paradigms on evaluation and assessment
at schools and beyond

Chapter 11

The U-curve going Dutch: Cultural differences in artistic
graphic development

Folkert Haanstra, Utrecht University/Amsterdam School of the Arts;
Marie-Louise Damen, VU University Amsterdam; Marjo van Hoorn, National
Knowledge Institute on Arts Education and Amateur Arts, Utrecht.

Abstract

The U-curve model of graphic development posits a decline in aesthetic production in middle childhood. This theoretical model has been criticized for having an underlying western and modernist bias and a number of empirical studies have tried to confirm or disprove its assumptions. This study is a partial replication of previous research that was done to challenge U-curve findings in order to show that the model reflects cultural-specific aesthetic judgements, rather than universal trends. To demonstrate this, artists and art educators from different cultural backgrounds judged a cross-cultural collection of drawings by children from different age groups (5-, 8-, 11-, and 14-year-olds), adult non-artists, and artists. The results indicate that differences in the cultural background of the judges generated different developmental patterns in aesthetic production.

Introduction

Studio work (making artworks) is central to art education in both primary and secondary education in the Netherlands. The assessment of the artwork of students produced as part of this curriculum is, however, often considered problematic (Haanstra and Schönau, 2007). This is especially the case in primary education, where achievement levels in art are difficult to make explicit as teachers have to take into account the large cognitive and psychomotor developmental differences of their pupils. A further complicating factor is the fact that teachers also have their own aesthetic values and preferences and these preferences can be different from what their pupils would consider good drawings and paintings. This is demonstrated in self-initiated art of students outside school, which often shows that students have wider visual repertoires and preferences than the ones that are taught and approved of in school (Haanstra, 2010).

Imaginative use of visual language and a unique personal expression are valued in western art. These characteristics can also be found in the unconventional graphic products of young children, which have led to comparisons being made between the work of pre-school children and the work of adult artists. This led Gardner and Winner to propose in 1982 the existence of a U-shaped developmental pattern which was based on the observation that young children's paintings and drawings possess an aesthetic merit similar to that of adult

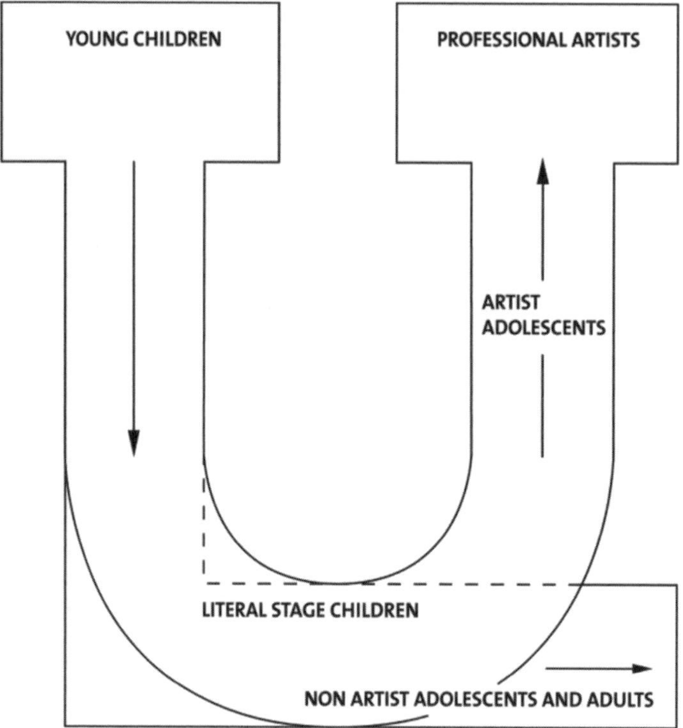

Figure 1: The U- and L-curve model of artistic graphic development (Davis, 1991).

artists whereas a decline in aesthetic merit could be seen in the artworks of older children. The upper-left point of the U represents the aesthetic value attached to drawings of young children (playful, direct, expressive, without inhibition) and is followed by a decline in middle childhood (the downward slope of the U). At this point in their development, Gardner and Winner stated, children are governed by the psychological principle of literalism, strive to acquire socially accepted skills, and wish to exhibit conventional adult behaviour. They start to copy, go in search of realism, or adopt a cartoon-like style. Children that are artistically persistent move forward in their development and ascend to the upper-right point of the U. However, as most people stop drawing and painting regularly after middle childhood they never make the ascent and their development can be characterized by an L (Literal) (Davis, 1991).

In terms of Goodman's art theory (1984), the drawings of middle childhood literally represent or denote objects. Such drawings hardly ever show expression or emotion through the use of symbols or the metaphorical use of line, colour, shape, and/or composition. The works of professional artists and young children show both literal denotation and metaphorical expression. According to Goodman, this sense of metaphorical expression is one of the aesthetic features that distinguishes art from non-art.

The U-shape hypothesis attracted a number of critics offering alternative hypotheses. Wilson (1981); Clarke (1981); Duncum (1986); and Korzenik (1995) argued that the assessment criteria used by Gardner and Winner seamlessly fitted the typical 20th century western conception of modernism, with its strong emphasis on formal and expressive elements. In his review of the then current material, Duncum (1986) concluded that the adherents of the theory not only disagreed on the actual period of decline but were also unclear about the purported decline manifested in the artworks of children. This led him to state that the U-curve represents aesthetic preference instead of artistic development and he therefore considered the model as being normative and based on western art traditions. This was a point recognized by Gardner and Winner (1982, p. 157), who called for studies in different cultures to put their findings in perspective and to determine whether the decrease in aesthetic quality in middle childhood is a genuine western or rather a universal phenomenon.

Growing body of research

In 1991, Jessica Davis finished her dissertation "Artistry lost: U-shaped development in graphic symbolization". She indicated the exact period and features of the decline and tested the theory in a cross-sectional study. Subjects from six age/expertise groups (5-, 8-, 11-, 14-year-olds, – both talented and non-talented – and adults, both non-artists and artists) were each given the task to make a "happy", a "sad" and an "angry" drawing. The drawings were judged by two experts against overall expression of the aesthetic dimensions, overall balance, use of line, and use of composition as appropriate to the emotion being expressed. On the whole, the results confirmed the hypothesis of U-shaped development.

Pariser and Van den Berg (1997) then challenged Davis's claim of a general pattern in artistic development six years later. They replicated her study using drawings by Chinese-Canadian subjects and called in the expertise of two American and two Chinese-Canadian judges. The US judges' appraisals fitted a U-curve, whereas the Chinese-Canadian judges consistently scored the drawings of the youngest group the lowest. In addition to Davis's protocol of judgement, they also gave the experts a less structured task. They had to sort the drawings into three piles: one pile for drawings they considered the best, another pile for the poorest, and a last one for average drawings. The results of the less structured task did not differ much from the results on the basis of the data collected with Davis's protocol. This led the authors to conclude that the replication study strongly suggested the U-curve model is indeed an artefact of the western modernist aesthetic values. They claimed that the Chinese-Canadian judges considered mastering graphic skills to be more important than developing artistic expression.

To test this hypothesis Pariser and Van den Berg set up a follow-up study in 2001. Two new experts had to sort the drawings by the criterion "technical skills". Pariser and Van den Berg subsequently calculated the correlations between the skill scores and the aesthetic scores.

The results showed a strong correlation between the Chinese-Canadian judges' aesthetic judgements and the measure of technical or graphical skill that was independently arrived at. As for the western judges, their aesthetic judgements of non-artists' drawings did not correlate with the scores they gave for graphical skill. However, when it came to judging the artists' drawings, the correlations between aesthetic judgement and the judgement of technical skills of the western judges are on a par with those of the Chinese-Canadian judges.

Two other studies, one in Taiwan (Kindler, 2000) and one in Great Britain (Jolley, Fenn and Jones, 2004) also failed to support the U-curve hypothesis. The difference between Kindler's study and the previous ones, was that Kindler did not have drawings made that expressed emotions (happiness, sadness, anger), but rather asked to make drawings of "a person", "a classmate sitting next to you", and a cartoon. Moreover, she not only used pairs of adult expert judges, but also pairs of judges representing the age groups of 8-, 11-, and 14-year-olds. Like Pariser she had the judges rate the drawings in three categories. The judges perceived a consistent increase in artistry with no decline in artistic skill in middle and late childhood. Unlike the young judges, the adults considered cartoon drawings significantly inferior to the other types of drawing. Kindler considers it pedagogically relevant that students' aesthetic criteria and artistic aspirations are at odds with those of their art teachers.

Jolley, Fenn and Jones (2004) had happy and sad drawings made by British 4–12-year-olds. Two pairs of judges rated the expressiveness of the drawings. Quantity of expressive devices was measured in the number of appropriate expressive content themes and formal properties evident in a drawing. Quality was measured on a Likert scale on the extent to which the drawing expressed the intended mood. No decline in expressiveness of the drawings of the older children was found. Instead both qualitative and quantitative expressiveness increased with age.

In their discussion of Davis's study, Pariser and Van den Berg concluded that the perspective of the study had changed from being about the "true" nature of the drawings to the assumptions of the judges in relation to differences in the judges' age, expertise, and cultural background. Given this change in perspective, it was considered crucial to ensure that the judges would be representative of the populations from which they were drawn and therefore future studies would have to be based on larger samples of culturally diverse judges. This was realized in a large scale study (Pariser et al., 2007) in which drawings were judged by 192 judges who differed in age and expertise (8-year-olds, 14-year-olds, adult non-artists, and adult artists) from Brazil, Canada, and Taiwan. Drawings were made by 360 children and adults (5-, 8-, 11-, and 14-year-olds, adult non-artists, and artists). Half of the subjects made happy, sad, and angry drawings (the Davis assignments) and the other half made an image that showed the route from home to school or work, a favourite cartoon figure, and a narrative drawing showing people.

An important finding was that the modernist aesthetic values are not widely shared. A U-shaped curve was produced by only 29% of the adult artists. Far more prevalent among all judge groups (regardless of country) was that aesthetic value is largely associated with technical skills that improve with age. The results also showed that on average all Brazilian judges preferred the drawings of their fellow countrymen whereas the Taiwanese judged precisely opposite. The Canadian judges showed no preferences in this respect.

The U-curve research provides opportunities to study the extent to which judgements might be influenced by an inherited intuitive sense, by culture as well as by education and experience. Starting with Davis's dissertation study from 1991 several U-curve studies with conflicting outcomes have been carried out. They were not exact replications, as there were changes in the drawing assignments, the judgement protocols, as well as variations in the age groups, the cultural backgrounds, and the number of judges. Davis trained two expert judges to use a number of formal criteria. The 2007 study by Pariser and others involved almost 200 judges who could choose their own criteria on which to base their judgement of the aesthetic value of the drawings. This change in approach mirrors the shift from studying the "true nature" of graphic artistic development to allowing variation in the ways in which judges conceive of artistic graphic development. We wanted to test the U-curve theory in a different context to contribute to the international debate on this topic and decided to do a replication study that was modelled after the latter design.

The Dutch context

The present study was carried out in the context of Dutch art education. An important recent change in Dutch education is the increase of students from different cultural backgrounds. This applies especially to schools in large cities where students of non-western backgrounds are in the majority in half of the primary and secondary schools (CBS, 2004). The premise of the research is to find out how art educators assess the artwork of these students. Do they judge their work according to modernist criteria or otherwise? And how would professionals, like art educators or artists with a different cultural background, assess students' artwork?

As in many western countries art education in the Netherlands is built on a strong modernist tradition with roots in both the formal and functionalist principles of the Bauhaus curriculum and starting from a child-centred approach which has creative self-expression as the principal goal. Art education has been renewing itself in the past few decades but nonetheless, many features of Efland's (1976) school art style can still be discerned in primary education. In secondary education, many art classes consist of studio art with skill-based exercises in elements and principles of design. Formal and expressive qualities prevail in assessments in both primary and secondary education (Haanstra, 2001).

In the Dutch case, it makes sense to compare both artwork and judgements from people with an Islamic background because this is the cultural background of two of the largest immigrant groups in the Netherlands – the Turkish and Moroccan communities. In Islamic culture a taboo on the portrayal of living beings exists, although this is by no means a universal taboo, as it differs depending on the time period and country being studied (e.g. De Groot, 2001). Cox (1993) claims that research shows that in cultures or communities "which have no established tradition of representational art", on average the "draw a man performances" are quite minimal. Research in Turkey unmistakably shows differences between drawings of children and adults coming from the city and the countryside. Cox adds that it is to be expected that "Muslim children perform relatively low on human figure drawing tasks" (p. 106) as there is a strong abstract decorative tradition in Muslim countries. However, it is important to note that the official Turkish art education curriculum does not propose a ban on images of living beings and figurative representation is generally accepted (Soganci, 2005). On the other hand, in the Netherlands several Islamic schools do prohibit making images of people and animals or at least try to prevent students from doing so (Paulides and Korthals, 2007).

There is hardly any controlled empirical data about the production and assessment of artwork made by Dutch population groups with different cultural backgrounds. There are, however, relevant studies concerning the so called "culture sensitivity" of the "draw-a-man test" – an updated version of the Goodenough test (1926). This test is being used to determine the cognitive development level of children and youngsters and is supposed to be "culturally fair". This hypothesis is not beyond reasonable doubt and therefore provoked a certain body of research. Van de Vijfeijken and Vedder (2000) examined if the assessed quality of drawings differed between children resident in the Netherlands of which both parents are born in the Netherlands, Turkey, or Morocco. In their study, quality did not refer to aesthetic merit but had to do with the representation of certain characteristics such as eyes, eyebrows, nostrils, ears, and the like. The number of characteristics present in a drawing was an indication for the developmental level. Their results showed no significant differences between Dutch, Turkish, or Moroccan children regarding the average number of items drawn. According to Van de Vijfeijken and Vedder this can be explained by the fact that all three groups grew up in the Netherlands and hence share the same experiences acquired in school and through the media.

The changing student population was one of the topics in a study investigating the current art education beliefs and practices in lower secondary education in Amsterdam (Haanstra, Van Strien and Wagenaar, 2006). Outcomes of interviews with teachers showed that although the increased diversity of cultural backgrounds is of influence on pedagogical practice, teachers neither changed subject matter nor assessment criteria. On the contrary, a substantial number of those teaching in schools with students of mixed cultural backgrounds expressly try not to address these differences. Their rationale stretches from the danger of stigmatizing to the fear of conflicts that might bubble up.

The influence of culture on the making and assessing of visual products can be examined in many different ways. We have taken the U-curve model of graphic development as our starting point for the purposes of this research. The study has two aims: firstly, to contribute to the international discussion concerning the model and secondly, to contribute to the still modest discussion concerning the aesthetic evaluation of children's and young people's artwork in an era in which Dutch schools show a growing culturally diverse population.

Research questions

Building on previous studies on the U-curve hypothesis, the first question of this study is:

1. What are the similarities and differences between Dutch, Moroccan, and Turkish judges if they respond to drawings of subjects from Dutch, Moroccan, and Turkish origin?

The drawings were judged on "overall aesthetic merit", according to the less structured task of Pariser and Van den Berg (2001). In the Pariser and Van den Berg study (2001) drawings were also judged on "technical skills" with a view to learning whether this particular criterion allowed for differences in aesthetic assessments. Technical skills are thought to be more traditional and conventional, referring to craftsmanship. Our second question is based on both the Davis (1991) and Pariser and Van den Berg (2001) studies:

2. What are the differences between judgements by Dutch, Moroccan, and Turkish judges based on the criteria "expression" and "technical skills" when judging drawings of Dutch, Moroccan, and Turkish subjects of different ages and expertise and how do these judgements relate to judgements of aesthetic merit?

Method

We gathered a collection of drawings from 162 children and adults with three different cultural backgrounds: Dutch, Turkish, and Moroccan, all living in the Netherlands. The subjects were – similar to previous research – 5-, 8-, 11-, and 14-year-olds, adult non-artists, visual artists, and art educators. Each of them made two drawings. The first was a replication of the "draw sad" assignment in the Davis study. The material constraints were similar too: make a drawing with a black medium-point felt marker on A4 white paper (8.5 × 11 inch). The second drawing was a self-portrait. Conditions were less constrained for this assignment, allowing subjects to choose both the materials and colour they wanted to use. Paper size was A3 (12 × 16.5 inch). Examples of six self-portraits and six "draw sad" drawings are shown below.

The drawings were judged on aesthetic merit by 133 Dutch, Moroccan, and Turkish artists and art educators. They gave the drawings that were perceived as "good" a score 5, "medium" a score 3, and "poor" a score 1. Additionally, a selection of 36 drawings was assessed on the criteria technical skills and expression. This selection consisted of one sad drawing and one self-portrait from 18 different people, representing all three cultural backgrounds and all six age and expertise groups. With this limited amount of drawings a more manageable judgment task was accomplished.

Judges did not judge the actual works; instead they reviewed scans of the drawings online. An Internet questionnaire proved to be more convenient than sorting the actual drawings. Furthermore, it was possible to involve expert judges living in Turkey and Morocco. The

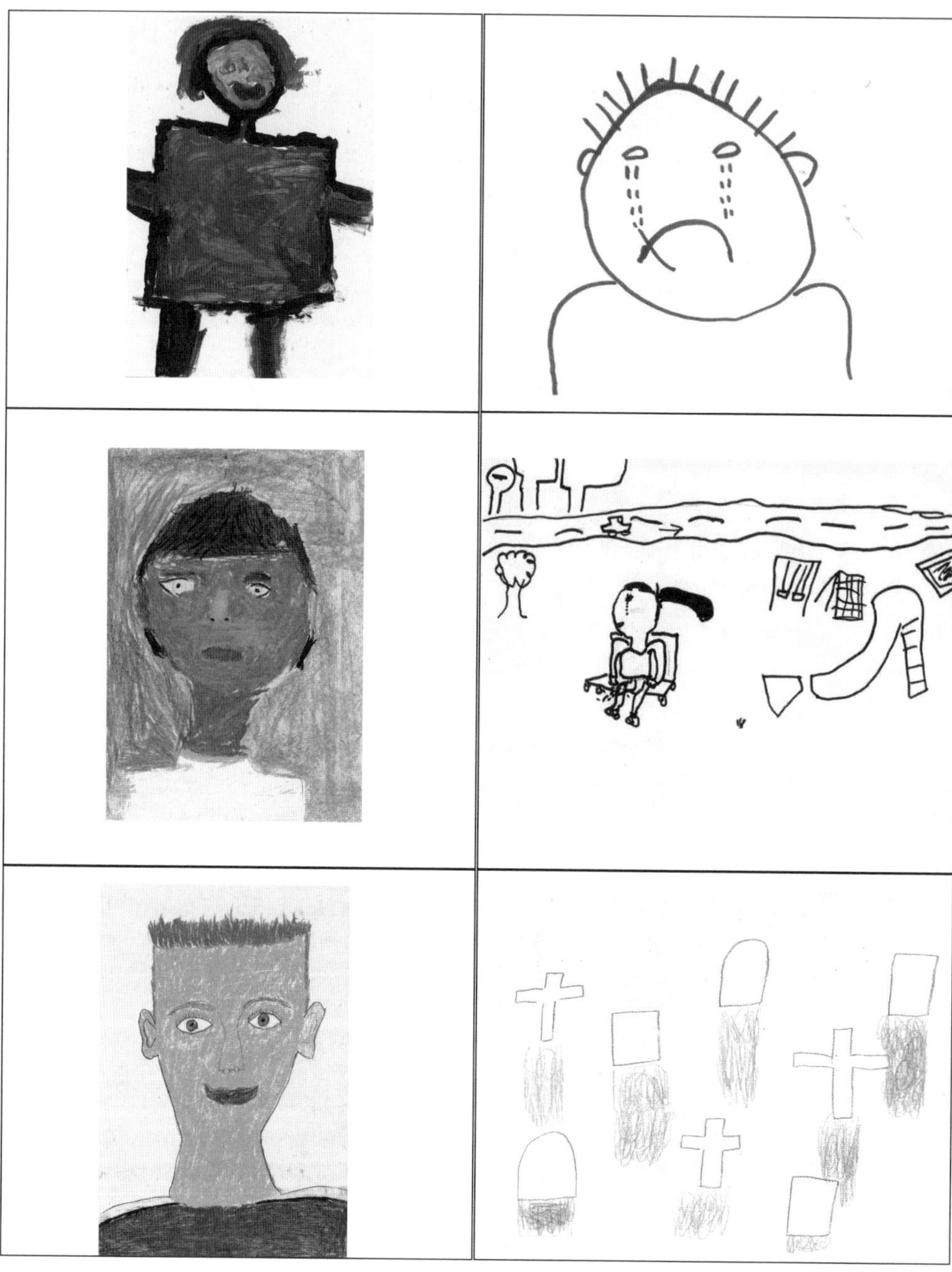

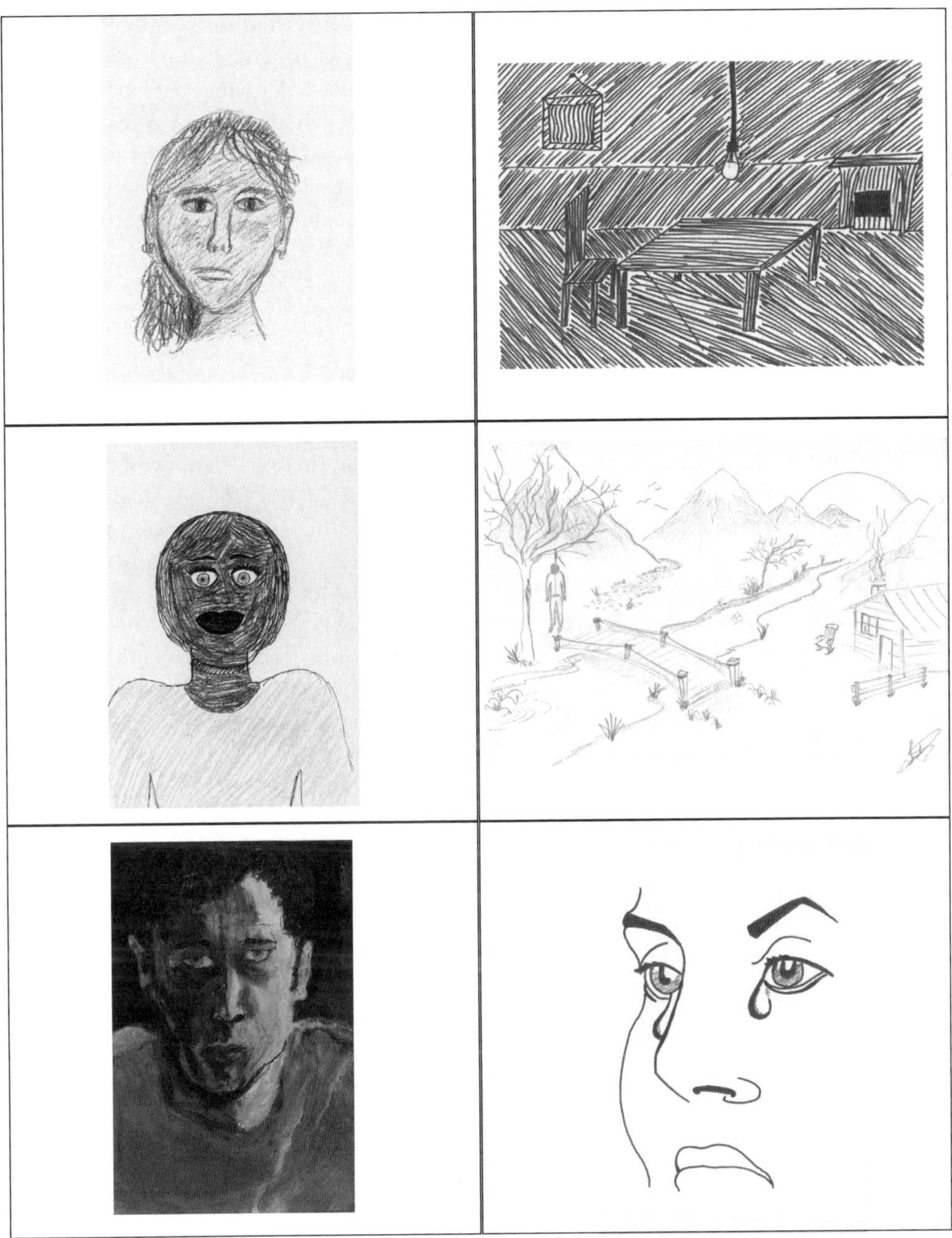

judges only received information on the drawing assignments. No information concerning age, expertise, or cultural background of the makers was provided, nor definitions of aesthetic value, expression, and technical skill. Analysis of Variance with Post Hoc tests were used to analyse the quantitative data. Lastly, qualitative data were gathered by interviewing a random sample of nine adult experts (three from each cultural background) on their judgement process. All nine graduated from art academies and are currently working as visual artists. Three of them were employed as art teachers in secondary education.

Patterns of aesthetic judgement

The first result concerns the average aesthetic judgement scores for both drawings of the six age/expertise groups by the judges. Self-portraits got a higher average rating than "draw sad", but their sorting patterns across the different age/expertise levels did not differ. Figure 2 illustrates the three general developmental patterns. There are significant differences between the age/expertise groups of the makers: $F (5, 22165) = 266.46$, p. < .001. The drawings from the professional artists are rated highest (mean 3.7). There are also significant differences between the cultural backgrounds of the judges: $F (2, 22165) = 90.24$, p. < .001. The Turkish judges are the most positive, whereas the Moroccan judges are the most critical group.

The drawings of the 5-year-olds are rated lower by the Moroccan judges than the drawings of the other age groups and their mean assessment pattern is an upward slope, whereas the Dutch and Turkish judges assess the drawings of the 8-year-olds and the 11-year-olds lower than the drawings of the youngest children. Their assessment patterns show the beginnings of a U-curve. In statistical terms: there is a significant interaction between age/expertise of subjects and cultural background of judges: $F (10, 22165) = 11.19$, p. < .001.

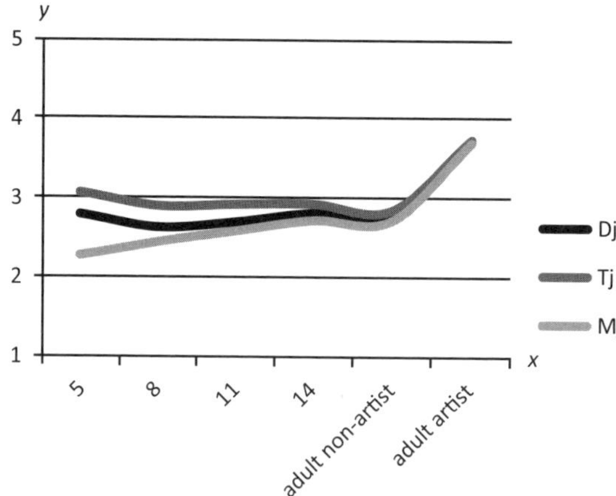

Figure 2: Mean assessment patterns of aesthetic value of drawings from six age/expertise groups by three groups of judges of different cultural background (Turkish, Moroccan, Dutch).

The average developmental patterns as shown in Figure 2 do not suggest that all judges from the same cultural background produce the same patterns. Pariser et al. (2007) distinguished four basic typical patterns based on the average scores of the drawings of the six age/expertise groups: the U-curve (the modernist view); the inverted U-curve (the anti modernist view), the linear upward slope (the traditionalist view), and the flat line (no aesthetic preference). The patterns were arrived at by operational definitions. For example, to be classified as a U-curve, at least three of the four intermediate average scores for drawings by 8-, 11-, and 14-year-olds and adult non-artists have to be both lower than those for drawings by 5-year-olds and by adult artists. In our study, 43% of the Dutch and 48% of the Turkish experts assess the drawings in line with the U-curve theory whereas only 8% of the Moroccan judges do so (Table 1).

In the next analyses not only the different cultural background of the judges is taken into account, but also the cultural background of the subjects who made the drawings. Figure 3 shows the mean assessment scores of the three groups of judges. It is based on the factorial ANOVA with both the cultural background of the subjects and the cultural background of the judges as sources of variation.

There is a significant effect of the cultural background of the subjects: the mean rating of the Dutch drawings is higher than the rating of the Turkish and Moroccan drawings: $F (2, 22174) = 71.3, p. < .001$. As we saw already in Figure 2, there are also significant differences between the cultural backgrounds of the judges: the Turkish judges are the most positive $F (2, 22174) = 95.6, p. < .001$. Apart from the significant main effects as a result of these factors, there is no significant interaction between the cultural background of the judges and

Table 1:   Percentages of judges' sorting patterns.

	Expert Judge Categories			
Sorting pattern	Turkish	Moroccan	Dutch	Average%
U-curve	48	8	43	41
Inverted U	3	-	2	2
Linear upward	10	17	17	14
Zig-zag	39	75	38	43
Total %	100	100	100	100

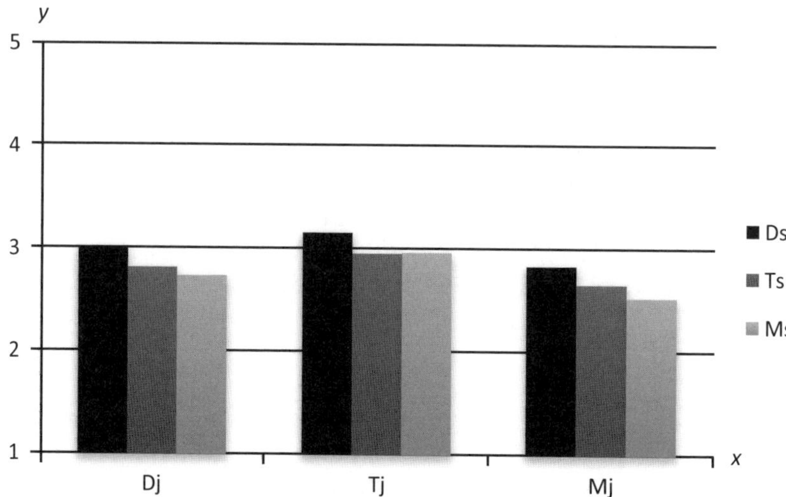

Figure 3: Mean assessments of aesthetic value of drawings from three groups of subjects of different cultural background (Turkish, Moroccan, Dutch) of all age/expertise groups by three groups of judges of different cultural background (Turkish, Moroccan, Dutch).

the background of the subjects who made the drawings, as Figure 3 shows. On average, the Dutch drawings are rated highest whatever the cultural background of the judges.

The comparison of the mean assessment scores of the Dutch, Turkish, and Moroccan drawings by three groups of expert judges can also be made for the drawings of the different age/expertise groups separately. The results show that significantly higher mean ratings for

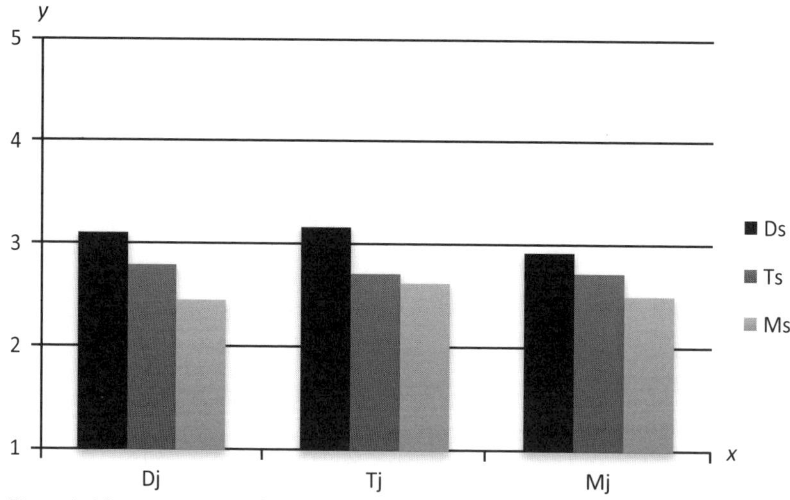

Figure 4: Mean assessments of aesthetic value of drawings from three groups of adult non-artists of different cultural background (Turkish, Moroccan, Dutch) by three groups of judges of different cultural background (Turkish, Moroccan, Dutch).

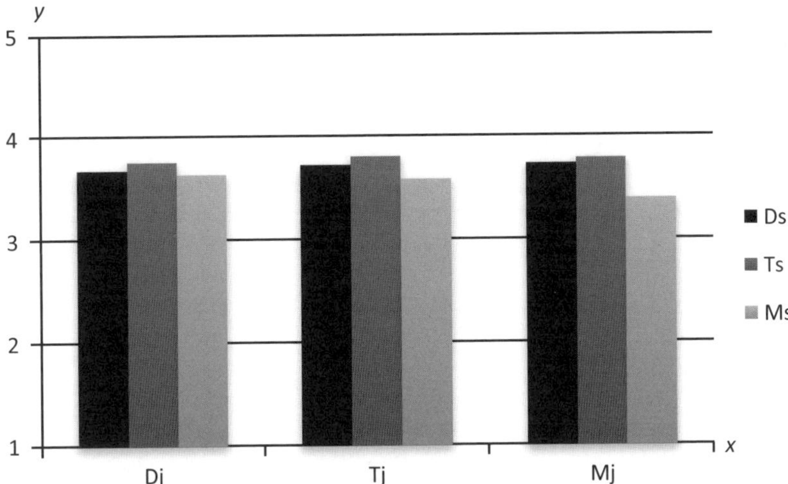

Figure 5: Mean assessments of aesthetic value of drawings from three groups of adult artists of different cultural background (Turkish, Moroccan, Dutch) by three groups of judges of different cultural background (Turkish, Moroccan, Dutch).

the Dutch drawings are given to the drawings of the 14-year-olds and the non-artistic adults, but no significant differences were found between the ratings of drawings from subjects' different cultural backgrounds for the 5-year-olds, the 8-year-olds, the 11-year-olds, and the professional artists. To show some examples, we have included the results of the mean scores for the drawings of the adult non-artists as well as those of the artists (Figures 4 and 5).

Assessment of expression and technical skills

Following the assessment of the drawings on aesthetic value, the 133 art teachers and visual artists judged 36 drawings on two additional criteria: expression and technical skills. A four-point scale was used, ranging from 1 (least expressive/least technical skills) to 4 (most expressive/best technical skills). To avoid any sequence effects in the results half of the experts first judged technical skills and after that, expression, and the other half vice versa.

The factorial ANOVA with assessment of expression as the dependent variable shows a main effect for the factor age/skill of the subjects (Figure 6): $F (5, 3834) = 51.66$, $p < .001$ as well as a main effect for the factor cultural background of the judges: $F (2, 3834) = 14.57$, $p < .001$. There is a significant interaction between the age/expertise factors of the subjects and cultural background of the judges: $F (10, 3834) = 4.31$, $p < .001$. The analyses of the Turkish and Dutch judges show no significant difference between Dutch average scores for the drawings of the 5-year-olds and adult artists. All other age groups show significantly lower scores. However, this does not apply to the Moroccan judges; they considered the 5-year-olds just as low on

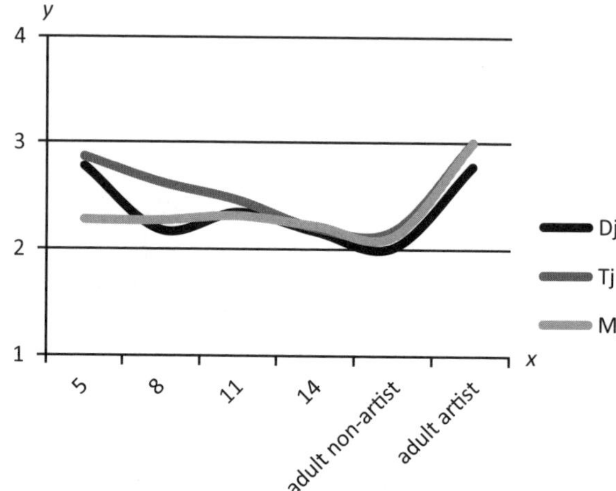

Figure 6: Mean assessments of expressive value of drawings from six age/expertise groups by three groups of judges of different cultural background (Turkish, Moroccan, Dutch).

expression as the 8-year-olds, the 11-year-olds, and the 14-year-olds. Neither the Dutch and Turkish assessment patterns, following a U-curve, nor the Moroccan assessment pattern are in line with the slow increase in expressiveness with age that Jolley (2010) found in his studies. The ANOVA with the assessment of "technical skills" as the dependent variable shows a main effect for age/expertise of the subject: $F_{(5, 3870)} = 157.23$, p. < .001. The assessment pattern (Figure 7) illustrates that the adult artists significantly differ from the rest with their highest mean score, while the 5-year-olds and 8-year-olds get the lowest scores. The 11-year-olds and 14-year-olds and non-artistic adults are in between those two low scores but

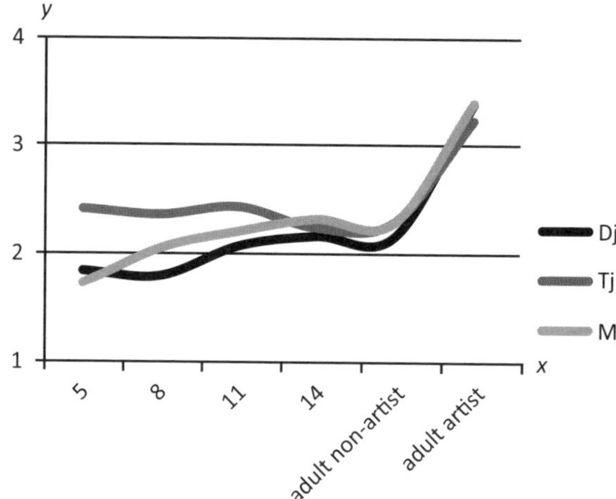

Figure 7: Mean assessments of technical ability of drawings from six age/expertise groups by three groups of judges of different cultural background (Turkish, Moroccan, Dutch).

Table 2: Correlations between aesthetic judgments and judgments on expression and technical skill.

	Expression and aesthetic judgment	Technical skill and aesthetic judgment	Technical skill and expression
All 36 drawings	.54	.56	.48
Drawings 5-yr-olds	.59	.43	.38
Drawings adult artists	.59	.57	.54

no progression is shown in these age groups. There is also a significant effect for cultural background of the judges F (2, 3870) = 32.51, p. < .001. The judges with a Turkish background again are the most positive while the Dutch judges are the most critical. There is also a significant interaction effect F (10, 3870) = 8.11, p < .001. The sorting patterns of both Dutch and Moroccan judges have a linear upward trend, whereas the pattern of the Turkish shows no difference between the three youngest age groups.

The dissimilar sorting patterns in Figures 6 and 7 illustrate that expression and technical skill are clearly distinctive assessment criteria. Table 2 shows the correlations between the two criteria and aesthetic judgement and it is clear that they are about equally as strongly related to aesthetic judgement as to each other. The strongest correlations between technical skills and aesthetic judgement for all three groups of judges are produced by the assessment of the adult artists' drawings. These correlations are lowest for the drawings of the 5-year-olds, with the Dutch judges marking the largest difference between the two groups. This means that, in line with the findings of Pariser and Van den Berg (2001), technical skills play a less significant role in assessing the aesthetic merit of the drawings of the 5-year-olds than in assessing those of the adult artists.

The experts who were interviewed as part of the project gave an overview of the criteria on which they based their judgement. For the first general exercise they indicated they were looking for originality as well as power of expression, which was directly linked to the broader criterion of expression. One expert summarized it as "uniqueness and expression, a feeling of genuineness: have the creators put something of themselves into their work".

The interviews also made clear that generally there was a distinct awareness of the different age groups that took part in the exercise. This factor played a role in the assessment of certain drawings, either leading to a milder or a more critical appraisal. For example, one expert's recognition of a self-portrait by a 5-year-old led to a higher rating of the drawing because the quality of the drawing was considered to be particularly high, given the creator's age. In another case, an expert remarked that he gave a milder assessment as it was clear that a child had made a particular drawing and put a lot of effort into his work. The youngest age-group were assessed highly, praised for the spontaneity of their work and the simple, but striking, manner of expression.

Conclusion and discussion

This study is a partial replication of previous studies on the U-curved pattern of artistic development, which posit a decline in aesthetic production in middle childhood. The original study by Davis (1991) supports the view of a "universal U-curve development", while later studies hold a relativistic position and indicate that differences in the age, expertise and cultural background of the judges lead to different developmental patterns. Outcomes of this study confirm the latter position: while a substantial number of Turkish and Dutch judges produce a modernist U-curve in their assessments, the vast majority of judges with a Moroccan background do not. The Moroccan judges on the whole rate the drawings of the 5-year-olds lower than the drawings of children in middle childhood. When asked to assess the drawings according to the criterion expression, the differences between the Turkish and Dutch judges on the one hand and the Moroccan judges on the other became even more obvious.

The question arises as to how we can explain the fact that the views of the Turkish judges are just as modernist as those of their Dutch colleagues, whereas Moroccan judges hold more traditional views. One explanation perhaps lies in the fact that although Islam has influenced the art of both Turkey and Morocco, there are substantial historical differences. The Turkish art world has been more orientated towards the West since the 19th century than the artistic community in Morocco. This western tradition in Turkey was strengthened after the foundation of the Turkish Republic in 1923. "Western iconography", for example, is dominant in art education in Turkish public schools (Soganci, 2005, p. 26). In Morocco, by contrast, the Islamic ornamental and decorative tradition remained dominant despite the western influence introduced into Morocco as a result of French colonialism (Benali, 2001). This is reflected in the teaching of art in all three countries. In the interviews several experts – based on their own experience – described the differences in the curricula of the contemporary art academies. They indicated that the School of Fine Arts of Casablanca (Morocco) still has a classical approach in comparison to the contemporary modern and postmodern approach in Turkish and Dutch art academies.

This fundamental difference between the different cultural notions comes through across the board. The judges had no information on the backgrounds of the subjects and that is clear in the results, which show no systematic bias of the art experts against drawings of people from a different cultural background. The fact that the Dutch drawings were rated higher was explained by some of the interviewees by the long tradition of the visual arts in the Netherlands and the resulting generally positive attitude towards drawing. Moreover, the assignments of drawing "sad" or drawing a portrait fit in the Christian western art tradition.

The results do not show significantly lower ratings for drawings of Turkish and Moroccan pre-schoolers and children in primary schools than for drawings of their Dutch peers, despite a different cultural background and drawing tasks that fit in the western tradition.

This could be explained by the fact that, through the media, Turkish and Moroccan children born in the Netherlands (the "second and third generation" immigrants) are immersed in the same, western visual culture as their Dutch peers.

Only the older age groups with a Turkish or Moroccan background, the 14-year-olds and the non-professional adults, seem at a drawback compared to their Dutch counterparts. This could be an issue for these students in secondary education as, unlike in primary education (Oomen et al., 2009), formal assessment and grading of art products forms an integral part of the curriculum. To reach more definitive conclusions on this, future research on this topic should include drawing tasks that represent a broader visual repertoire, such as an ornamental, decorative task.

We did not collect data on background variables, such as educational level and the socio-economic status of the people who made the drawings or of their parents. As these variables are related to cultural background (Van den Broek, 2006), in future research these factors ought to be collected in order to control their effects and get a more direct view of possible cultural differences.

On a final note, it is important to touch upon the fact that the use of cultural background as a variable raises certain ethical questions. Art museums and galleries in the Netherlands have become reluctant to organize exhibitions of Turkish or Moroccan contemporary art as such. This is primarily due to the fact that many artists do not want to be lumped together as "Turkish or Moroccan" artists because they believe that their country of birth has little impact on their work and identity. The marker of being primarily a Turkish or Moroccan artist does not do justice to the differences in content and style of their works (Buikema and Meijer, 2004; Thijsen, 2006). Similarly, many art teachers who teach classes with students from various different cultural backgrounds stress that all students are equal to them and that they are afraid of stigmatizing students by addressing them as representing the Turkish, Moroccan, or another culture (e.g. Haanstra, Van Strien and Wagenaar, 2006).

Nevertheless, even though one acknowledges that cultural background is neither something static nor deterministic, there is no "faceless universalism" (Lavrijsen, 1999, p. 15) in art either. Land of birth, or the country of origin of an artist's parents, and its cultural tradition do, to a greater or lesser extent, play a role in someone's identity and therefore in their art.

Wilson (2009) states that in art education research it is rare that a theory formulated on the basis of testable hypotheses gives rise to a subsequent series of empirical studies. It is clear that the theory of the U-curve is an exception to this general rule. This invites researchers who hold different paradigms on art and artistic development to study the impact of different cultural background of the judges in relation to different drawing tasks and different assessment criteria. The results of this study further underline that cultural background does – in some respects – make a difference concerning aesthetic judgements and this strengthens the call for further research into the U-curve hypothesis to gain a deeper understanding of the cultural dimension of assessment and its implications to art education practice.

References

Benali, D. (2001). *De kunst van in- en uitsluiting: De relatie van beeldende kunstenaars van Surinaamse, Turkse en Marokkaanse afkomst tot de Nederlandse gevestigde kunstwereld/The relationship between artists from Surinam, Turkey and Morocco the Dutch art world.* (Master thesis Art and Culture Studies, Rotterdam: Erasmus University, 2001.)

Buikema, R., Meijer, M. (Eds.) (2004). Kunsten in beweging, 1980–2000. *Cultuur en migratie in Nederland/Culture and migration in the Netherlands.* The Hague, the Netherlands: SDU.

CBS (2004). *Allochtonen in Nederland 2004/Ethnic groups in the Netherlands 2004.* Heerlen, the Netherlands: CBS.

Clarke, E. C. (1981). Response to Winner and Gardner. *Review of research in art education, 7* (14), 34–35.

Cox, M. (1993). *Children's drawings of the human figure.* Hove: Lawrence Erlbaum Associates Publishers.

Davis, J. (1991). Artistry lost: U-shaped development in graphic symbolization. (Unpublished Dissertation, Graduate School of Education, Harvard University, 1991.)

Duncum, P. (1986). Breaking down the U-curve of artistic development. *Visual Arts Research, 12* (1), 43–54.

Efland, A. (1976). The school art style: A functional analysis. *Studies in Art Education, 17* (2), 37–44.

Gardner, H., Winner, E. (1982). First imitations of artistry. In S. Strauss (Ed.). *U-shaped behavioral growth.* New York: Academic Press.

Goodenough, F. (1926). Measurement of intelligence by drawings. New York: World Book Co.

Goodman, N. (1984). *Of mind and other matters.* Cambridge, MA: Harvard University Press.

Groot, I. de (2001). Kunst en de Islam/Art and Islam. *Maandblad voor de beeldende vakken, 122* (3), 16–17.

Haanstra, F. (2001). *De Hollandse schoolkunst: Mogelijkheden en beperkingen van authentieke kunsteducatie/The Dutch school art style: Possibilities and limitations of authentic arts education.* Oratie. Utrecht, the Netherlands: Cultuurnetwerk Nederland.

——— (2010). Self-initiated artwork and school art. *International Journal of Art and Design Education, 29* (3), 271–282.

Haanstra, F., van Strien, E., Wagenaar, H. (2006). *Docenten en leerlingen over de lespraktijk beeldende kunst en cultuur/Teachers' and students' perceptions of art lessons and art teaching.* Amsterdam, the Netherlands: Lectoraat Kunst en Cultuureducatie AHK.

Haanstra, F., Schönau, D. (2007). Evaluation Research in Visual Arts Education. In L. Bresler (Ed.). *International Handbook of Research in Arts Education.* Dordrecht, the Netherlands: Springer. 427–442.

Jolley, R.P., Fenn, K., Jones, L. (2004). The development of children's expressive drawing. *British Journal of Developmental Psychology, 22* (4), 545–567.

Jolley, R. P. (2010). *Children & Pictures: Drawing and understanding.* Chichester, UK: Wiley-Blackwell.

Kindler, A. (2000). From the U-Curve to dragons: Culture and understanding of artistic development, *Visual Arts Research, 26* (2), 15–28.

Korzenik, D. (1995). The changing concept of artistic giftedness. In C. Golomb (Ed.). *The development of artistically gifted children*. Hillsdale, New Jersey: Erlbaum Ass. Inc, 1–30.

Lavrijsen, R. (1999). *Culturele diversiteit in de kunst/Cultural diversity in the arts*. Den Haag, the Netherlands: Elsevier.

Oomen, C., Visser, I., Donker, A., Beekhoven, S., Hoogeveen, K., Haanstra, F. (2009). *Cultuureducatie in het primair en voortgezet onderwijs: Monitor 2008–2009/Arts and heritage education in primary and secondary education: Monitor 2008–2009*. Utrecht, the Netherlands: Oberon/Sardes.

Pariser, D., Van den Berg, A. (1997). The mind of the beholder: Some provisional doubts about the U-curved aesthetic development thesis. *Studies in Art Education, 38* (3), 158–178.

—— (2001). Teaching art versus teaching taste: What art teachers can learn from looking at a cross cultural evaluation of children's art. *Poetics, 29* (6), 331–350.

Pariser, D., Kindler, A., Van den Berg, A., Dias, B., Chen Liu (2007). Does practise make perfect? Childrens' and adults' constructions of graphic merit and development: A cross-cultural study. *Visual Arts Research, 33* (65), 96–114.

Paulides, J., Korthals, H. (2007). *Kunst met de Islamitische klas / Art in Islamic schools*. Master thesis Theatre Studies, Utrecht University

Soganci, I.Ö. (2005). Mom, why isn't there a picture of our prophet? *International Journal of Education through Art, 1* (1), 21–27.

Thijsen, A. (2006). De paradox van de kunstmarokkanen/The paradox of Moroccan art. Amsterdam, the Netherlands: Stichting Upstream.

Van den Broek, A. (2006). *Comparing cultural practices: content and context of cultural activities of ethnic groups in The Netherlands*. Paper presented at Changing Cultures ESA Conference, Ghent, Belgium.

Vijfeijken, K. van de, Vedder, P. (2000), De cultuurgevoeligheid van de mens-teken-test/The cultural sensitivity of the human figure drawing test. *Pedagogische Studiën, 77* (3), 167–172.

Wilson, B. (1981). Response to Winner and Gardner. *Review of research in art education, 7* (14), 32–33.

—— (2009). Artistic development, judgements of aesthetic merit, and the U-curve: A perfect storm. In Haanstra, F.; Hoorn, M. van (Eds.). *Culturele invloeden op de esthetische beoordeling van beeldend werk/Cultural influences on the aesthetic judgement of visual arts*. Cultuur+Educatie 24. Utrecht, the Netherlands: Cultuurnetwerk Nederland.

Chapter 12

Subject- and process-oriented competencies in visual arts education

Edith Glaser-Henzer, University of Applied Sciences Northwestern Switzerland, School of Education, Switzerland

Abstract

Spatio-visual competencies form an essential basis for the development of perceptive and creative capacities in children and teenagers. They control and steer not only the perception of objects and phenomena, but also their further processing in students' individual artistic activities.

This chapter introduces the research project "raviko", a qualitative-empirical study, which identifies spatio-visual competencies and specifies levels of competencies relevant for visual arts education. It is based on innovative data-collection methods and modes of triangulation. The core finding of our analysis is the reconstruction and definition of what we term "processing competency", i.e. visual, creative, cognitive, and affective processing competencies that form the basis of children's spatial representations.

This approach permits a better understanding of children's spatial imaginations and a precise description of their artistic and representational intentions. It enables us to explain both students' heterogeneous problem-solving methods and learning strategies, and the resulting drawings. Consequently, individual strength/weaknesses can be detected, students' learning performance can be assessed, and their achievements adequately graded.

With its innovative shift from cognitivist stage models to subject- and process-oriented competencies, the findings of "raviko" connect with and contribute to the pedagogical and educational discourse around competencies and educational standards.

Introduction and research question

The project reported here,[1] to which the results of this report refer, examines the visual and spatial competencies of pupils in respect to the aesthetic experience and learning processes in art lessons of fourth- to sixth-year level. In the context of the discussion on educational standards it was necessary to define, through empirical methods, the teaching and learning targets concerning the visual and spatial perception and representation as well as their respective growth. In particular, there was a need to develop more precise criteria, which govern the discovery and invention of a personal pictorial language on the one hand, and on the other hand, characteristics of the levels of development of spatial and visual competencies.

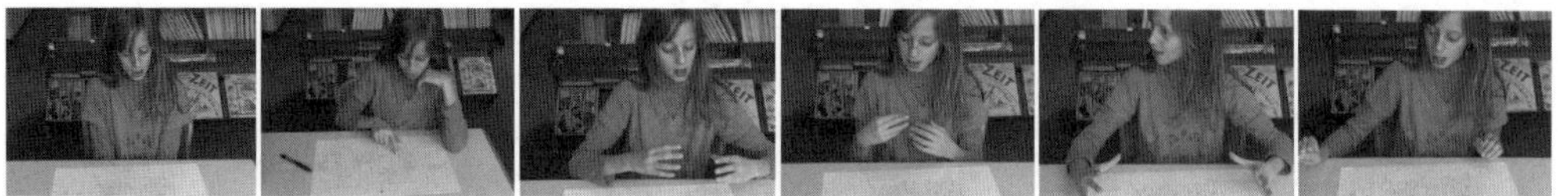

Figure 1: Interview with Enia (age 10; 10) commenting on her drawing.

Research of children's drawings (Mühle, 1955/1971; Reiss, 1996; Richter, 1997; Schuster 1993; Willats, 1997, 2005) is based, with few exceptions, on the final product. This focus ignores the connection between the aesthetic experience and the spatial and visual competencies. The complex interaction, between the perception of emotional as well as cognitive processing and the act of drawing (Glaser, 2006, p. 22), however, requires research methods that focus on this process. Some research methodical experience has already been gained in the qualitative research of children's painting and drawing processes (Dietl, 2004; Mohr, 2005). These are taken up and further developed in the present investigation.

Research method

The focus shift from the product of children's drawings (Mosimann, 1979; Schütz, 1990; Schoppe, 1991, 1992; Reiss, 1996; Richter, 1997; Schuster, 1993) to the creative process of a drawing (Dietl, 2004; Mohr, 2005) is central in this research project and requires new methodological procedures such as the combination of several elicitation methods. In the context of this qualitative empirical investigation, various data types are used and *an innovative triangulation form has been developed*. In addition to the children's drawings during an educational intervention,[2] drawing process as well as a narrative-focused guided interview was videotaped. These three data sets – drawing, creative process of the drawing, and interview – were analysed and triangulated depending on the form of material and varying on the basis of the "Grounded Theory" model (Glaser and Strauss, 1967; Strauss and Corbin, 1996; Strübing, 2004). The "triangulation as empirical approach to the fields and objects researched [provides] a way to further understanding" (Flick, 2004, p. 11). The phenomena that are investigated can be analysed from various angles and thus interpretations can be compared, extended or specified. In making the drawing process visible, the following aspects can be observed: the spatial concept that the pupils resort to and work on, if and where critical moments occur and how they are mastered, and how something new emerges or a concept changes. The videotaped interview (Figure 1) sheds light on how adolescents reflect and comment on the experiences made during the lesson and their drawings. By means of these various data sources, pictorial thinking, the development of the presentation idea, and the formation of aesthetic judgement can be reconstructed.

Result A: Determining spatial representation types and their levels

In the anlaysis of the children's drawings, the research team draws on the repertoire and terminology of cognitive-oriented children's drawing research. The analyses of the children's drawings are carried out with theoretically coined categories based on the Grounded Theory Model (Glaser and Strauss, 1967). The systematic clarification of the previous categories from the various sources of literature about children's drawings leads to evaluation forms and innovative categorizing.

Phases and phenomena of spatial representation

The phases of spatial representation are connected with the cognitive-oriented-phase model (Mosimann, 1979, Schütz, 1990, Reiss, 1996, Richter, 1997, Schuster, 1993 Willats, 1997, 2005), in which the change of pictorial language correlates with the cognitive development. The structural changes are attached to three phenomena: spatial-situational relations, total space, and representation of objects. The first phenomenon shows the *spatial connections between two or more objects* and refers to the manner in which the views of the objects are combined and the objects relate to each other in respect to their representation on the picture (cf. Schütz, 1990, p. 108). *Total space* refers to the representational form of the spatial extension, which is filled with and delimited by objects. *Representation of objects*, finally, refers to the single object and its representational form. The morphological changes within the three phenomena were observed in the material collected, and were organized and categorized from the point of view of *increasing complexity of spatial representation*. It is assumed that behind more complex spatial representations there are also cognitively more sophisticated mental concepts. Compared to the above-mentioned previous investigations the representational forms in the 500 children's drawings of 10–13-year-old pupils show a great variety of manifold combinations of these structural phenomena and therefore require clarifications and amendments leading to *new categories*.

Establishing the types of spatial representation and their levels

To characterize the spatial representation types aimed at, features of the three phenomena are combined with each other. Basically, the degree and the combination of the three phenomena, within a defined phase of spatial representation, determine the following *four types of spatial representation*: two-dimensional, including the third dimension, three-dimensional, three-dimensional projective (Subgoal 1). With this formally oriented arrangement ideal types are formed, which are not absolutely selective. The problem is due to the fact that the three phenomena – spatial–situational relation, total space, and

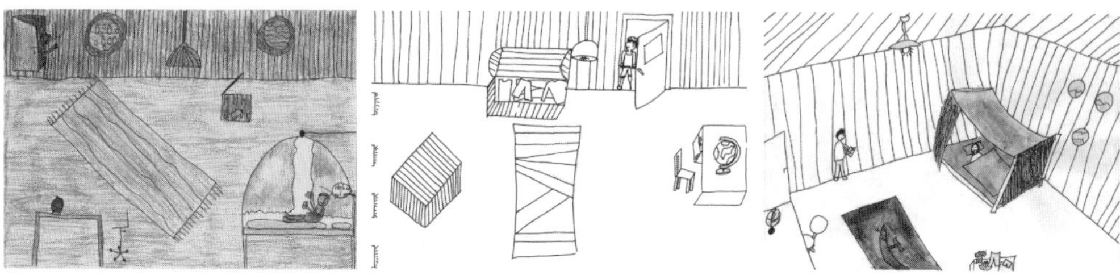

Figure 2: III.57_Anthony/Level 1   **Figure 3:** III.66_Markus/Level 4   **Figure 4:** III.67_Lisette/Level 5

representation of objects – do not develop in step and in parallel time. To attribute a drawing to a type, one phenomenon, total space, is laid more weight on than the other two.

In addition the individual types of spatial representation are differentiated to varying levels on the basis of the observed type-immanent phenomena (Subgoal 2). These levels are paradigmatic and differentiated by features as distinct as possible. Apart from those drawings, which represent an ideal type of spatial representation, in this study there are many various examples of mixed forms and of different qualities. This clearly deviates from results presented in earlier research literature. They are type-overlapping in the combination of the phenomena, i.e. the representations can be de- or increased respectively in their spatial complexity, by including a formal characteristic of the previous or subsequent type of spatial representation.

An example based on three case studies on the differentiation of levels is introduced in the context of the ideal type "including the third dimension" (III.57; III.66; III.67, Figure 2–4).

Description of the sample cases (cf. task S4_"In the boat's cabin")

Anthony (age 11; 1)/Ill.57/Level 1 (Figure 2)
In Anthony's example, fore- and background are easily distinguished. These two zones are linked in the middle by the coloured floor and the slanting rug. In the foreground there is a table, chair, and canopy on a standline. In the background a panelled wall with two portholes and a door, through which a person is looking into the room, is visible. The objects in Anthony's example are drawn in a basic shape (a category assigned to the two-dimensional type) with partly carefully embellished features (cf. canopy).

Markus (age 10; 5)/Ill.66/Level 4 (Figure 3)
By positioning the trunk askew (picture left), and with the door, clearly reaching into the room, Markus manages an *attempt* at an illusionistic depth of the room. The desk, moved to the right margin of the picture and the bird's-eye perspective of the portholes on the left – thus indicating the left wall of the room – complement the floor and back-wall zone and enhance the spatial complexity.

Lisette (age 11; 1)/Ill.67/Level 5 (Figure 4)
Lisette leads two sides of the floor zone askew into the picture space. The bed is clearly drawn on the floor zone in the corner of the room. The ceiling with parallel panelling over the entire picture space is less obvious. In this zone there is a lamp. Objects such as the desk, the carpet, and the trunk are pictorally cut and in their orientation correspond partly with the floor zoning. The canopy emphasizes the spatial clarity of the foot of the bed, but obscures, however, the head of the bed. The person who has entered the room stands on the floor in front of the side-wall making towards the person lying on the bed.

Consequences A

Findings of previous, cognitivist-oriented theories of the children's drawing research, namely those about the three-dimensional projective representation form (vanishing point perspective) – in which the entire space and its spatial elements are seen from one consistent angle – it is presumed that spatial representation of this type is not possible before age 13/14 (Reiss, 1996, pp.117–118). The sequence of spatial stages is thus dependent on the cognitive development (cf. chart). *However, the frequency and quality of so-called mixed forms of spatial representation are noticeable.* They show surprisingly varied combinations of the three investigated space-related, structural pictorial phenomena beyond the literature-based (ideal) types. These mixed forms of spatial representation do not only differ from child to child, but also occur very often in different variations within the six collected drawings of each individual case. The pictorial solutions make obvious that the pupils do not draw on a single mental spatial concept, but on several variants, which belong to the individual repertoire and are combined with each other or altered. Some evidence indicates that these mixed forms are evoked by the didactic settings and impulses. They may also be the effect of the increased consumption of pictorial media of young people of this generation. Our proposition is *that the various forms of spatial representation offered by the media are to a large extent used value-freely and pluralistically in reception and production.*

For art education didactics, this means that judging the aspiration level of a pictorial representation does not primarily depend on the spatial complexity of the representation. Fundamentally, it is a question of how far the choice of the form of pictorial representation is suitable for the intended effect, or respectively, for the function opted or given. More precise criteria for judging the quality of a pictorial solution are then provided by the representational levels established within the traditional types of spatial representation. A high aspiration level can be recognized by the characteristic and the combination of the three structural pictorial phenomena (total space, representation of objects, spatial relations), which are for the first time consistently separated in this investigation. A drawing can thus make use of various functions of representation and at the same time achieve its task at a high level. The determination of structural pictorial phenomena with the appropriate chart is above all also a basis for a differentiated appreciation of the various mixed forms of the children's spatial representations.

The permeability of spatial representation types and their levels is an indication of the fact that it is not only a question of linear development. The forms of representation in a drawing are rather influenced by other factors in addition to the chosen function of the drawing – an irritation, which leads to the discovery of the processing competencies in the course of the investigation.

Result B: The processing competencies

Prompted by the process-orientation and the frequently occurring mixed forms in spatial representation, this investigation includes *processing competencies of children as a new element of an empirically more precise model to explain the spatial representation in children's drawings* for the first time. This had not been anticipated at the time of application, for these competencies were not taken into account in the earlier schema of cognitivistic-oriented stage models (Schütz, 1990; Schoppe, 1991, 1992; Reiss, 1996; Richter, 1997; Schuster, 1993; Willats, 1997, 2005). Thanks to the audio recordings of the interviews and the videotaped drawing processes, pictorial, creative, cognitive, and affective aspects of the processing forms in the children's spatial perception – and above all representation – can be reconstructed. The processing competencies are based on spatial representation forms and influence these substantially. From the collected data material of several case studies a theoretical–interpretive frame is gradually formed, which is based on the Grounded Theory model (Glaser and Strauss, 1967; Strauss and Corbin, 1996; Strübing, 2004) with an originally open and later more precise coding. The interpretations are contrasted and related to each other again and again and lead to the new result: *processing competencies.* The competencies established for the first time are: *pictorial reification* (e.g. depicting, copying a model, creating imaginatively), *pictorial solution process, discrepancy experience, imagination, self-positioning in the space/spatial apprehension,* and *aesthetic judgement.* In the present final report they are introduced and discussed in connection with several case studies.

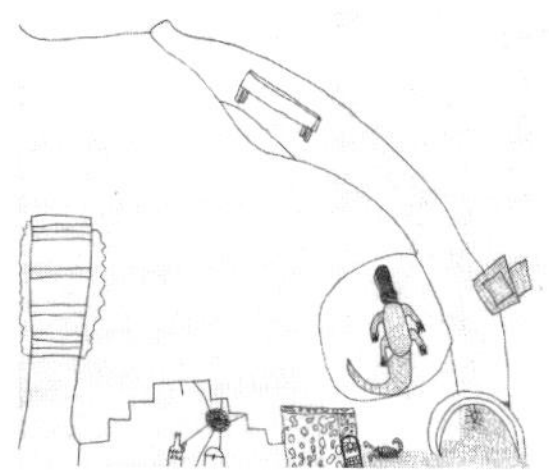

Figure 5: S1_Enia (age 10;10)

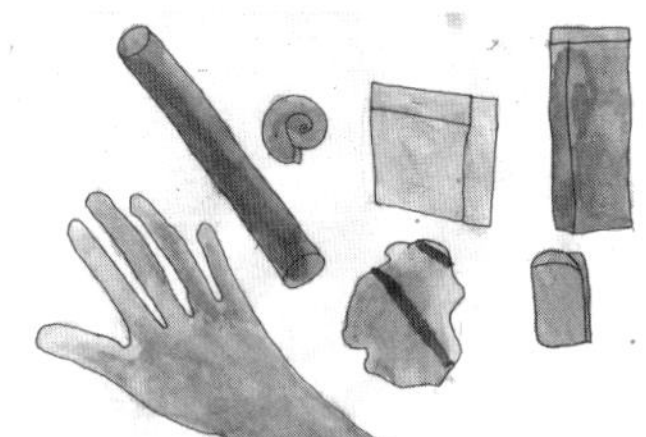

Figure 6: S2_Enia (age 10;10)

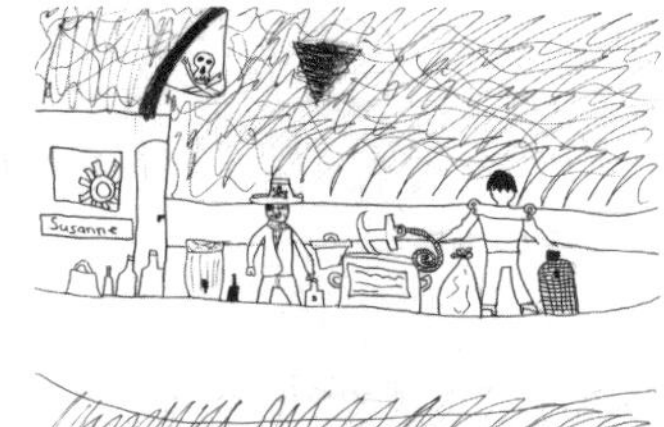

Figure 7: S3_Enia (age 10;10)

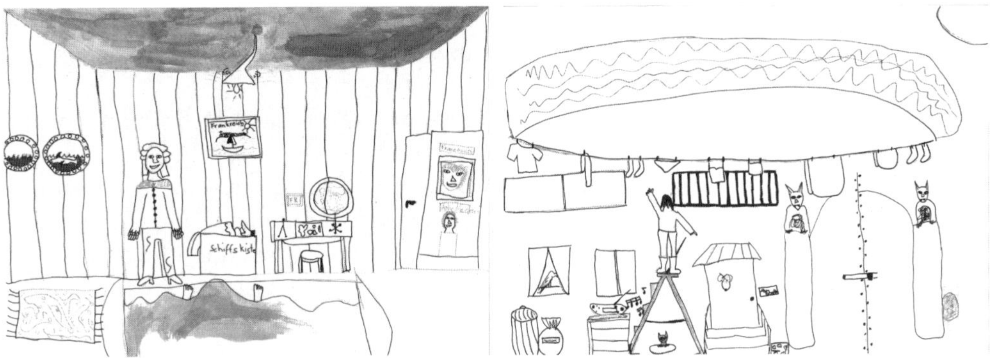

Figure 8: S4_Enia (age 10; 10)   Figure 9: S5_Enia (age 12; 0)

To illustrate the investigated processing competencies two case studies – Enia (age 10;10, Figures 5–9) and Mina (age 9;11, Figures 10–14) – are presented. Again the interpretation is based on the three data materials: the interview, the children's drawing (cf. note 2), and the videotaped drawing process.

Enia

Basic motivations and attitudes

Enia's reaction to tasks is extremely motivated and confident. She expects interesting challenges. She possesses to a high degree the quality of being open to new aesthetic experiences. She has a say in the quality of the experience by actively exploring her surrounding or by combining a tale/verbal instructions with associations and personal experiences.

Case specific competencies

Aesthetic judgement
Enia judges her drawings by means of clear criteria. Her reflections are sophisticated and she describes and justifies pictorial decisions. She realizes in S4 (Figure 8) that her pictorial solution (cf. bed) differs from that of her classmates and she is proud of her achievement.

Pictorial solutions and reifications
During the lesson her experience is "not a fateful irruption of something new, but the consequence of purposeful doing – i.e. acting" as Duncker (1999, p. 12) following Dewey (1934/1980, p. 9–11) formulates it. Traces of her mental acting are found in her drawing, e.g. in S4 (Figure 8) the tools on the table for navigating the ship or the deposited clothes in the trunk. The unexpected irritates her, but at the same time triggers associative, pictorial action.

Thus Enia interprets the tip of the groped cloth in S1 (Figure 5) as the tail of a crocodile, or in S4 (Figure 8) she expands the story by the presence of the ship owner in picture and sculpture (cf. to the right side of the picture).

Almost all the drawings show complex mixed forms (cf. "Result A: Determining spatial representation types and their levels") of spatial representation, which are both the results of concerns of contents and narrative as well as of formal nature. Enia plays with representation conventions and can rely on a good pictorial memory and a pronounced imagination. The interest in cultural products, historical and topical, concerning both form and contents, which was mentioned again and again, finds its expression in the drawings. In a communicative intention Enia displays formal features of Playmobil figures in S3 (Figure 7) or characterizes the invented figure as a French servant of the ship owner in historical costume and wig in S4 (Figure 8). She draws the ceiling with the foreshortening of central perspective, whereas the trunk and the table are standline-oriented without volume. In S5 (Figure 9) she remembers a picture of the atrium in Augusta Raurica and quotes – cognitively not yet understood – the representation of the roof, which delimits all around the courtyard from the open sky.

Enia welcomes demanding cognitive challenges. In S4 (Figure 8) e.g. she quickly realizes that she cannot do justice to the given situation with her usual pictorial repertoire – her view from the bed into the room. She tenaciously pursues her own solution process, on which phases of successive development (ceiling, trunk, desk) are followed by phases of pausing and reflection (bed with identification figure and floor stripes). In the process Enia specifies her perception and understanding of space and discovers a new viewer-centred total space representation.

Self-positioning in the room and spatial apprehension

By only drawing her feet, sticking out from under the bed cover (Figure 8), she combines the view of the person in the picture with her own as drawer. With this new conceptual element she enhances the complexity of the spatial representation and also shows a highly reflexive competence in the interview comments.

Imagination

Enia's imagination has variations of shapes as well as narrative aspects of representation. In order to illustrate the rocking of the ship in the storm, she does not only draw high waves in the porthole but changes the form of the lamp by adding elements of movement borrowed from comics, visualizing the to-and-fro of the lamp (Figure 8). Above all Enia enjoys moments of surprise and sometimes tries to intensify this pleasure by complementing the aesthetic experiences with eerie pictures, both attractive and scary (cf. S1, Figure 5). The didactic setting gives her a frame of reference, which she expands imaginatively with scenes and situations "hardly bearable in real life" (Duncker and Neuss, 1999, p. 16). In S1 (Figure 5) she shows relief that the expected appearance of a skeleton did not materialize. Her ambivalent attitude, however, leads her to imagine a new danger straight after her relief, to which she exposes herself playfully, experiencing a "crumby" feeling. In the interview she is very aware of the change into the phantasy world. In the interview she creates a distance by changing the formulation of "I noticed" into "well – I thought so". The 11-year-old Enia changes naturally from depicting outer reality to personal constructs, which contain possible elements. She loves designing phantasies and combining objectively perceived elements with pictures from a self-created world, identifying herself with these, only to distance herself again as the observer.

Mina

Basic motivation and attitude

Mina experiences and conceptualizes the story. She tells the events in her drawing in a self-motivated way, rich in details and with individual preferences. Her interest is aimed at the people in the picture and she is concerned to show clearly how they act and relate to each other. Mina obtains her drawing skills mainly from outside the normal lessons and learns independently.

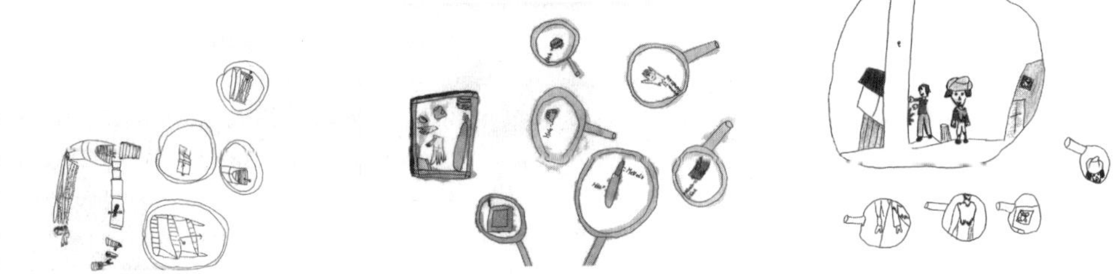

Figure 10: S1_Mina (age 9;11)   **Figure 11:** S2_Mina (age 9;11)   **Figure 12:** S3_Mina (age 9;11)

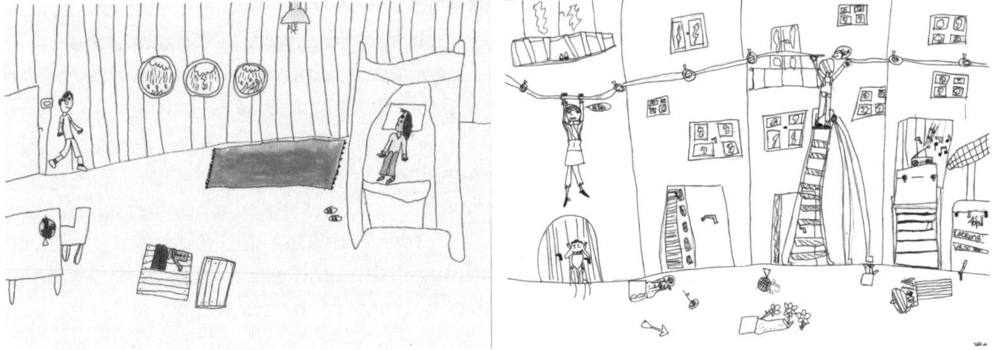

Figure 13: S4_Mina (age 9; 11)   **Figure 14:** S5_Mina (age 11; 1)

Case specific competencies

Aesthetic judgement
Mina has a clear idea of a good – i.e. readable and understandable – representation of people. Her models are based on comics or, a year later, on mangas. She expresses criteria-oriented pleasure with the people in her picture. For her representation of objects and their spatial relation she does not draw on models, however, but on personal visual experiences and judges her pictorial rendering on this background.

Pictorial solutions and reifications
In the drawing process and interviews it becomes obvious that Mina is interested in the pictorial language of comics and likes adopting formal aspects of "how to do". In S1-S3 (Figure 10–12) for example, she uses the possibility to magnify selected objects of the total pictorial situation and thus make them more readable by means of "detail drawing". In S4 and S5 (Figure 13–14), she takes a lot of time and care to represent people, whom she is particularly interested in, according to the interview statements. The attention to people, the predilection to present feelings and postures could be explained by Mina's great interest in social matters. Furthermore she explains how she has learned from comics to draw people in various poses and movements (sitting in bed with tucked up legs). However, she is not interested in pictorial problems of spatial representation. For the motif of the closed room in S5 (Figure 14) her attention is directed towards single, object-related features such as windows and doors. Problem awareness and reflexivity are largely focused on formal aspects of representing people, and contextual, narrative intentions. This is done in a very differentiated and skilful way. During the drawing process, Mina draws on her usual pictorial repertoire both in S4 and S5 (Figure 13–14), which she modifies slighltly as needed. She attributes the pictorial solution in S4 (Figure 13) confidently to her own abilities, which she acquired independently. A year later she is not absolutely convinced of her representation of the courtyard any more, (S5, Figure 14), as one might think the row of houses was standing along a street. Mina seems to suspect that for a solution of the pictorial task both the manifestation and the arrangement of all pictorial elements – living beings and artefacts – are essential and that the spatial situation could be represented more clearly. She reacts very positively to didactic input in S5 (Figure 14), such as the guided observation of a stepladder, implements what she perceived in her drawing, and comments on her attempt critically in the interview.

Self-positioning in the room and spatial apprehension
Mina feels mentally in the centre of the pictorial events and does not position herself outside the picture. In S4 (Figure 13) she draws herself as a figure looking into the room, her head turned to the side and thus visible in profile. Although Mina can assume the observer point of view of the interviewer, she does not (yet) reflect her view of the drawer, but feels one with the person in the picture and draws all pictorial elements "object-centred" (cf. Willats, 1997, 2005; Aissen-Crewett, 1986 ["*anordnungsbezogen*"]).

Imagination

Mina extends the story by specifying, for example, the relationship between the two people in the drawing, achieving this by turning the head of the figure in the bed and the leg movement of the person entering the room. A pictorial overlapping – trunk and clothes – she compares with an everyday situation, when she hangs her clothes over her bed and only sees part of her trousers afterwards. Mina's narrative imagination is unspectacular. It is based on personal, reflected, everyday experiences and precise observations stored in her memory.

Consequences B

Individual strengths and weaknesses of the pupils in connection with spatial perception and representation can be appreciated more widely and more precisely by means of the processing competencies. Explanations can be found for differences in the drawings as well as the different strategies and learning paths, which lead to pictorial solutions. By taking these facets of processing competencies into consideration, methods of individual advancement can be systematized and expanded and effective advancement models can be developed.

For art teaching, these results mean taking leave of the simplified, linear progression model for perception and above all spatial representation in the plane. They mean replacing it by a model, which does justice to the increase of complexity, especially those features related to the children's thoughts and actions in dealing with structural pictorial phenomena. Increase of complexity can be achieved by reflexivity, for example, by a playful as well as tenacious attitude to problem solving, or by learning about additional pictorial possibilities of spatial representation.

With the *focus shift from cognitivistic-oriented stage models to subject and process-oriented competencies*, the results of the present investigation can be connected with the current scientific discussion around the notion of competencies and its multi-variant application in practice (e.g. Swiss-German Curriculum 21). The present results contain aspects of cognitive as well as "the attached motivational, volitional and social skills" (Weinert, 2001, p. 27f.), which, according to F. E. Weinert, ought to be used for a responsible and successful solution in variable situations. The results form a starting point for the development of tasks, which lead to the classification of types and levels, and can be used in future output- and longitudinal-oriented tests for impact research. The collected material, the evaluation charts, and the categorizations, are essential for further investigations and offer many possibilities for new issues. Above all the interaction of spatial representation competencies and processing competencies requires further clarification and the development of praxis-oriented consequences.

For the first time, subject-related competencies of spatial perception and representation have not just been deducted from didactic literature, as authors of previous standards have done, but have been determined empirically and can be reconstructed on the basis of investigation material. This has also led to new, surprising insights and competencies incongruent with previous assumptions. This offers great potential for further research questions and projects.

Acknowledgements

I would like to thank Professor Dr Georg Peez, Goethe-Universität Frankfurt am Main, for his scientific advice and persistent support; Dr Jörg Berger and Verena Matter (MA) for the English translation; my team, Luitgard Diehl Ott and Ludwig Diehl; Professor Christiane Maier Reinhard and Professor Hermann Graser for their valuable contributions; and all students and their parents and teachers for their enthusiastic participation.

References

Aissen-Crewett, M. (1986). Räumliche Vorstellung und Darstellung bei Kindern. [Children's spatial imagination and representation], *Kunst+Unterricht*, (105). 14–19.

Dewey, J. (1980). *Kunst als Erfahrung*. Frankfurt a.M., Germany: Suhrkamp. 9–11. [engl. 1934. *Art as Experience*. New York: Minton, Balch; London: Allen & Unwin]

Dietl, M-L. (2004). *Kindermalerei. Zum Gebrauch der Farbe am Ende der Grundschulzeit. [Children's painting. About the use of colours at the end of elementary schooling.]* Münster, Germany: Waxmann.

Duncker, L., Neuss, N. (Eds.) (1999). *Ästhetik der Kinder. [Children's aesthetics.]* Frankfurt a.M., Germany: GEP. 12.

Flick, U. (2004). *Triangulation*. Wiesbaden, Germany: VS Verlag für Sozialwissenschaften. 11.

Gardner, Howard (1998) *Abschied vom IQ. Die Rahmen-Theorie der vielfachen Intelligenzen*. Stuttgart, Germany: Klett-Cotta. pp. 9, 163–174. [engl. 1983. *Frames of Mind, The theory of multiple intelligences*. BasicBooks (Harper Collins), New York]

Glaser, B. G., Strauss, A. (1967). *The Discovery of Grounded Theory: Strategies for Qualitative Research*. Chicago, IL: Aldine.

Glaser–Henzer, E. (2006). Vorstellungsbildung im Unterricht. [The development of imagination in art classes.] *BDK Mitteilungen, Fachzeitschrift des BDK Fachverband für Kunstpädagogik*, 42 (4). 22–26.

Glaser-Henzer, E., Diehl Ott, L., Diehl, L., (2011). *Forschungsprojekt ‚raviko' – Schlussbericht. [‚raviko' – Final Report.]* http://www.kunstunterricht-projekt.ch. Accessed 20 February 2011.

Glaser-Henzer, E., Diehl Ott, L., Diehl, L., Peez, G. (2012). *Zeichnen: Wahrnehmen, Verarbeiten, Darstellen. Empirische Untersuchungen zur Kinderzeichnung und zur Ermittlung räumlich-visueller Kompetenzen im Kunstunterricht. [Drawing: Perceiving, assimilating, representing. Empirical studies of children's drawings for the purpose of identifying spatial and visual competencies in art lessons.]* Munich, Germany: Kopaed.

Mohr, A. (2005). *Digitale Kinderzeichnung. Aspekte ästhetischen Verhaltens von Grundschulkindern am Computer. [Digital children's drawings. Aspects of aesthetic behaviour of elementary school children on the computer.]* Munich, Germany: Kopaed.

Mosimann, W. (1979). *Die Darstellung von Mensch, Tier, Baum, Haus, Raum und Farbe in Kritzel, Zeichen, Bildzeichen und Bild. [The representation of human figure, animal, tree, house, space and colour in a scribbling, sign, icon and picture.]* Bern and Stuttgart, Germany: Verlag Paul Haupt.

Mühle, G. (1955/1971). *Entwicklungspsychologie des zeichnerischen Gestaltens. [Developmental psychology of drawing.]* Berlin, Germany: Springer.

Peez, G. (2005). *Evaluation ästhetischer Erfahrungs- und Bildungsprozesse: Beispiele zu ihrer empirischen Erforschung. [Evaluation of aesthetic experiential and educational processes: Examples of empirical research on this subject.]* Munich, Germany: Kopaed. 13–17.

———— (Ed.) (2007). *Handbuch Fallforschung in der Ästhetischen Bildung/Kunstpädagogik. Qualitative Empirie für Studium, Praktikum, Referendariat und Unterricht. [Handbook of case research in art education. Qualitative empiricism for study, practical training, internship, teaching.]* Hohengehren, Germany: Schneider Verlag GmbH.

Reiss, W. (1996). *Kinderzeichnungen: Wege zum Kind durch seine Zeichnung. [Children's drawings: Understanding children through their drawings.]* Berlin, Germany: Luchterhand. p. 7, pp. 107–136.

———— (2000). Die Darstellung des Raumes bei Kindern und Jugendlichen. [Representation of space by children and adolescents.] *Kunst+Unterricht*, (246/247). 56–59.

Richter, H-G. (1997). *Die Kinderzeichnung: Entwicklung, Interpretation, Ästhetik. [The child's drawing: Development, interpretation, aesthetics.]* Berlin, Germany: Cornelsen.

Schuster, Martin (1993). *Die Psychologie der Kinderzeichnung. [The Psychology of children's drawings.]* Berlin, Heidelberg, Germany: Springer. 67–71.

Schoppe, A. (1991). *Kinderzeichnung und Lebenswelt: Neue Wege zum Verständnis des kindlichen Gestaltens. [Children's drawings and living environment: New ways of understanding children's creative work.]* Herne, Germany: Verlag für Wissenschaft und Kunst.

———— (1992). Kinderzeichnung und Lebenswelt: Eine neue Sichtweise zeichnerischer Entwicklung und ihre Konsequenzen für den Unterricht. [Children's drawings and living environment: A new view of the development of drawing skills and the consequences for art classes.] *Kunst+Unterricht*, (63). 38–39.

Schütz, N. (1990). *Die Raumdarstellung in der Kinderzeichung: Eine empirische Studie an vier- bis sechsjährigen Kindern zur Erklärung der Entwicklungsphänomene. [The representation of space in children's drawings: An empirical study of four- to six-year-old children to explain developmental phenomena.]* Essen, Germany: Die Blaue Eule.

Strauss, A., Corbin, J. (1996). *Grounded Theory: Grundlagen qualitativer Sozialforschung.* Weinheim, Germany: Beltz/Psychologie VerlagsUnion. (engl. 1990. *Basics of Qualitative Research: Grounded Theory Procedures and Techniques.* Sage Publications, Inc.)

Strübing, J. (2004). *Grounded Theory: Zur sozialtheoretischen und epistemologischen Fundierung des Verfahrens der empirisch begründeten Theoriebildung.* Wiesbaden, Germany: VS Verlag.

Swiss-German Curriculum21, http://www.lehrplan.ch. Accessed 31 October 2012.

Weinert, F. E. (Ed.) (2001). *Leistungsmessungen in Schulen. [Performance assessments in schools.]* Weinheim, Germany: Beltz.

Willats, J. (1997). *Art and Representation: New Principles in the Analyses of Pictures.* Princeton NJ: Princeton University Press.

———— (2005). *Making Sense of Children's Drawings.* Mahwah, NJ: Lawrence Erlbaum Associates.

Notes

1   Project information: "raviko" – visual and spatial competencies concerning aesthetic experiences in art lessons; a qualitative-empirical investigation relating to the didactic development of competencies levels teaching standards of school years 4–6 (2007–2010). Team of the final report: Edith Glaser-Henzer, Ludwig Diehl, Luitgard Diehl Ott (University of Applied Sciences Northwestern Switzerland, School of Education, Switzerland) and Georg Peez (Scientific Adviser, Goethe-Universität Frankfurt am Main, Germany). Further financial support was given by the Jacobs Foundation and Association of Teachers of Art Switzerland (LBG-EAV). Publication in German, kopaed-Verlag, München 2012. www.fhnw.ch/ph/ip/forschung/raviko. Correspondence address: em.glaser@bluewin.ch. http://www.kunstunterricht-projekt.ch

2   These data were collected during the art classes. A story on the subject of pirates is the basis for the first four tasks S1–S4 (task S5 was carried out one year later):

    S1_ Escape in the ship's hull (completing a perception course with blindfolds on)

    S2_ Feeling around at the bottom of the sea.

    S3_ Seen through the telescope

    S4_ In the boat's cabin

    S5_ Chaos in the courtyard

Chapter 13

Considering the effects of metacognition on the process of writing about art

Kazuhiro Ishizaki, University of Tsukuba, Japan; Wenchun Wang, Independent Scholar, Japan

Abstract

The purpose of this study was to assess the effects of metacognition on the process of writing about art and to consider the relationship between metacognition and appreciation skills. Twenty-four undergraduates in an Introduction to Art Appreciation class were encouraged to express their reflections through the process of writing. The indexes to metacognitive knowledge and metacognitive experiences concerning art appreciation were categorized and the metacognitive scores were calculated on the undergraduates' reflective descriptions. We defined art-appreciation skills in terms of the combination of two factors: the elements of artworks that viewers pay attention to and how they respond to them. Appreciation skills were extracted from five pieces of writing written by each undergraduate in the class. We rated the level of each skill, the diversity of skills used by the viewers, and the contextual cluster in the writing, and these three indexes were considered as the proficiency of viewers' writing. In comparing five written art appreciation tasks, the scores of the fifth task were significantly higher than in the first task. Especially, there was a significant correlation between the metacognitive score and the ratio of the skills used by the viewer to all defined skills. The metacognitive scores of the group that showed a steady increase in scores of appreciation skills in the five writings, tended to be higher than those of the group that didn't show an increase. The result suggested that encouraging metacognition could be effective in improving writing about art.

Purpose of the study

This study examines the correlations between metacognition and the learning effects of appreciation skills for the purpose of analyzing the effects of metacognition in the process of writing about art.[1]

We have developed software for instructing writing about art to examine effective learning methods (Ishizaki and Wang, 2004). Recent researchers of learning sciences have considered learning methods that encourage metacognition in the learning process alongside computer-assisted instruction (Bransford, Brown, and Cocking, 2000; Dunlosky and Metcalfe, 2009; Hacker, Dunlosky, and Graesser, 2009). Supporting methods for encouraging metacognition are thought to enable active learning and have effects on learners' positive attitudes and thoughts, and motivation toward learning (Sannomiya, 2008).

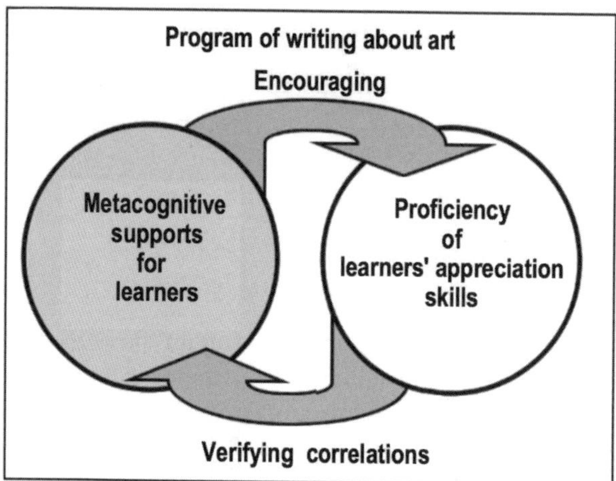

Figure 1: Research image map.

The hypothesis of this study is "metacognitive supports in the process of writing about art have effects on learning appreciation skills".

As Figure 1 illustrates, we designed and implemented a program of writing about art, encouraging metacognition and verifying correlations between metacognition and the learning effects of appreciation skills.

Background and definition

Flexible thinking and art-appreciation education

Recent educational reform in the world calls for responses to these rapid social changes. Sato (2003) indicates that literacy education in the present post-industrial society should heighten the effects of reflective thinking and communication abilities. Also, Efland (2002) indicates the importance of learners' cognitive flexibility and ability to apply their knowledge in their daily lives. In other words, the more complex a society grows, the greater the importance of flexible thinking. In fact, fostering flexible thinking is one of the important goals of present educational reform in Japan (Central Council for Education, 2008). What is now questioned is how to foster flexible thinking in art education. We hope to illustrate a possible contribution to fostering flexible thinking, through the learning of art appreciation.

In order to appreciate diverse and multiform artworks, the tolerance and flexibility of the thinking process is essential. Logical and critical attitudes are of additional importance. Stout (1995) placed emphasis on critical thinking as higher-order thinking, when instructing writing about diverse artworks in her college class. It is notable that she encouraged students to comprehend metacognition for critical thinking.

Perkins, Jay, and Tishman (1993) regarded metacognition as a reflective intelligence. They considered that the strategies and attitudes gained through metacognition could also function in different fields, which was one of the reasons why they highly valued metacognition. The effects of metacognition in the learning of school subjects are of great interest. In Japan, related researches have been advanced in such areas as reading and composition in Japanese classes, problem solving in arithmetic and math classes, and observation and experiment in science classes (Kato, 1997; Kiyokawa and Inuzuka, 2003; Matsuura, 2003).

Definition of appreciation skills

In this study, we use the term "appreciation skills" as one of the strategies of art appreciation and focused on two factors: the elements of artworks that viewers pay attention to and how they respond to them. We defined appreciation skills in terms of the combination of these two factors (Ishizaki and Wang, 2006, 2010b; Ishizaki, Wang, and Parsons, 2008). In order to define art-appreciation skills by combining them as shown in Table 1, A1–D6, we used the *elements of artworks* and *response behaviours* as indexes. We also identified that specific appreciation skills, such as *appreciation repertoires*, had been repeatedly used and familiarized by the viewers. In reference to elements of artworks, we proposed four frames –*subject matter, expression, elements of art*, and *style*– based on Parsons's developmental theory (1987). For response behaviours, we proposed six frames – *association, observation, impression, analysis, interpretation*, and *judgment* – referred to as the 14 domains in Housen's developmental theory (1983).

The relationships of elements of artworks with response behaviours are actually not only one-to-one relationships. They are also combined to form multiple combinations, resulting in diversity. The expansion of such diversities is a characteristic of appreciation skills and appreciation repertories.

Table 1: Framework of appreciation skills.

		Response behaviours					
		1 Association	2 Observation	3 Impression	4 Analysis	5 Interpretation	6 Judgment
Elements of artworks	A Subject matter	A1	A2	A3	A4	A5	A6
	B Expression	B1	B2	B3	B4	B5	B6
	C Elements of art	C1	C2	C3	C4	C5	C6
	D Style	D1	D2	D3	D4	D5	D6

Definition of metacognition

Metacognition is often defined as "cognition about cognition" or "thinking about thinking". According to Flavell (1979), metacognition consists of both *metacognitive knowledge* and *metacognitive experience*. Metacognition is thought to be an interaction with both. Further, metacognitive knowledge is divided into three categories – *knowledge about persons, knowledge about tasks*, and *knowledge about strategies*– and metacognitive experience is divided into *metacognitive monitoring* and *metacognitive control* (Sannomiya, 2008). Based on this classification of metacognition we proposed examples of metacognitive knowledge and metacognitive experience related to appreciation skills, as in Table 2 (Ishizaki and Wang, 2010a).

Table 2: Examples of metacognition related to appreciation skills.

		Classification	Examples related to appreciation skills
Metacognitive knowledge	Metacognitive knowledge about persons	Knowledge about an individual's cognitive characteristics	Where are my points of interest? What kinds of appreciation skills do I often use?
		Knowledge about the cognitive characteristics between individuals	What commonalities or differences are there between myself and others in art appreciation?
		Knowledge about the cognitive characteristics of humans in general.	How do people, from children to adults, look at artworks? How about specialists?
	Metacognitive knowledge about tasks		Why do I write about art? With whom do I want to communicate?
	Metacognitive knowledge about strategies	Declaratory knowledge: what are the strategies?	What are the elements of artworks? What kinds of appreciation behaviours exist? What kinds of combinations of elements of artworks and appreciation behaviours make it easier to communicate one's thoughts to other people?
		Procedural knowledge: how to use the strategies	Which types and methods of appreciation skills are more effective than others?
		Conditional knowledge: when to use the strategies and why?	Which appreciation skill is more effective and when is it most effective? Why do I use this particular appreciation skill?
Metacognitive experience	Metacognitive monitoring	Recognition, perception anticipation, examination, and evaluation of cognition	What kinds of appreciation skills am I using now? Are the appreciation skills effectively composed? Can I communicate my thoughts to readers?
	Metacognitive control	Establishing aims, planning, and modifying cognition	Are there more effective appreciation skills? How can I incorporate appreciation skills to deepen my thoughts?

Methods of the study

Outlines of the program "Writing about Art"

The writing about art program was composed of six units as shown in Figure 2. This program was incorporated into a college class called Introduction to Art Appreciation (15 weeks, 30 hours). A total of 24 college students (7 freshmen, 11 sophomores, and 2 auditors) participated in the class from April to July, 2009.

Comprehension of appreciation skills was attempted in Units 1 and 2. In Unit 1, students were encouraged to write freely about their favourite artworks, and about Andrew Wyeth's *Christina's World* (1948). Later, they were introduced to the definitions of appreciation skills using worksheets, and asked to make a self-analysis of what types of appreciation skills were used in their own writing. By producing analysis maps of appreciation skills, they were urged to understand more about the different kinds of appreciation skills and the possibility of the skills combining flexibly.

In Unit 2, students used the software *Art Reporter* (Ishizaki and Wang, 2004), to write about *Christina's World*, and analyzed the appreciation skills they used in their own writings.

Thus, in Units 1 and 2, students utilized their perspectives on appreciation skills as metacognitive knowledge in order to make self-analyses of their own writings. In other words, they were encouraged to monitor their skills. Later, students had a group (four members) discussion on what kinds of skills they used.

In Units 3 and 4, students were instructed to give careful thought to constructing their writing plans. In Unit 3, students visited a local museum that permanently exhibited René Magritte's *The Great Family* (1963). They were expected to use as many appreciation

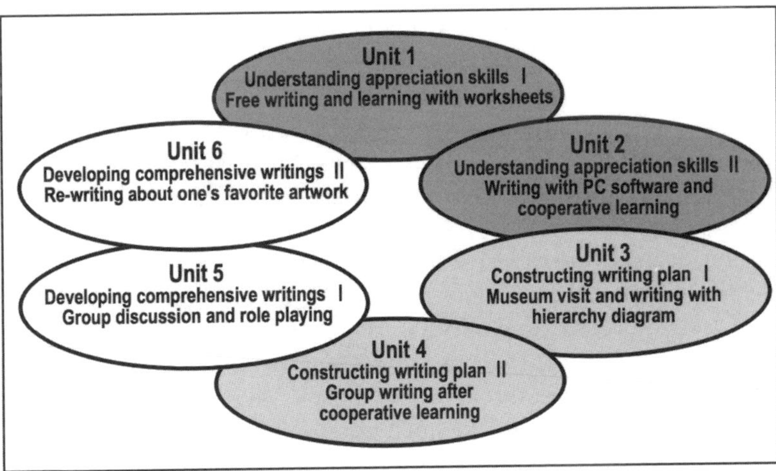

Figure 2: Diagram of writing program.

skills as they could by using the worksheets we had prepared. Furthermore, students were required to ask questions regarding the artwork and use the given materials to seek a basis for their thoughts toward such questions. Students used hierarchy-diagram worksheets to put their thoughts in logical order, and figure out the composition of their writings. Finally students were required to present their writings at a pseudo-contest.

In Unit 4, students had another chance to use the software *Art Reporter*, and wrote about Pablo Picasso's painting *Guernica* (1937). After students gave individual presentations of their writings in their groups, they worked together for their group writings.

In Units 5 and 6, we expected students to develop comprehensive writing skills and attempt to enhance the quality of their writings. In Unit 5, the "situated learning" strategy was undertaken and students worked in their groups to write about Georges Pierre Seurat's painting *Sunday Afternoon on La Grande Jatte* (1884–86), to apply for a curatorial post. The students gave presentations of their writings.

In Unit 6, a group discussion on "What is a profound understanding about artwork?" and "What is comprehensive writing" was carried out. Later, writing task about the artwork that individuals chose at the beginning of the program was assigned as a final assignment.

Concrete metacognitive supports during the learning process are described below.

First, we prepared 20 types of worksheets for learning appreciation skills. The worksheets designed so that the students could complete them while they wrote, by filling in the blanks at different points during the class, allowed them to reflect on their learning. For example, in the worksheet for understanding appreciation skills the learners analysed what types of appreciation skills they used based on their own writings, and then they were encouraged to conduct monitoring activities. We also prepared worksheets to support writing and gave examples of compositional methods in order to support the students' control activities. There were other types of worksheets where students had to apply a hierarchy diagram. Another task targeted reading and summarising / quoting skills. Students were also mentored on how to improve comprehensive writing and develop amore profound understanding of artworks through group discussions, and therefore they were able to modify their writing plans. We also prepared "Reflection Memo" worksheets (see, e.g. Figure 3). After students gave presentations of their writings in groups, they wrote down comments about other group members' writings on labels (Post-its) and exchanged them with group members. Then, they stuck the Post-its onto their own reflection memos, and wrote in response to the comments for further reflection.

In cooperative learning, learners are expected to grasp the situation and problems fully through mutual interaction with others (Johnson, Johnson, and Holubec, 1993). In a situation where learners remain considerate of each other, metacognitive monitoring and metacognitive controlling activities are activated through the presence of others. During our learning process metacognitive activities through other people were actively encouraged. It was so arranged that students were placed in small groups of four at the beginning of the class and were asked to exchange ideas with each other. In the small-group activities, opportunities to reflect on learning were provided as often as possible.

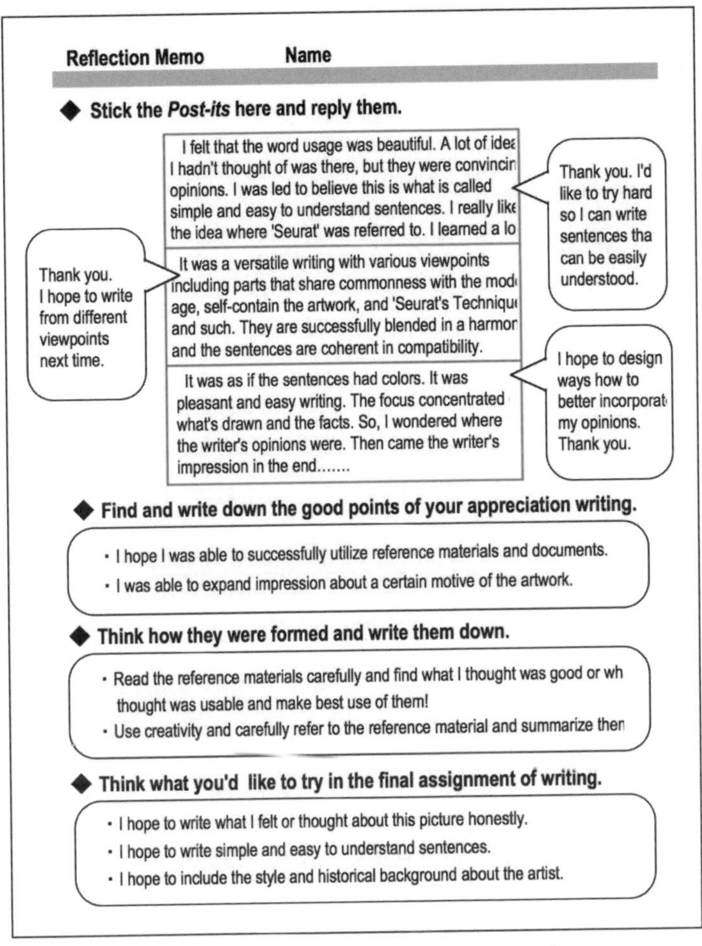

Figure 3: Reflection Memo, Unit 5 (an example of memo writing).

In Unit 4, after developing group activities suitable for four members, *group-writing* exercises were undertaken. First, students were required to write down their thoughts on Post-it labels while they read the reference material. Then, during the group discussions they started to group all their thoughts together and classify them into several themes. Based on these themes they considered the structures of writing, divided writing tasks amongst themselves, revised them as a group, and completed the multi-author writings. While carefully and closely examining their thoughts with each other, they were encouraged to express their individual appreciation methods in words and graphs, and share what they had learned from each other in the study groups. We devised these kinds of activities for group writing to encourage metacognitive monitoring and metacognitive control.

Table 3:   Analysis of five selected writings

Writings	Artworks and exercises
# 1	In Unit 1, students wrote about their favourite artworks freely.
# 2	In Unit 2, students wrote about *Christina's World* using the software *Art Reporter*.
# 3	In Unit 3, students wrote about *The Great Family* for a pseudo-contest.
# 4	In Unit 5, students wrote about *Sunday Afternoon on La Grande Jatte* for the role-play activity of applying for a curatorial position.
# 5	In Unit 6, students wrote again about their individual's favourite artworks where each was the same artwork as in writing #1.

Scoring appreciation skills and metacognition

We quantified the data as follows. First, the learning effects were assessed by analysing the proficiency of the appreciation skills evident in the writings. Based on *proficiency indexes* that we devised, students' writings were judged for each of the following: *level of response behaviour, skill rate,* and *contextual rate* of the appreciation skills (Ishizaki and Wang, 2008; Wang and Ishizaki, 2009). As shown in Table 3, five types of writings were selected as the subjects for analysis.

Next, in order to quantify metacognition, we produced an assessment sheet based on the classification of *metacognitive knowledge* and *metacognitive activities*. We selected 14 descriptions for analysis from among the texts that students had written on the worksheets and reflection memos. The descriptions were analysed to determine which metacognition could be recognized. Each description was rated from 0 to 4 according to the number of metacognitive sentences and the total was calculated as *a metacognitive score*.

Results

Proficiency indexes in appreciation skills

Figures 4–6 indicate the changes in the three indexes for writings #1 through #5. Students chose their favourite artworks at the beginning of the program and wrote about the same artworks for writing #1 and #5. Writing #1 was written before learning about appreciation skills and writing #5 was written at the final stage of learning. We compared writing #1 with #5 in the mean score of each index.

It was found that writing #5 was rated significantly higher in each index than writing #1: level of response behaviour ($p < .01$), skill rate ($p < .01$), and contextual rate ($p < .01$). The increases in these indexes showed the learning effects of appreciation skills introduced in this program.

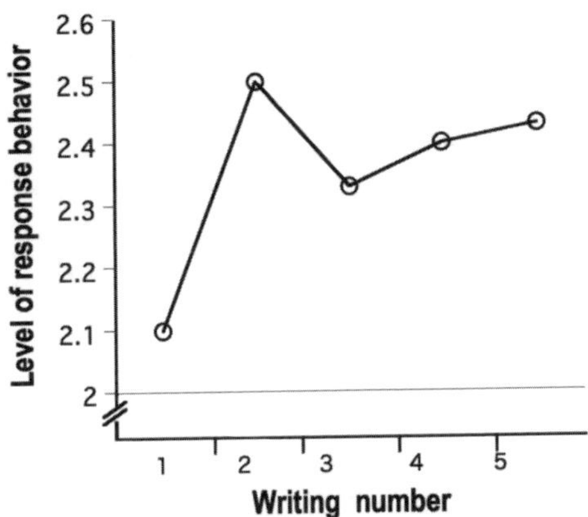

Figure 4: Level of response behaviour.

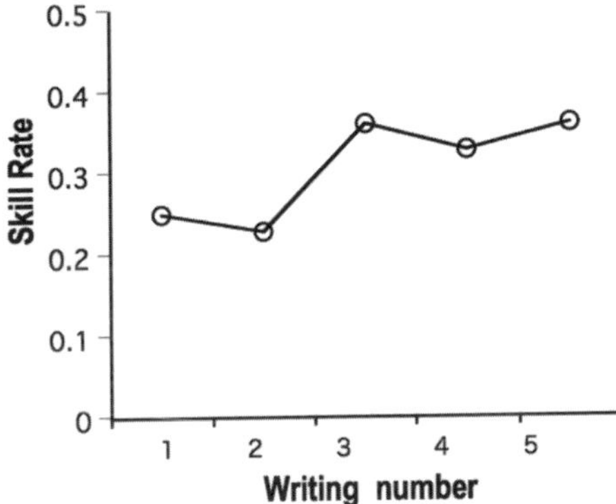

Figure 5: Skill rate.

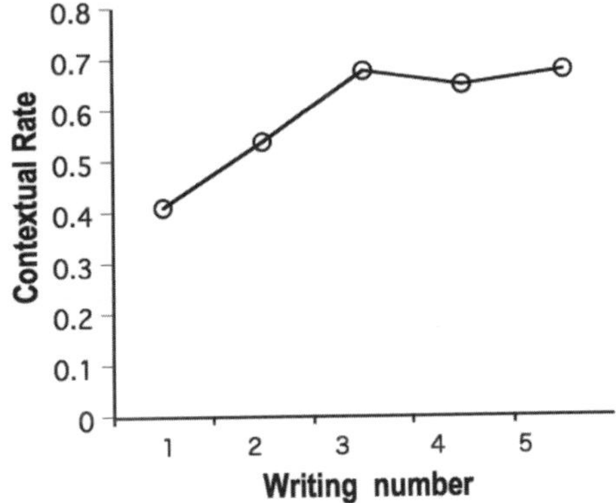

Figure 6: Contextual rate.

Correlation between metacognitive score and learning effect scores of appreciation skills

The increased scores of writings #5, in comparison to those of writings #1, were calculated for each of the three indexes as *learning effect scores*. As a result, there was a significant correlation between the metacognitive score and the learning effect score of skill rate ($r = .467$, $p< .05$), one of *the learning effect scores* of the three indexes which is described previously (Figure 7).

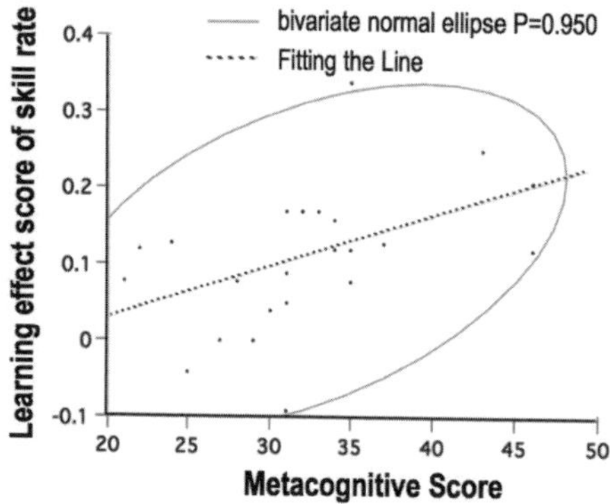

Figure 7: Correlation between metacognitive score and learning effect score of skill rate.

We then made a comparison between each of the index scores for writing tasks #1 and #5 of individual students and classified them into two categories: *large increase* and *small increase*. The scores of 0.3 or higher for level of response behaviour, 0.1 or higher for skill rate, and 0.3 or higher for contextual rate, were categorized as large increase, and those below were categorized as small increase. Students whose three scores were categorized as two or more large increases constituted the *large learning effect group*, and the others constituted the *small learning effect group*. Then, the metacognitive scores between the large learning effect group (16 students) and the small learning effect group (8 students) were compared. As shown in Figure 8, the metacognitive score for the large learning effect group tended to be higher than that of the small learning effect group, but the difference did not reach the level of statistical significance (N.S., $t = 1.54$, $p = 0.14$).

Metacognition among different proficiency groups

We focused on the relation between metacognition and learning effects when students had differences in the proficiencies of their appreciation skills at the beginning of the program.

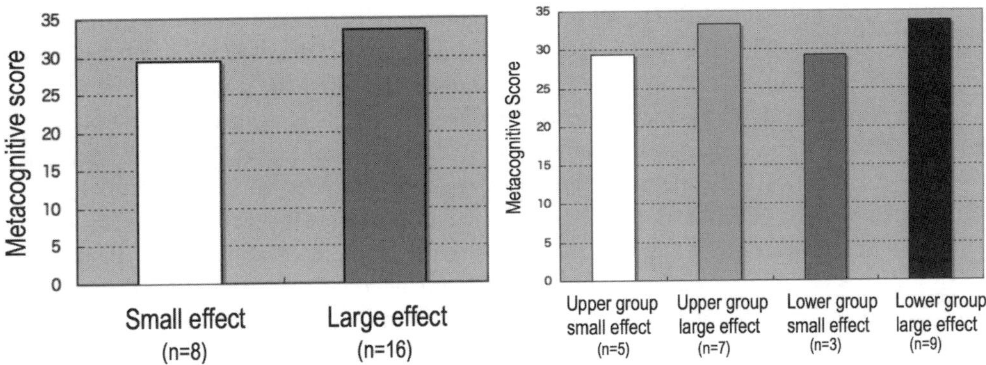

Figure 8: Learning effect and metacognition.　　Figure 9: Comparison among four groups.

Each score for the three indexes in writing #1 was classified into two categories: *above average* and *below average*. When two or more of the index scores were above average, the students were categorized as *upper group*, otherwise they were categorized as *lower group* at the beginning of the program. In accordance with this judgment, 12 students were placed into the upper group and 12 into the lower group. Further classification was made by crossing the previously mentioned learning effect quantities: the small learning effect and the large learning effect, which resulted in the following four classifications: *upper group small learning effect* (5 students), *upper group large learning effect* (7 students), *lower group small learning effect* (3 students), and *lower group large learning effect* (9 students). Metacognitive scores were then compared among these four groups.

The resulting metacognitive scores tended to be higher in both the upper group large learning effect and the lower group large learning effect (Figure 9). However, analysis of variance (ANOVA) among the four groups suggested no statistical significance (N.S., df = 1, F = 0.72, p = 0.55). Our analysis did not show whether differences in proficiencies in the students' appreciation skills at the beginning of learning had an obvious relation with metacognition and consequent learning effects.

Discussion

Effects of metacognitive supports and the verification methods

Yoshino (2006) reported that metacognitive supports for practicing a musical instrument helped beginners enhance their metacognitive responses more than they did for skilled learners. However, Yoshino did not verify the learning effects of metacognitive supports. Beyond Yoshino's results and limitations, we attempted to examine these learning effects. The increases in the scores of the appreciation skill proficiency indexes indicated positive learning effects in the program, and a significant correlation was observed between the skill rate and the metacognitive score. Since control experiments were not used in this study, we cannot conclude metacognitive supports as the fixed primary factor of the learning effects. Thus it was suggested they could be one of multiple factors.

Similar to this study, in the earlier literatures where the effects of metacognitive supports on art appreciation were studied, quantitative analysis using control experiments was attempted; however, no statistically distinctive differences were indicated between the experiment groups and control groups (Dennis, 1995; Shin, 2002). For educational practice there are ethical problems for verifications using control experiments. Limitations also exist in quantitative verifications where data from a limited number of subjects is used. In order to overcome such problems, close cooperation between study and practice and multiple considerations of practical data are required. Stokrocki (1997) predicted that compound study methods including qualitative and quantitative analysis would increase as methods of study in art education in order to resolve complex and difficult problems. The qualitative considerations in particular should be focused on as study methods for integrating various data for future studies of metacognition. Below we show some qualitative considerations by case analysis.

Significance of metacognitive supports in the learning of art appreciation

In general, logic has been valued as one of the cognitive characteristics of thought. Today the cognitive domain extends to a large area including intuitive, creative, and emotional acts (Parsons, 1998). How are the cognitive characteristics of thought considered in art? Efland (2002) concludes that the cognitive features provided by the arts are cognitive flexibility, integration of knowledge, imagination, and aesthetic experience. Parsons (1992) argues that interpretation in art appreciation is a cognitive activity related to language and culture. Perkins (1994) discusses why looking at art requires cognitive operations, and indicates that art appreciation promotes cognitive activities. The appreciation experiences that we have categorized include *association, observation, impression, analysis, interpretation,* and *judgment.* They have been fractionalized into cognitive characteristics. Metacognition by art viewers involves self-analysis of the cognitive characteristics of their own appreciation experiences.

On the other hand, it can be considered that metacognitive supports were more meaningful for the novice learners in particular, because beginners in art appreciation are, in general, less experienced in reflecting on the cognitive characteristics of art appreciation. We have reported, in previous research (Wang and Ishizaki, 2009), a case where the writer was too preoccupied with quoting given materials to show their own viewpoint and was overwhelmed by knowledge. Therefore, there has been apprehension as to whether or not an excessive exposure to knowledge and information for beginners might hinder their sensibility. Such apprehension suggests a need to study how beginners should cope with newly acquired knowledge of art appreciation.

The next two cases show how students handled their knowledge of given materials differently, and had different ideas about intuitive sense while reflecting on their own learning process with the metacognitive supports.

In the first case, a positive attitude towards knowledge of art appreciation was expressed when learning was reflected upon:

"All that I had to work with was what I could perceive from the painting, so learning about Vincent van Gogh's thoughts enabled me to think more profoundly about the painting, and I felt my thoughts were empowered by this. Through learning about background I was able to acquire further sensitivity to the artwork, which helped me to reflect more deeply about the picture."

The student made the following statement as a general theory of art appreciation:

"I felt a strong difference in my art-appreciation ability after gaining greater knowledge. By realizing the state of my mind both before and after gaining knowledge I was able to further deepen my thoughts. If an artwork is viewed with background knowledge, there are greater possibilities for discovery, which might be missed when an artwork is viewed without this knowledge."

On the other hand, there is another case where a student continued to maintain their intuitive impression of an artwork even after they had gained further information and knowledge about it. For instance, a straightforward feeling towards the painting is described in the initial writing.

"I learned the pleasure of viewing something that could be thought of as simply beautiful. For me the painting, *Primavera,* has become a symbol of beauty."

Though in the student's final writing knowledge seemed slightly undigested, a lot of information about the artwork; its historical values and positioning and so forth, was presented. In addition, a part of what was written in her initial writing was quoted, and her initial thoughts were highly valued. She expressed her thoughts as follows:

"After learning about methods of appreciation of artwork and how to write about artworks in this class I feel my viewpoint on the artwork has changed and I have a deeper perception now. I came to realize more varied things than before when I looked at the artwork again. However, I am surprised that my feelings about and impression ofthe artwork remained unchanged from the beginning."

It can be said that this student is prepared for experiencing various appreciation methods in the future, without being overwhelmed by knowledge.

From the cases above, it was observed that students showed their attitudes of self-direction while reflecting on their own appreciation experiences. It would probably be rather difficult to bring out this kind of student initiative with a one-sided presentation of the viewpoints and methods of art appreciation by the teacher. We consider that metacognitive supports functioned as one of the factors contributing to the promotion of student initiative.

Conclusion

We examined the relations between the learning effects of appreciation skills and metacognition in the program of writing about art. It is reasonable to suggest that the enhancement of metacognition can be one of multiple factors related to learning effects. We would like to focus attention on one of the statistical results, in which a significant correlation can be seen between skill rates, one of the proficiency indexes, and metacognitive scores. However, it was difficult to overcome all the limitations of quantitative study, and reach a sufficient conclusion, without using control experiments. Alternatively, the important point to note is that we offered qualitative consideration by case analysis. On the grounds that students initiatively studied various methods of art appreciation, by reflecting on their experiences, providing metacognitive supports should be considered as an effective approach to the challenge of the teaching of art-appreciation writing.

Our metacognitive supports were designed to make the students conscious of their own cognitive abilities from the viewpoint of art-appreciation skills. In light of this concept, we presumed that such metacognitive supports would be more effective for beginners who have limited opportunities for thinking about the characteristics of art in their daily lives. According to our investigations, it is likely that beginners will be able to continue learning during a challenging task if they are more prepared. However, if we hope to clearly verify the effects of metacognitive learning, particularly for beginners, our study needs to incorporate other teachers' experiences of teaching art appreciation. Since we are convinced that quantitative studies will encounter difficulties when ethical issues and other limitations are taken into consideration, the future direction of this study would be to include other teachers' experiences of metacognitive teaching in art writing, and develop these methods to assess the qualities of metacognition in more detail.

References

Bransford, J. D., Brown, A. L., Cocking, R. R. (2000). *How people learn: Brain, mind, experience, and school.* Washington, DC: National Academy Press.

Central Council for Education (2008).*Report of improvements to the courses of study for elementary, lower secondary and upper secondary schools,* http://www.mext.go.jp/a_menu/shotou/new-cs/news/20080117.pdf. Accessed 24 January 2013.

Dennis, F. C. (1995).Aesthetic perception, metacognition and transfer: Thinking in the visual arts. (Unpublished doctoral dissertation, University of California Los Angels, 1995).

Dunlosky, J., Metcalfe, J. (2009). *Metacognition.* Los Angeles, CA: Sage.

Efland, A. D. (2002). *Art and cognition: Integrating the visual arts in the curriculum.* Williston, VT: Teachers College Press.

Flavell, J. H. (1979). Metacognition and cognitive monitoring: A new area of cognitive-developmental inquiry. *American Psychologist, 34* (6), 906–911.

Hacker, D. J., Dunlosky,J., Graesser, A. C. (2009). *Handbook of metacognition in education.* New York: Routledge.

Housen, A. (1983). The eye of the beholder: Measuring aesthetic development. (Unpublished doctoral dissertation, Harvard University, 1983.)

Ishizaki, K., Wang, W. (2004). A study on the *Art Reporter* program using multimedia CD-ROM. *The Bulletin of the Faculty of Education, Utsunomiya University, 54,* 115–130.

—— (2006). Study of repertoires in writing about art.*BijutsuKyoikugaku [The Journal for the Association of Art Education], 27,* 29–41.

—— (2008). An analysis of expertise in writing about art.*BijutsuKyoikugaku [The Journal for the Association of Art Education], 29,* 49–60.

—— (2010a). The role of metacognition in art appreciation learning.*BijutsuKyoikugaku [The Journal for the Association of Art Education], 31,* 55–66.

—— (2010b). Considering the framework of art appreciation repertoires. *International Journal of Education through Art, 6* (3), 327–341.

Ishizaki, K., Wang, W., Parsons, M. (2008). Learning about "appreciation skills": Case study of two teenagers. *Proceedings* [CD-ROM].*The 32nd International Society for Education through Art (InSEA)World Congress 2008*, Osaka, Japan, 5–9 August, 1–10.

Johnson, D. W., Johnson, R. T., Holubec, E. J. (1993). *Circles of learning: Cooperation in the classroom* (4th ed).Edina, MN: Interaction Book Company.

Kato, H. (1997). Study on the role of metacognition in mathematical problem solving: The effectiveness of metacognitive supports. *Journal of JASME: Research in Mathematics Education, 3,* 81–89.

Kiyokawa, S., Inuzuka, M. (2003). Interactive explanation: Teaching reading by dividing activities into object-level and meta-level. *Japanese Journal of Educational Psychology, 51* (2), 218–229.

Matsuura, T. (2003). Study on instructional strategies to develop metacognition in science education: Scientific observations and experiments. (Unpublished doctoral dissertation, Hiroshima University, 2003.)

Parsons, M. J. (1987), *How we understand art: A cognitive developmental account of aesthetic experience.* New York, NY: Cambridge University Press.

—— (1992).Cognition as interpretation in art education. In Reimer, B.; Smith, R. A. (Eds.). *The arts, education, and aesthetic knowing (National Society for the Study of Education Yearbooks).* Chicago, IL: National Society for the Study of Education. 70–91.

—— (1998).Child development in art [Review of the book by Kindler, A.]. *Studies in Art Education, 40* (1), 80–91.

Perkins, D. N. (1994). *The intelligent eye: Learning to think by looking at art.* Santa Monica, CA: Getty Center for Education in the Arts.

Perkins, D. N., Jay, E., Tishman, S. (1993). Beyond abilities: A dispositional theory of thinking. *Merrill-Palmer quarterly, 39* (1), 1–21.

Prawat, R. S. (1989). Promoting access to knowledge, strategy, and disposition in students: A research synthesis. *Review of Educational Research, 59* (1), 1–41.

Sannomiya, M. (2008). Metacognition and intelligence in learning. In Sannomiya, M. (Ed.), *Metacognition: higher-order cognitive function supporting learning ability.* Kyoto: Kitaojishobo. 17–37.

Sato, M. (2003). Concept of literacy and its redefinition.*The Japanese Journal of Educational Research, 70* (3), 292–301.

Shin, S. R. (2002). The effects of a metacognitive art criticism teaching strategy that incorporates computer technology on critical thinking skill and art critiquing ability. (Unpublished doctoral dissertation, The Florida State University, 2002.)

Stokrocki, M. (1997). Qualitative forms of research methods. In La Pierre, S. D.; Zimmerman, E. (Eds.).*Research methods and methodologies for art education.* Reston, VA: National Art Education Association. 33–55.

Stout, C. J. (1995). Critical conversations about art: A description of higher-order thinking generated thought the study of art criticism. *Studies in Art Education, 36* (3), 170–188.

Wang, W., Ishizaki, K. (2009). The expertise and transfer in learning about "appreciation skills". *BijutsuKyoikugaku [The Journal for the Association of Art Education], 30,* 465–476.

Yoshino, I. (2006). The effect of metacognitive support to the musical instrument practice and the learners' thinking: Comparison between experts and novices. *Proceedings of the 70th Annual Convention of the Japanese Psychological Association,* Fukuoka, Japan, 3–5 November, 720, http://www.sap.hokkyodai.ac.jp/yosino/rsrch/JPA06pp.pdf. Accessed 8 January 2011.

Note

1   This study was supported by the Japan Society for the Promotion of Science, Grant-in-Aid for Scientific Research (C), #22530950.

Chapter 14

Research on visual literacy meanings with students and teachers

Ricardo Reis, University of Barcelona; i2ADS, School of Fine Arts, University of Porto

Abstract

In Portugal, research in art education does not reveal narratives that show us what visual literacy is; what skills are included in the concept; what its importance is; or what its significance is to teachers and students. This research project intends to discover the narratives made by students and teachers and also the narratives made by institutions and the scientific field of art education. This could give relevance to the role of schools in the development and social appreciation of visual literacy. In this chapter I will focus on one specific area of our study: the collection of teacher and student discourses on art education. Discourses are just one of the vertices of the triangle (see Research Scheme, Figure 1) which, articulated with the others, will help to understand the problem. I intend to begin with discussing issues about research on visual literacy and then I give a general overview of the research project, the methodology, and also my personal development as a researcher. I will present the problems and the research aims, as well as the criteria for the sample and the predicted difficulties related to the study of teachers and students. I will talk about the use of visual research methods and present some of the activities, suggestions, methodological and ethical questions that arose when we used these methods. I will also talk about the problems that emerged when we analysed visual data and the difficulty of writing about the research. The conclusion will provide a synthesis of problems developed through the chapter and also reflect my doubts about the conception and application of a research methodology about the visual skills and abilities of young people.

The state of the art: Visual literacy at glance

There are multiple notions of literacy, but some are more consensual than others. Literacy, in a large sense, is based on the competences people achieve in the school context and, in general, it refers to the ability to read and write, although there are other skills associated with these. (UNESCO, 2005).

The globalization of social and cultural relations and the different forms of knowledge and communication have contributed to extend the concept of literacy. (Hernández, 2007; Hong, 2006), and allowed for reflection on the skills, knowledge, and our understanding of the development of literacy in modern societies (Hong, 2006). In the late 1960s the concept of "visual literacy" was devised by JonhDebes (1969, p. 27), and the concept of "multiliteracies" arose in the 1990s (The New London Group, 1996).

When we talk about "literacy in arts", Livermore (1997, p. 8) refers to two dominant perspectives: one related to the domain of technical terms associated with the basic visual elements of art and the structures that organize them; the other related to people's ability to read and write in the course of analysis of different art forms. Hong (2006) refers to the expansion of the concept in three stages: (1) as coding and decoding of symbolic notations; (2) as a response to artworks; (3) as a consequence of making and creating; a reflection of the aims, processes, and contexts of art.

In the last two decades studies and reports have been carried out in the sphere of literacy in the arts. As an example is the report by McIntosh et al (1993), *The state of the art: Arts literacy in Canada*, which defines a literate person as one who shows a level of knowledge, comprehension, and highlighting aptitude in one or more of the arts. This idea has been confirmed by different institutions in the United States, such as the Getty Institute for the Arts and the Arts Education Partnership. In 1994, the National Standards for Arts Education were accepted in the United States. They define literacy in arts as the comprehension of and ability to work with artistic elements and the structures that organize them. The Guggenheim Museum carried out the study *Teaching Literacy through Art*,[1] evaluating the ability of students to describe and interpret art as well as apply these competences to the comprehension of written texts. In 2010, the Partnership for 21st Century Skills brought about a new idea about the concept, with the publication of *Skills Map for the Arts*.[2]

In Portugal, the concept of literacy was used for the first time by Ana Benavente (1996), and some years ago a department of Ministry of Education (GEPE) published a report about the economical dimension of literacy (Data Angel Policy Research Incorporated, 2009). In 2001, the concept of "literacy in arts" appeared in the *Currículo Nacional do Ensino Básico: CompetênciasEssenciais* [*National Curriculum of Basic Education: Essential Skills*] (Departamento de Educação Básica, 2001, p. 151). It had never before been stated or considered in the practices of visual arts teachers. 'It is unknown whether there has been a study into teacher comprehension of the concept of visual literacy, the level of concept comprehension of teachers and their use of the concepts in their teaching practices. The way students incorporate and mobilize the concept is also unknown. The proposed study aims to fill in these gaps.

The research project and the methodological approach

This study will contribute to the comprehension of the concept of visual literacy and to the role of school in its development and social appreciation through the application of a constructionist methodology. This will be a contribution to the scientific updating of art education in Portugal. It will also bring about a complete vision of the concept, based on three main perspectives (see Research Scheme, Figure 1):

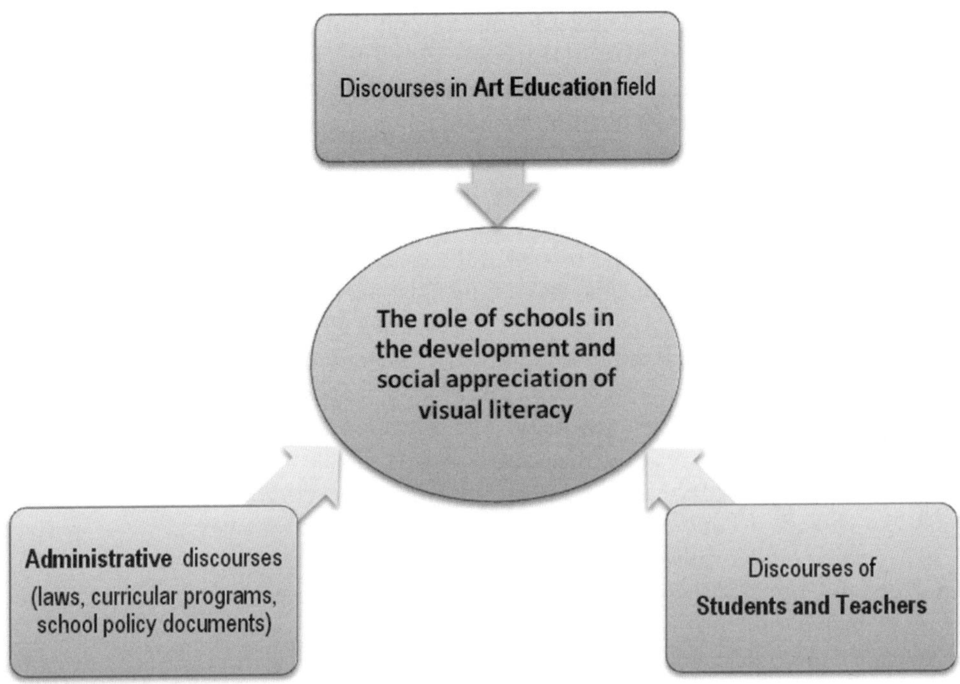

Figure 1: Research Scheme.

(1) The discourses of the scientific field of art education, with their different international approaches;
(2) The administrative discourses provided by laws regulating education, curriculum programs, and school policy documents that organize the work of educators;
(3) The discourses of students and teachers.

In this project, school will be the centre of the research and, inside it, students and teachers will be the most important actors in the research. Somers (1994) said that we need to give importance to the social aspects of the narratives about the process of identity construction. If I want to know how students build up their own narratives (*ontological narratives*) about visual literacy, I also have to know teacher and school narratives (*public narratives*), and the narratives of the Ministry of Education and the field of art education, which besides being considered *conceptual narratives*, may also be considered as *metanarratives*, because they determine the other narratives. Thus, I intend to research *with* students and teachers, and in a larger way, *with* schools, too.

An analysis of the discourses in the field of art education revealed the types of narratives that have been made concerning "what is visual literacy", and helped to build a broader vision of the concept by enlarging and updating the concept that is in the *National Curriculum of Basic Education: Essential Skills* (Departamento de Educação Básica, 2001)[3], without forgetting that the concept of literacy is socially constructed and based on a particular vision of the world. It was used to found the idea of "social stratification and delinquency" (Wortham and Jackson, 2008).

The Ministry of Education's and schools' perspectives discerned in this study will be based on analysis of the administrative discourses that we found in official documents: the curricular programs of subjects related to the visual arts, laws, and school educational projects. The discourses of students' and teachers', who are the main actors in school and society, will hold great importance in this study because they can clarify the professional and technical perspectives on the concept through teachers' discourses, as well as the social perspective through students' discourses. This kind of study requires a narrative approach with mainly qualitative, but also quantitative data collection. Some projects will be defined by students (see Table 1), where visual materials and texts will be made in different forms. This evidences are what I want to collect. The teachers were informed about the research process and artworks were produced by the students. Through collective analysis of the material, we expected emerging categories and dimensions, connections, and relationships, which allow for a definition of the role of the school in the development and social appreciation of visual literacy.

We expect the results will support the reflective processes of teachers and the awareness of the importance of visual literacy as a key competence by students. This competence may be acquired and useful in different social and professional contexts.

We want to contribute to the reinforcement of professional competence and to the improvement of the pedagogical practices of visual arts teachers; and to the creation of a curriculum for visual arts capable of promoting the development and knowledge of competences adapted to the characteristics of contemporary society, not only at school, but also in the public space of education (Nóvoa, 2009).

From positivism to constructionism: A personal path through methodology

The main problem we faced was within the dialogue of the research methodologies related to constructionist learning. Adopting these methodologies meant changing the discourse: I must stop using "we", and I have to start using the term "I". Changing the discourse is a long process. However, I have to change not only the way I write but also the way I think. Every day I try to look at images around me in a different way: my vision of the world is changing continuously.

In some aspects the positivist perspective is "user friendly" because it guarantees the achievement of expected results; similar to a user manual or recipe book that assures the correct use of equipment or a delicious meal. In the constructionism research paradigm, the personality of the researcher, his actions and himself as a person are most important.

Methodology is constructed by me and that allows me to adopt my decisions on route and forces me to relate with the object being studied; it is something that does not exist but is designed and built by me.

However, this change is difficult to interiorize: it is like losing directions; references that ensure and predefine a path. My path through the methodology involved a constant change of my concepts and of my prejudices against the research, as well as my understanding of the role of the researcher and the object under study.

Research problem

The main research problem is:

- What relationships can be established between the discourses and practices of students and teachers, the administrative discourses and the field of art education in order to understand the role of schools in the development and social appreciation of visual literacy?

Other questions also have to be answered in order to help understand this problem:

- How socially constructed is the concept of visual literacy?
- What kind of knowledge/skills have been constructed by the different discourses in order to allow a citizen to be considered visually literate?
- What are the impressions students and teachers have of the social recognition of citizens as capable in the area of visual literacy?
- What types of discourses are constructed about the importance of visual literacy in jobs and/or daily life by research groups?

The aims of the research procedure

The most important aims and objectives of the research project are listed below:

- To create and apply a constructionist research methodology that allows for collection and analysis of different narratives about visual literacy;
- To know the way the concept of visual literacy is constructed in our society;
- To analyse the narratives that define the content, knowledge, and competences considered necessary in order for a person to be considered visually literate;
- To decide, through the narratives collected, what students and teachers consider to be visual literate and how it is shown.

Research with young people

Research with students appeared at the beginning of the 20th century with the "discovery" of adolescence which unleashed studies about psychological development. Since then, research with students has been applied to other areas, such as educational research, cultural studies, transition to adult life (research politically-directed with a great tradition in the United Kingdom), social and cultural geography, and "girls studies" (Brooks et al., 2009). All these researches contributed to the revision of the social perspective on young people, and from this has emerged two beliefs in society which have had a great impact on the way we do research: the ability of young people to speak and their right to do so (Thomson, 2008, p. 2).

There is no biological reason to believe that young people have nothing to important to say. The idea that connects age with the ability to make decisions and have responsibilities is socially constructed because we see children and young people as immature, and so we do not take them seriously. I have no doubt that children and young people are capable of giving important testimonies about their experiences and way of life.

The right of young people to speak (and have adults listen to them) appeared in the Convention on the Rights of the Child in 1989, which says that children who are capable of forming their own views have the right to express those views freely in all matters affecting them, and that those views should be given due weight in accordance with their age and maturity (Nações Unidas, 1989). This point is very important because it allows children and young people to be heard and to participate in decision making, and institutions have to ensure that that happens.

The consequence of these changes is that young people became social actors, with rights and responsibilities (Brooks et al., 2009, p. 58). This change led to the production of research that went from an external and colonialist vision of youth to a collaborative and participant vision, where young people are actors and partners.

This type of research is common in anglophone countries, namely the United Kingdom, Australia and the United States, but not in Portugal. In these countries, people speak about "student participation", "taking the advice of students", or the "students' voice" when considering research in education (Thomson, 2008, p. 2). The degrees to which young people participate and are involved vary from involvement in the research design to involvement in the collection and production of data; realization of task-based activities; and involvement in data interpretation, or involvement in all the processes of investigation.

However, we cannot talk about "one voice"; we must talk about several voices, an idea that comes from postcolonial and feminist theories. It is not admissible to consider a social group as unique and indivisible if we do not pay attention to its different voices. The idea of a representative voice still remains in the social sciences, where it is possible to find examples of the often quoted requirement, "give students a voice", but in reality students fill in the surveys and researchers analyse the data (in Portugal this kind of research is the most used, especially in the field of educational science).

Researching groups

The research took place in two public schools in Portugal. Schools were chosen according to the following:

- School, teacher, and student interest in participation in the study;
- Parental consent to carry out a research study with students;
- Authorization to accede to school documents;
- Demography of the school and ease of access;
- Local curricula of visual arts education exist in the area.

I will also choose which students can participate in this study. Only students that cumulatively fulfil the following criteria can participate:

- Young people aged 15 who should have capacity for initiative, reflection, argumentation, and concretization;
- Students in the ninth grade (because it is the end of a cycle and students must select a field of specialization for secondary school or decide to start working);
- Students attending the same school or group of schools (it is a guarantee of having a pedagogical continuity: teaching based on the same local curriculum orientations).

According to the structure of the Portuguese educational system most students should meet these criteria. However it is important to ensure voluntary participation free of charge, that is to say, students do not have to pay and do not receive any payment for participating. The question the researcher should consider is: will the social and intellectual compensations be enough to motivate the students to participate in this research?

Visual methods in visual literacy research

The use of visual methods is considered less intimidating by some researchers, because they are less directive and are capable of reaching young people and adults directly, through the technologies used, even during the process, which allows changes to be made (Brooks et al., 2009, p. 124). Visual research methods are also used because young people are very interested in images: they live in a world full of images and they even produce some of them. Images have a way of communicating that is different from words, because they unleash not only aesthetic and emotional responses, but also intellectual. When young people are involved in image research, they feel more motivated because it is something different from what they are used to: they are used to dealing with words (Thomson, 2008, p. 12).

In the context of this project, research *with* students represents only a small part. The project's aim is to contribute to a fuller comprehension of what visual literacy is and how it has been constructed and socially recognized. Students' discourses will be collected through some activities (see Table 1). The project is carried out in phases – over two weeks – to allow breaks between sessions according to the complexity of the activities

Methodological questions

I will address two questions: the first is related to the technical competences of the researcher in using and demonstrating visual methods; the second is related to the technical competences of the students to produce visual products.

Concerning the first question, Thomson (2008, p. 15) says we do not need to be artists or art teachers to undertake research with visual methods, but it will help if we consider visual methods not only as a technique, but also as a social practice with traditions, genres, discussions, grammar, and hierarchies. This question is relevant to the analysis of visual material.

Concerning the second question, we cannot accept that young people are technically capable in any visual environment just because technology is available. To involve them, we must ensure they are familiar with the equipment; its capacities and limitations and the way to handle it, because the use of these methods requires specific competences as well as knowledge and personal sensitivity (Thomson, 2008, p. 12–14).We should be aware that the technical domain can influence the collected data and, consequently, the results (Brooks et al., 2009, p. 128).

I believe students must use the available technological mediums and the ones that they can easily handle, because I want to survey their competences. However, I can participate in some of the activities but without providing specific training or solving technical problems, because that could slant the results.

Students must be empowered to decide over the study themes, but I will propose one challenging task for the students: to pretend to apply for a job in any of the branches of the creative industry. Despite the "creative industries" being a generalized concept, it is possible that students are not familiar with it, or at least do not have the same ideas about it. I will provide the following definition of the creative industries to guarantee that everyone involved comes to the same understanding: the creative industries are activities which are inspired by cultural and artistic creativity and have the potential to create economic value through the generation and exploitation of intellectual property.[4] They include sectors such as architecture, design, advertising, cinema and television, radio, fashion, audio-visual and interactive media, software, music, performing arts, visual arts, and cultural heritage.

Brooks et al. (2009, p. 128) refer to an important research problem: the lack of student interest in the purpose of the tasks, regardless of whether or not they decided to participate. They suggest that it is easier for students to "default" during the summer, because activities inherent to this time of the year are much more desirable. Thus, I decided to start the study during the third term, in May, as a matter of agenda and strategy: it is before examinations, the days are longer, and the climate is better; all beneficial conditions to carrying out the tasks.

Ethical questions

It is particularly important to discuss ethical questions in research that uses images because, depending on the type of data collected, it may be difficult to ensure anonymity and confidentiality. This is why it is extremely important that all participants are well informed about the data I intend to collect, how I am going to collect it, and how the data are going to be diffused. It is beneficial to involve young people in the collection/creation of images because then they can decide which images to collect, reveal their perspective on the images, and what they want to show or hide; thus the images correspond to their point of view, their sensitivity, and their own ethic (Brooks et al., 2009, p. 129). Another ethical consideration regards who made the images (Thomson, 2008, p. 14), if they are not made by the students, but this could be a question to discuss with the students during analysis of the produced materials.

Parental consent will be necessary because the participants will be young people 15 years old. I will obtain authorization not only from the parents but also from the Portuguese Ministry of Education, the Portuguese Data Protection Authority (CNPD), and the Executive and Pedagogical Boards of the schools where the studies are being carried out.

Activities oriented towards a certain purpose

The visual methods will be privileged in the activities oriented towards a certain purpose, and, in some specific activities, students will choose the best way to express themselves; the way in which they feel most comfortable, because "traditional" methods are usually guided by adults and people must have some level of knowledge, articulacy, and confidence (Brooks et al., 2009, p. 124).

Evaluation of visual data

Evaluating visual data can raise some methodological and ethical problems, but it is the most important consideration in this project because it is related to data interpretation and results.

Objectivity, reliance on facts and data as essential concepts of scientific effort, were affected by the idea that oral expression depends on culture and its meaning changes according to the time and place. That is why I need to think about other ways of research. The realization that knowledge is culturally constructed and the researcher and its social environment as importance in the research has interference in the research with images: (1) an image is not neutral, its meaning is socially and culturally constructed; (2) an image can be interpreted in many different ways (Thomson, 2008, p. 9–11).

Table 1:   Development plan of the research activities with students.

Session	Activities
1	Presentation of the study and its aims: What do we expect from each actor? Activity 1: Where do we come from? Next session: Bring three images related to you and write a short report explaining why you chose them.
2	Presentation of the images and texts: What do we learn about ourselves? Can we connect the issues confronted with each other? Activity 2: "Images of Visual Culture and I" Next session: Bring three images that you have seen which have had an impact on you. It could be photos of what you saw in the street, in a magazine or newspaper, in a film, etc. Then write a short report explaining your choices.
3	Presentation of the brought materials and reports: What kind of discussions could the brought materials unleash? Are we capable of finding any relation between them? Which categories become visible? Activity 3: Presentation of the concept of the creative industries and their sectors. Would you like to work in any of these areas? Next session: Imagine there is a company (from an area you would like to work in) that is recruiting young people of your age. This company is selecting people not according to their curriculum vitae, but through the creative ways candidates introduce themselves. You have to create a product (such as a video, blog, portfolio, website, poster, book, performance, etc.) through which you introduce yourself as the "right person in the right place". You have to show all your skills and knowledge to get the job.
4	Discussion of presentations to the group: Which competences do students highlight most? Activity 4: You have shown everything you can do in the previous task. Now you have to make an exhaustive list of all the things the "right collaborator" in this company should be able to do. Now write "I know" or "I don't know" in front of each sentence. For those who wrote "I know" explain where you learned to do it, e.g. "at school in Visual Education class", "on a course", "with friends" or "alone". For those who wrote "I don't know" say if you are interested in learning and where can you learn it.

Visual expression can be evaluated at different levels. Brooks et al. (2009, p. 126) state that first we must consider the difference between realist and constructivist approaches. A realist approach to images tends to understand them as evidence of the real world; places, events or objects; a constructivist approach gives emphasis to the context in which the image was created and in which it is seen, as well as to the power relations involved in its production. It may analyse visual material from different points of view: producer, reader/observer, and the image itself.

The use of visual methods in research with young people is especially relevant because it allows researchers to explore some different features. Images can reveal the parts of young peoples' lives that they do not talk about, and images can also provide access to private spaces that researchers would not normally have access to, and this raises ethical questions.

For this study I want the analysis of the visual material to be conducted with the students in order to identify the differences between spoken messages and visual messages to dispel or to confirm their doubts.

Research with teachers: Two different moments in the researching schedule

The research is developed with teachers in two different phases and with different collaborators. The aim of the first phase is to collect the images (and information related to them) that the teachers and educators share with their students, during the classes. To know this information will enrich the research process because it will allow us to collect data that will help us to understand the concepts teachers have about visual literacy, and predict the implications for students' development in visual literacy as well as their conceptions of art and visual culture. When all the information about the school year has been collected it will be possible to have a larger perspective on the kinds of images that students see at school and how these images are shown. The results of this research action will allow us to adjust subsequent research actions with students.

The data were collected on the Internet, making use of web-based applications such as Google Docs. The advantages of using these kinds of resources are obvious: open use; free of charge; personalization of layout; user-friendly interface; teachers' familiarity with web questionnaires, which, because of their ubiquity online, can be filled in at any time and from any place; speed of completion; opportunity to diversify the sample thanks to the participation of people with different professional experiences; ease of sharing images and information related to pedagogical materials or the museums visited, for example, through creating links; possibility for automatic statistical treatment of data; and last but not least, data can be kept safe, ensuring they are classified. Thus, I made the questionnaire online and the answers were ordered into a database that uses online storage space.[5] Thus, collaborating teachers can upload the images shown to their students. However, there are disadvantages of using this technology: first, teachers that have no e-mail account and do not know how to use Google Docs are unable to participate; second, sharing data is impersonal and some participating teachers prefer to give up during the research process. To address these problems, I sent e-mails regularly to all collaborators, shared information about the evolution of the research, and clarified doubts that may have arisen. It was important to ensure teachers' anonymity by sending all the collective e-mails in *blind carbon copy* to protect their identities and addresses.

I sent e-mails inquiring about the research procedure to a selection of my contacts and 90 responded. They were all teachers of different educational levels and most of them participated in the research. My first intention was to have weekly participation, but I soon realized that that would be impossible because teachers said they did not have the time and they could not show images to the students every week. So, I decided they could fill in the form whenever they had relevant material to share, giving them the opportunity to decide what and when to share.

The second phase, when teachers are called in to participate, happens after the collection of the materials produced by the students in each participating school. In each school there should be a group of five teachers from different cycles (from Grade 1 to Grade 9). All the teachers should be employed by the school and responsible for implementing school educational projects. The group should meet in a work session in order to analyse and discuss the methodology of the research project and the material produced by their students. This action is intended to verify the relationship between students' and teachers' concepts of visual literacy and to come to an understanding about the art education concepts that guide teachers' practice at school.

Conclusion

According to Lather (cited in Thomson, 2008, p. 3) qualitative researchers are becoming obsessed by voices; prioritizing what participants say during the research and defending the idea of "confessional stories, self-revelation [...] [and the] reinscription of a non problematic reality". She speaks about "complexity, partial truth and multiple subjectivities". This almost extremist way of formulating the question, causes me to doubt, or, in this case, worry: how do I present what happened during the research? How do I write without fancying? How do I explain consciously why I make these interpretations? Another question is about the predictability of my professional view of the material collected: how can I deal with my subjectivity as a teacher, when I interpret students' tasks and produced visual materials?

The real purpose of this chapter, and the presentation of this project at the research pre-conference of the 33rd *InSEA World Congress*, is the possibility of these raising questions can be discussed by a group of people interested in the topic and in the research methodology, not sufficiently explored in Portugal. This needs a great deal of reflection and uses methods of data collection, little used with this aim. The questions that emerged are related not only to the research design, but also to methodological, ethical, and operational worries, namely, related to the practice of instructing on the spot in a school environment, which as a researcher is not my normal practice. I am also aware that the success of the study depends on its dissemination and visibility. Involving young people in this task could be a good strategy because it would empower them and ensure that the results, more than promote comprehension and knowledge about their lives, will also have an impact on them. The evaluation of young people participation in this study is important and they should also participate in the evaluation. Young people should have a say the whole of the research process.

Acknowledgements

A research project is done with the support of many people that generously share their knowledge through the books they wrote or just by spending time on hearing, criticizing or helping us. I would like to thank to all those people, especially to Fernando Hernandez for his orientation, to my PhD colleagues for their share, to all participants in the research, and to Cristina Sério for the translation of this text. I would also like to thank the opportunity that has been given to me to discuss this project with a large group of specialists in the Research Pre-Conference of InSEA World Congress, at Budapest, and the possibility of sharing it now with much more people, through this publication. This chapter was possible with financial support from the Foundation for Science and Technology (FCT), SFRH/BD/72980/2010, co-financed by the European Social Fund (ESF).

References

Benavente, A. (Ed.). (1996). *A literacia em Portugal: resultados de uma pesquisa extensiva e monográfica [Literacy in Portugal: results of an extensive and monographic research]*. Lisbon, Portugal: Fundação Calouste de Gulbenkian.

Brooks, R., Heath, S., Ireland, E., & Cleaver, E. (2009). *Researching Young People's Lives*. Thousand Oaks, London, New Deli: SAGE Publications Ltd.

Data Angel Policy Research Incorporated. (2009). *A Dimensão Económica da Literacia em Portugal: Uma Análise [The Economic Dimensions of Literacy in Portugal: A Review]*. Lisbon, Portugal: GEPE.

Debes, J. (1969). The Loom of Visual Literacy. *Audiovisual Instruction, 14* (8), 25–27.

Departamento de Educação Básica. (2001). *Curriculo Nacional do Ensino Básico: Competências Essenciais [National Curriculum of Basic Education: Essential Skills]*. Lisbon, Portugal: Ministério da Educação.

Hernández, F. (2007). *Espigador@s de la cultura visual: otra narrativa para la educación de las artes visuales [Gleaners of visual culture: another narrative for visual arts education]*. Barcelona, Spain: Octaedro.

Hong, C. (2006). Developing literacies in postmodern times: the role of arts in education. *UNESCO World Conference on the Arts in Education*. Lisboa: UNESCO. Retrieved March 4, 2006, from http://portal.unesco.org/culture/en/file_download.php/47472850f65e46872ccc81 181610c94aChristina+Hong.htm

Livermore, J. (Ed.). (1997). *More Than Words Can Say: A Set of Arts Literacy Papers*. Melbourne: Australian Institute of Art Education.

McIntosh, D., Hanely, B., Verriour, P., & Van Gyn, G. (Eds.). (1993). *The state of the art: Arts literacy in Canada*. Victoria, British Columbia: Beach Holme Publishers.

Nações Unidas. (1989). Convenção sobre os Direitos da Criança [Convention on the Rights of the Child].*UNICEF web page*. Retrieved May 10, 2011, from http://www.unicef.pt/docs/pdf_ publicacoes/convencao_direitos_crianca2004.pdf

Nóvoa, A. (2009). Educação 2021: Para uma história do futuro. [Education 2021: For a history of the future]. *Revista Iberoamericana de Educación*, (49), 1–18. Retrieved from http://www. rieoei.org/rie49a07_por.pdf

Somers, M. R. (1994). The narrative constitution of identity: a relational and network approach. *Teory and Society, 23* (5), 605–649.

The New London Group. (1996). A Pedagogy of Multiliteracies: Designing Social Futures. *Harvard Educational Review, 66* (1), 60–92.

Thomson, P. (Ed.). (2008). *Doing visual research with children and young people.* London: Routledge.

UNESCO. (2005). *EFA Global Monitoring Report. Education for all: Literacy for life.* (N. Burnett, Ed.). Paris: UNESCO Publishing.

Wortham, S., & Jackson, K. (2008). Educational Construccionisms. In J. A. Holstein & J. F. Gubrium (Eds.), *Handbook of Construccionist Research.* New York, London: The Guilford Press. 107–127.

Notes

1   Available at: http://www.guggenheim.org/new-york/education/school-educator-programs/learning-through-art/research-findings.

2   Available at: http://arteducators.org/research/21st_Century_Skills_Arts_Map.pdf.

3   "Literacy in arts assumes the ability to communicate and interpret meanings using the languages of the arts disciplines. It implies the acquisition of competences and the use of particular signals and symbols, distinct in each art form, in order to perceive and convert messages and meanings. It further requires an understanding of a work of art in the social and cultural context that surrounds it and the recognition of its functions within it"(Ministério da Educação, 2001, p. 151).

4   This is Chris Smith's definition, from the United Kingdom's Department of Culture, Media and Sport. This concept appeared in the 1990s in Australia, but it was developed by the Creative Industries Taskforce, created by Tony Blair's government in 1997.

5   The questionnaire and the online storage folder are no longer online.